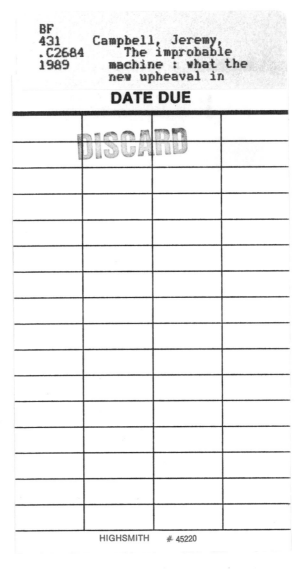

45209

THE IMPROBABLE

MACHINE

WHAT THE UPHEAVALS IN
ARTIFICIAL INTELLIGENCE RESEARCH
REVEAL ABOUT HOW THE MIND
REALLY WORKS

JEREMY CAMPBELL

SIMON AND SCHUSTER   NEW YORK   LONDON   TORONTO   SYDNEY   TOKYO

Simon and Schuster
Simon & Schuster Building
Rockefeller Center
1230 Avenue of the Americas
New York, New York 10020

SIMON AND SCHUSTER and colophon are registered trademarks
of Simon & Schuster Inc.

Designed by Karolina Harris
Manufactured in the United States of America

10 9 8 7 6 5 4 3 2 1

Library of Congress Cataloging-in-Publication Data

Campbell, Jeremy
The improbable machine : what the upheavals in artificial
intelligence research reveal about how the mind really works /
Jeremy Campbell.
p. cm.
1. Intellect. 2. Artificial intelligence. I. Title.
BF431.C2684   1989
153—dc20   89-36916
                CIP
Illustration on page 211 reproduced by permission of the American Institute of Physics.

ISBN 0-671-65711-9

FOR PANDORA
THE MIND THAT REALLY WORKS

CONTENTS

INTRODUCTION

WHEN the curtain goes up in a theater, and the stage is peopled with characters who are familiar yet foreign, like us and unlike us, larger than life, strange, almost as if they were visitors from another planet, the hush of anticipation is only in part a sign of eagerness on the part of the audience to be drawn into the narrative of the play. It is also due to the expectation that, watching these exotic creatures of a playwright's imagination, we may learn more about ourselves. Onstage, invented men and women walk and talk, making sense of an invented world, and yet, sitting in the darkness of the theater, we can use the artifice of those ingeniously fabricated minds to obtain new insights into our own.

The computer, in its own special way, has also forced us to think afresh about the nature of human thought, because it, too, is like and at the same time unlike our own intelligence; similar enough to furnish a metaphor for certain operations of reason, but so radically different in other respects as to make it abundantly obvious that this is not the way the mind is made. Because of these differences, the computer cries out for the creation of more realistic and illuminating theories of the natural mind.

A popular myth says that the invention of the computer diminishes our sense of ourselves, because it shows that rational thought is not special to human beings, but can be carried on by a mere machine. It is a short step from there to the conclusion that intelligence is mechanical, which many people find to be an affront to all that is most precious and singular about their humanness.

In fact, the computer, early in its career, was not an instrument of the philistines, but a humanizing influence. It helped to revive an idea that had fallen into disrepute: the idea that the mind is real, that it has an inner structure and a complex organization, and can be understood in scientific terms. For some three decades, until the 1940s, American psychology had lain in the grip of the ice age of behaviorism, which was antimental through and through. During these years, extreme behaviorists banished the study of thought from their agenda. Mind and consciousness, thinking, imagining, planning, solving problems, were dismissed as worthless for anything except speculation. Only the external aspects of behavior, the surface manifestations, were grist for the scientist's mill, because only they could be observed and measured. As for the notion that human beings are somehow exceptional by virtue of their unique mental powers, that too was thrown overboard. The behaviorist, declared John Watson, one of the school's founding theorists, "recognizes no dividing line between man and brute."

It is one of the surprising gifts of the computer in the history of ideas that it played a part in giving back to psychology what it had lost, which was nothing less than the mind itself. In particular, there was a revival of interest in how the mind represents the world internally to itself, by means of knowledge structures such as ideas, symbols, images, and inner narratives, all of which had been consigned to the realm of mysticism.

The idea that the mind is irrelevant to a theory of human behavior was linked early on to what was known—or rather what was not known—about the brain and nervous system. Scientists who studied the nervous system maintained that the neuron, the basic unit of the brain's operations, conducts signals in one direction only, and initiates no activity of its own. It seemed reasonable, then, to suppose that mental activity is simply a direct response to events that impinge on the brain from outside. The brain, and by implication the mind as well, could not be regarded, in the light of science, as a creative organ, originating thoughts and ideas; in the fashionable metaphor of the day, it was no more than a telephone switchboard, transmitting information, a most uninteresting role to play.

In this way brain science put its imprimatur on the behaviorist doctrine that what a person does is rather predictably shaped by events in his or her immediate vicinity, especially rewards and punishments, without the intervention of a "brain-mind" that, true to its switchboard character, is essentially uncreative. By the 1930s scientists knew that the neuron is capable of firing spontaneously, which suggested that the brain is an originator and not merely a transmission device, but by that time behaviorism, which took no interest in how the brain works, had gained such a stranglehold on American psychology that the new discoveries in neuroscience were largely brushed aside.

In the 1950s, the computer began to undermine the empire of behaviorism, because it manifestly did contain internal structures, in the form of components and circuits. It was not a mysterious black box. It represented aspects of the world to itself by means of symbols. The machine's behavior was driven by an interior information-processing system that was describable in scientific terms and was completely understood. All this was an invitation to take the architecture of the mind seriously.

The new emphasis on the mind, however, still did not come to terms with the physical reality of the brain. Apart from the fact that it processes information, a digital computer bears little resemblance to the brain. It works in serial fashion, manipulating symbols step by step, one after another, under the control of a central processing unit, according to explicit rules. Using components that are very fast and reliable, and a code consisting of only two letters, it performs long and intricate arithmetical calculations at high speed, much faster and more accurately than any human being can.

The brain is another kind of device altogether. It has roughly as many processing units as there are stars in our galaxy, and is so profligate it lets millions of them be destroyed, without any noticeable loss of efficiency. Yet in spite of this profusion of processors, most of the brain consists of "wires"; a single unit may have thousands of connections with other units and with itself. That is not the case in a standard computer, where a chip usually has less than six connections. Moreover, neurons are much, much slower than the switching elements of the computer. It seems likely that the brain can accomplish its complex feats of perception and thought by means of millions of connections acting in parallel. The connections as a whole define the information content of the system. In this way a vast amount of knowledge can be brought to bear on a decision all at once. The brain seems to be able to perform as many as two hundred trillion operations in a second; not serially, but simultaneously.

The brain and the digital computer both have speed and power, but they are speedy and powerful in quite different ways. At certain tasks, such as recognizing faces, understanding language, making agile movements of the body, the brain is superior to a thousand supercomputers, and yet when it is called upon to multiply large numbers together without using pencil and paper it is a cognitive wimp, outperformed by the simplest, cheapest microprocessor.

At the dawn of the age of artificial intelligence, scientists did start to build machines that were inspired by certain features of the brain, but their rivals, who threw in their lot with the unbrainlike digital computer, made more rapid headway and were amply rewarded with funds. It was a case of history repeating itself. Whereas behaviorism took on a life of its own as it got into its stride in the 1930s, neglecting the new discoveries of brain science that contradicted its claim that the mind cannot be studied scientifically, artificial intelligence made the study of mind respectable again, but still divorced it from what was known about how the brain works. Once more, brain and mind drifted apart, partly because the digital computer is much easier to understand than the brain, and partly because the brain itself was supposed to be general and powerful enough to support any theory of thinking, perceiving, learning, or remembering that psychologists might dream up. After all, programs of astonishing versatility and variety simulating aspects of human thinking could all be run on the same, biologically implausible serial computer, so why worry about the brain? The fact that the brain appears to have no internal programs of the kind that exist in standard artificial-intelligence systems made it all the more mysterious and remote from what computer scientists were doing.

Philosophy could not challenge such views directly because it has never managed to sort out the vexed and tangled question of how the mind stands in relation to the brain. There are almost a dozen different theories from which to choose, some purporting to show that states of mind are merely complex states and operations of a physical device we call the brain, others that the mind is radically different from the brain, and cannot be understood in physical terms.

In the 1980s, however, the whole landscape of artificial intelligence and cognitive science in general was thrown into convulsions by a revival, in a much stronger and more compelling form, of the early attempt to build thinking machines that are influenced by the physical design, the actual hardware, of the brain. This movement, known as "the new connectionism," takes the brain seriously. It does not require us to believe that the mind *is* the brain; but it does suggest that what the brain is, how it evolved, constrains in interesting and important ways the sort of theories we can reasonably entertain about how the mind works. If the brain is a parallel device without programs, in which massive amounts of knowledge, implicit in the connections that make up the bulk of the brain's volume, are brought to bear on a problem simultaneously, then this must surely affect our ideas about the whole of mental life, including such high-level activities as thinking and reasoning.

Far from "reducing" the mind to the brain, the new connectionism is likely to enlarge and enhance our understanding, because it *adds* to what we know about the mind, rather than subtracting from it. Connectionism explores the hidden machinery underlying the surface appearance of thinking, remembering, and perceiving. If we analyze thought on a large scale, from the top down, pretending that the hidden machinery is of no importance, then we are likely to mistake thought's essential nature. A theory of reasoning that takes reason at its face value might assume that when people think, they arrive at a conclusion serially, by means of step-by-step deduction, from a set of premises. If the brain is regarded as an inscrutable black box, or a device so powerful it can implement any kind of thinking whatever, then we are free to theorize (incorrectly) that someone who decides, for instance, not to ride the New York subway at three o'clock in the morning, did so by silently rehearsing the following chain of inferences:

1. All trains are dangerous at night.
2. It's dark outside.
3. Therefore, it's better to take a taxi.

At this level of description, which is brain-indifferent, it is easy to fall into the trap of believing that commonsense thinking is inherently logical. The standard digital computer, being essentially a logic machine, helped to perpetuate this myth. Recently, however, some compelling research in cognitive psychology has shown that we are logical only in a superficial sense; at a deeper level we are systematically illogical and biased. Our everyday reasoning is not governed primarily by the rules of logic or probability calculus, but depends to a surprisingly large extent on what we know, on the way our knowledge is organized in memory, and on how such knowledge is evoked. Highly intelligent people, asked to solve a simple problem calling for the use of elementary logic, are likely to behave like dunderheads unless the problem is couched in such a way as to trigger networks of knowledge that are organized in logical fashion. Content is of critical importance in deciding whether we think rationally or not, whereas in logic exactly the reverse is true: content is supremely unimportant, and form is everything.

It would be nice for scientists if common sense were based on logic, because logic is a system of knowledge that is thoroughly explored and understood. As it is, common sense remains something of a dark continent, mysterious and uncharted. Building a machine that has common sense, once thought to be a straightforward undertaking, turns out to be fraught with unsuspected difficulties, and is not one of the great success stories of the sciences of the artificial.

Among the main ingredients of common sense are not only the possession of vast amounts of varied knowledge about the world, but also the ability to mobilize, quickly and easily, parts of that knowledge that are relevant to the problem at hand. A serial computer can store tremendous quantities of data, but trouble begins when scientists try to make what the machine "knows" play an active, integral part in interpreting new and unforeseen information.

Connectionism looks beneath the surface of common sense, to the hidden machinery. Some, though not all, connectionists commit themselves to a theory of the nature of the hardware of the human computer. They propose that the architecture of the brain, with its Milky Way–like galaxy of units and its spectacular web of connections, naturally, as a result of its basic design, mobilizes the knowledge needed for commonsense thinking; the knowledge determines directly and actively how the processing units interact. Knowledge *is* process, memory *is* reason—a startling departure from the standard serial computer, where data sits inertly in a memory cell, waiting to be looked at by a central processing device.

Connectionist models are not exactly like the brain; they are cartoon versions of it, simplifying the complexities, exaggerating certain features and ignoring others, even building in devices, like the back-propagation of errors, which do not seem to exist in the brain at all. But the models do behave in lifelike ways. In general, they are bad where we are bad and good where we are good. They mimic some of the mind's actual strengths and weaknesses. A connectionist model is not inherently logical, but rather statistical, synthesizing swarms of ideas, weighing a myriad of choices all at once, "settling into" the solution to a problem rather than deducing the answer by means of explicit rules of inference; nevertheless, it may seem to be making logical deductions if we consider only the final outcome of the settling process and ignore the process itself; the same is true of human beings.

Taking the brain seriously means recognizing that there are limits to what the mind can do, but the limits are radically different from those suggested by the metaphor of the serial computer. Under the influence of this metaphor, whether they realized it or not, psychologists often took a cramped and niggardly view of the mind by portraying it as a system in which a central device with a limited capacity processes information a few digits of code at a time, searching a separate, passive memory, only a small fraction of which is active at any given moment. Sometimes, it was suggested that consciousness is a central processing device of this sort, a narrow channel through which all thoughts must pass. In an eloquent manifesto, the psychologist Ulric Neisser has shown how prevalent and at the same time how terribly wide of the mark such a notion is.

Throwing out the metaphor of the serial computer and replacing it with the metaphor of a brain which is not a logic machine but a knowledge medium, in which immense amounts of knowledge are active simultaneously and so much happens in so short a time we are not aware of how it happens, leads to a considerably more expansive and generous view of the mind. Complex forms of thought go on below the level of awareness, so that conscious deliberation may be only a tiny part of intelligence, and perhaps the least interesting part; the tip of a huge iceberg whose existence we overlook because we have almost no insight into the hidden machinery of thought that connectionism posits. Moreover, the essence of connectionist systems is that they learn, continuously and as a matter of course, rather than being programmed, and so they are always changing, always breaking through the limits previously set.

Nobody, Neisser points out, has succeeded in relating the sheer size of the brain, the number of its neurons and connections, to the limits on its performance. When a complex new mental skill is learned, it is performed almost unconsciously, leaving the conscious mind free to attend to other matters. A good musician can sight-read at the piano while listening to someone reading aloud from a novel, and a seasoned secretary can type a letter at high speed while carrying on a sharp-witted conversation. There seems to be no way to set hard and fast boundaries to the ability of the mind to do more than one thing at a time and to pursue multiple goals, because it never stays still long enough for anyone to define the limits. "The question of capacity looks very different if we consider it from the perspective of biology rather than of engineering; if we regard the mind as something living and growing (which it is) rather than a machine (which it is not)," Neisser believes. A mind is more like a seed than like a mechanical device, bursting into flower if its potentialities are realized in the right environment.

Limits on cognition, from the connectionist standpoint, are more likely to affect precision than capacity. The serial computer is most at home in a world very unlike our own, a world of well-defined puzzles having clear solutions, exhaustive descriptions, lists, explicit rules, literal meanings, perfect information. The world in which the brain evolved is a great deal more untidy and less circumscribed, full of ambiguity, deceit, problems that sprawl in ungainly fashion and have no firm boundaries, words with multiple meanings, faces that send enigmatic messages, information that is incomplete or contradictory, answers that breed endless families of further questions.

In that sort of world, exactness and fixed rules are poor strategies for survival. The brain evolved in such a way that it thrives on imperfect information, generalizing, filling in the missing parts from its large reserves of worldly knowledge, making plausible guesses, "recognizing" answers to problems rather than deducing them from premises, being satisfied with fast, approximate solutions. We use clues to construct plausible stories.

Logic works only if information is complete, and for a real brain in a real world, it is seldom or never complete. We pay a price for acting on limited information, however. We extend and amplify impoverished data on the basis of what we know about how the world typically behaves, and the result is that prejudice becomes a natural part of "rational" thought. Avoiding the risk of prejudice involves the greater risk of being innocent about the world. Worldly innocence is not a hallmark of our species.

Connectionist models are not magic, nor do they even come close to duplicating human intelligence. They are least impressive in what they have to say about the deliberative, serial type of thinking that is an important part of intelligence, even though some psychologists believe it amounts to only about three percent of our mental life. But the models do suggest that no theory of the mind can afford to ignore the fact that we are creatures who evolved in a real world, so that the design of our brains, and therefore the architecture of our intelligence, is not arbitrary, but is dictated at least in part by our need to make sense of a particular world, and to be engaged with it.

Certainly one key to understanding the weaknesses and strengths of natural intelligence is to consider what sort of world produced the brain. Building machines that can do justice to the complexity of the human surroundings is one of the most formidable challenges facing scientists who try to model the mind. It has proved enormously difficult to scale up a machine that inhabits a sparse, cramped, impoverished environment into one that can make sense of a larger, richer, more untidy world like our own. Human beings *never* lived in a world as simple and as artificial as those of today's intelligent machines, which may explain why our "mental computers" do not resemble the standard man-made kind. We can understand the close link that exists between mind and world only if we recognize that what the mind does has something to do with what the brain is; with its biology and the way it evolved.

This book is about the worldly brain and what its worldliness means for the mind. The very fact that an intelligence is embodied forces us to see it not in terms of abstract, Olympian rules of perfect rationality, but instead as a system with a certain design, and with weaknesses and strengths that arise from that design. An ancient philosophical definition of God is "something than which nothing more perfect can be conceived." If we, in our skeptical age, have put nature in the place of God, then we should beware of making the mistake of defining nature in the same way. Nature is imperfect, and we gain insights into her workings by taking her imperfections seriously. Natural reason is both worse and better than the classical tradition would lead us to believe. That is a key to understanding how the mind works, and a reason why no machine has yet come near to modeling human thought.

1: THE WORLDLY BRAIN

When Galileo made a telescope and invited members of the Venetian senate to peer through its lenses at ships sailing far out at sea, the dignitaries who climbed the many steps to the high campanile in St. Mark's Square were vastly impressed. They realized that this "new spyglass," as Galileo called it, was a military asset, an early-warning device that could detect sailships a full two hours before they were visible to the naked eye. In time of war, the artificial vision of the telescope would give navies and armies a useful edge over an enemy equipped with nothing but natural vision. With shrewd generosity, Galileo made a free gift of his instrument to the doge, and the grateful senate showed its appreciation by awarding him tenure at the University of Padua, doubling his miserably small salary.

In Galileo's hands, however, the telescope did more than improve the military security of Venice. It ushered in a new age of intellectual insecurity, in which all the comfortable ideas, developed over many centuries, about the universe and man's privileged place in it were suddenly out of date. For years, Galileo had accepted as correct the theory of Copernicus, that the earth revolves around the sun, but he regarded it as too abstruse, too abstract, for minds accustomed to the established system of Ptolemaic astronomy. People would not accept something that might be a mathematical trick. They needed a shock, an intellectual shakeup if they were to come round to a totally different way of thinking. What Galileo saw through his spyglass when he aimed it at the heavens provided just such a jolt. As he looked at the sky, an immense number of new stars swam into his view, overthrowing the prevailing view of mankind as uniquely situated in the cosmos. The stars newly visible were incontrovertible evidence that the earth floated on a limitless ocean of space, and if there were no boundaries to space, it could have no defined core, in which case human beings could no longer be sure they were the center of the universe, with the special status that implied. Galileo's artificial eye detected four planets, never seen before in the whole history of the world, revolving around Jupiter, suggesting a similar motion around the sun for the very globe on which Galileo stood. As for the supposed perfection, the divine, unspoilable sheen of the celestial bodies, thought to be utterly different from the domain of earth, that notion, too, had to go overboard. In closeup, the sun had spots on it and the moon's surface, instead of being smooth, like an apple, was pitted with hollows and jagged with hills; its rough skin, unsightly as teenage acne, showed that it was made of the same imperfect stuff as our own world. Previously, the faint smudges on the moon visible to the naked eye had been thought to represent the stains of Adam's sins.

Galileo did not invent the telescope, nor was he the first to turn it on the open sky, but he presented his discoveries so vividly, with such literary flair and infectious excitement, that people could not help but take notice. At first, philosophers were more scandalized than theologians. Some simply refused to put their eye to the fearful instrument. Others dismissed it as a deceiver, a producer of optical illusions. Martin Horky, a rival astronomer, ostensibly scorned the discovery of new stars as a hallucination, but secretly took wax impressions of the lenses of Galileo's spyglass in order to pirate his own version. As for reports of sunspots, the philosophers took refuge in the explanation that Galileo had been misled by the sight of planets passing in front of the sun and blocking his view.

What particularly vexed Galileo's critics was that he had overthrown the order and beauty of the universe, established by astronomers and thinkers over thousands of years, with a machine, a mere toy, no more than a tube and a couple of pieces of glass. Such a great tradition had been upset by an almost laughably simple device. Spectacle-makers were selling such gadgets to shoppers as playthings in the streets of Venice and other cities, and here was Galileo using one to bring down a whole edifice of thought, to shatter ancient certainties. The toy wreaked metaphysical havoc. It forced the viewer to confront new truths. It suggested that human beings were no longer the point, the meaning of the universe.

There are certain parallels between the story of Galileo's telescope and the arrival of the modern electronic computer some three and a half centuries later. The telescope amplified a part of the human nervous system, enlarging the power of the eye. It gave Galileo artificial vision, making the celestial bodies appear a hundred times larger than when they were seen by the naked eye. At the same time, his artificial-vision machine revealed philosophical truths. It showed that the senses are untrustworthy. They are limited, and their limitations may bamboozle the mind into entertaining false ideas about the world. The telescope suggested that while the naked eye can dupe and deceive, reason, exemplified by the Copernican theory, which was so difficult, so implausible, so foreign to commonsense and ordinary observation that for years leading thinkers of the day had dismissed it as a mathematical caprice, leads the mind to truth. It was the "unnatural" device of the telescope, combined with the artificial system of mathematics, that replaced an attractive fiction with a difficult truth. Western thought itself underwent a crisis, in which it became increasingly clear that our direct experience of the world need not correspond with the knowledge we obtain by computation.

The computer, too, is an amplifier of the nervous system. Where Galileo's spyglass gave him artificial vision, the computer has given us artificial intelligence—of a sort. It enlarges certain of our mental powers. Like the telescope, the computer in its early days was an item in a defense budget, a war machine, part of the US and British military effort. It broke secret codes, calculated artillery firing tables, and computed airplane wing flutter. As time went on, however, the new machines became instruments for imitating, extending, and understanding the human mind.

In the beginning, the computer exaggerated just one aspect of human thought: the power to calculate. At this early stage, engineers were interested in any device that would help them to answer certain practical questions that were solvable, but horrifyingly complicated, requiring vast amounts of calculation of almost inhuman length and tediousness. The mathematics needed to find the stresses on the roof of a railroad station, for example, involved thirty equations in thirty unknowns, and the work took human beings several months to complete. Military problems, such as calculating the angle at which to set a gun so that it would hit a target under particular conditions, occupied teams of workers, mostly young women with college degrees, for several hours. The electronic computer was a heaven-sent amplifier of the weak power of the "naked mind" to undertake such marathon ventures in manipulating numbers.

Paul Ceruzzi has described how the power of mechanical computing machines, precursors of the electronic computer, was measured in terms of how many human brains they could replace, as if they were labor-saving devices, pulling thought along like a locomotive dragging a heavy load of freight cars uphill. Just as the selling price of the first steam engines was based on their horsepower, or how many live horses they could replace, so the early calculators were rated according to their "clerkpower," an index of their speed and efficiency. A radical change took place, however, when the first electronic computers came on the scene. These machines were different creatures; they were able to perform calculations so immense that no conceivable collection of human brains, writing on paper or cranking the handle of a mechanical device, could possibly accomplish them. It is meaningless to equate "five hundred clerkpower" in an electronic computer with five hundred human beings working on a given task, for the same reason that it makes no sense to suppose that a team of five hundred horses could pull a train as efficiently as a five-hundred-horsepower diesel engine. There is no way of coordinating the efforts of each member of such a large team, whether of horses or of human beings, so that they contribute fully to the work of the team as a whole. They would get in each other's way, pull in different directions, cancel out the efforts of the rest of the team. Today, artificial intelligence researchers are discovering that it is not possible to speed up the writing of the huge and incredibly complex software programs needed to make a machine clever, just by increasing the number of writers. The optimum size of a modern software-writing team is only about five people, which means that if the programs are to become even longer and denser, some way must be found to make the machine do its own learning.

The early electronic computers amplified the power of calculation to such an extent that the correspondence with human thought, with clerkpower, broke down. Computers were so superior to the brain in this one respect that nobody could seriously claim that they imitated human thinking or could unravel any deep mysteries of the mind. Soon after the end of World War II, however, two American scientists, Herbert Simon and Alan Newell, who have been described jointly as the "Galileo of artificial intelligence," realized that a computer is not just a superfast calculator, but a processor of symbols of all kinds. This was not a brand-new idea. In the 1930s, the young English logician Alan Turing, sprawled on his back in a grassy meadow at Granchester, near Cambridge, in a sort of daydream, imagined a machine that would operate on symbols, using a small number of simple logical rules that were so general they would apply to symbol sequences of whatever sort: not only numbers, but also propositions or statements such as "Socrates is mortal." Because symbolic logic is the epitome of a general-purpose reasoning system, it was chosen as the language for this fantasy machine, which was really the first computer. Symbolic logic had been invented in the nineteenth century through a marriage of logic and algebra, in such a way that symbols that traditionally used to stand for numbers were made to encode ideas, and these could be manipulated as if they were numbers. The rules could be applied by a complete simpleton, or by a machine, since they were indifferent to what the symbols mean. Such a machine—the one Turing envisaged while lying prone in his meadow—though simple, would be universal, able to do the work of any other computer, no matter how complex. In fact, Turing believed that logic is general enough to simulate human thought.

At first, American engineers, intent on bringing clerkpower to bear on their diabolically complicated sets of equations, replaced Turing's logical rules by numerical operators because they were not interested in making general-purpose machines that could juggle ideas. But Herbert Simon and Alan Newell were different; they began to think about the computer along the lines suggested by Turing, as an embodiment of intelligence. Simon had been especially impressed by a computer model of an air defense center created by the Rand Corporation, which generated not numbers, but points on a map representing the various positions of fighter planes. He realized that the new machines were able to manipulate representations of the real world, which is what the brain does. In January 1956, Simon announced to a bemused class of students that he and Newell had spent the Christmas holidays inventing "a thinking machine."

The program for this new machine, Logic Theorist, was not written out of a desire to surpass human computing power, as had been the case with the wartime supercalculators. In this sense, it was a radical departure, and marked the beginning of a new science. Simon and Newell wanted to understand how the human mind works. Logic Theorist, which was able to prove theorems in symbolic logic, and its successor, General Problem Solver, a less austere program that played chess and solved puzzles, were deliberate attempts to discover and describe universal laws of thought, laws that supposedly underlie human intelligence. They used rules of thumb as well as formal principles of logic, and allowed for a certain amount of muddling through. Logic Theorist could reason backward, just as a person often starts with a glimmering of the answer to a problem and then considers what needs to be true if that answer is the correct one.

A paradox lurked in the modest success of these first "thinking" machines, however. By amplifying what seemed to be the quintessence of human intelligence, the ability to manipulate symbols by means of rules, finding a way through the maze of possible pathways toward the answer to a problem, Newell and Simon's programs actually showed that there is no such thing as the quintessence of human intelligence, and that if there were, logic would not be a leading contender for the title. The early artificial-intelligence programs did not discover what natural intelligence is fundamentally like, so much as demonstrate what it is unlike, which is their peculiar service to the understanding of the mind.

Simon and Newell did not aim to invent a thinking machine that would be superrational to an extent impossible for humans. Simon, in particular, was deeply interested in how people actually solve problems. His doctoral thesis at the University of Chicago in 1943 was based on an investigation into the way bureaucrats in Milwaukee's city government made decisions. Extending those studies to people working in firms and private industry, Simon developed his theory that people are rational only within certain limits, which won him the Nobel Prize for economics in 1978. When writing the programs for General Problem Solver, he and Newell asked people to think aloud while they worked on various puzzles and games, so as to be able to capture their actual thought processes in the machine.

Simon maintained that a core criterion of intelligence, whether in a human or in a machine, is the ability to reduce the complexity of the choices confronting the mind when it is considering a problem. It is useless to search all possible paths toward a solution, wasting time in blind alleys and fruitless choices. His heuristics, or rules of thumb, were intended to find shortcuts through the forest of branching ways, and such shortcuts were universal, necessary devices, which could not be dispensed with by building larger computers or breeding smarter people, because complexity is deep in the nature of things. Yet the Simon and Newell programs, for all their muddling through, did rely on massive search of possibilities by trial and error, because the computer's great asset is that it can run through lists of items at a fantastic speed. The project also reflected a belief that simple logic and a limited number of universal principles can be used to solve a wide variety of problems.

There was no doctrinaire assertion here that formal logic is the essence of thinking. Traditional artificial-intelligence research contains a fairly small number of people who believe the fabric of thought is held together by threads of logic, and a fairly large number of people who do not. An ideal reasoner, according to the first view, thinks by deducing new, valid conclusions from previous conclusions, according to the rules of logic. Newell and Simon were in the second, majority camp. Thinking, for them, was not especially concerned with "truth," or with logical deduction, but rather with goals and subgoals in solving problems. The interesting relationships were not between premises and conclusions, but between goals. An intelligent system of this sort behaves rationally, since it is deciding on appropriate goals, but the system is not an ideal reasoner, in the sense of deducing new beliefs from old ones.

Certainly Newell and Simon did not believe in an "intelligence principle," a single idea that accounts for thinking in all its manifestations. But they did insist that there is no intelligence without symbols. In their view, any physical symbol system that is large enough can be organized in such a way as to become as intelligent as a human being. All rival theories of what cognition is, from the Gestalt school of psychology to behaviorism, are so vague that they, too, can be interpreted in terms of symbol systems. To this Newell and Simon added the "law of heuristic search," which states that a symbol system solves problems by generating possible answers, one after the other, and then searching until it finds the correct answer, making the search as brief as possible by looking at the most likely answers first.

Newell and Simon's doctrine was profoundly influential. It pervaded the thinking of computer scientists for nearly twenty years. Since the doctrine applied to human and machine intelligence alike, the mind itself was regarded as a physical symbol system that made sense of its world by searching a "problem space" of possible answers to whatever puzzle the world may present. The real begetters of the doctrine were the three chief founders of modern mathematical logic, Gottlob Frege, Bertrand Russell, and Alfred North Whitehead, who made it possible to think about symbolic reasoning as a game played with meaningless tokens according to rules that are not "about" anything but the formal properties of the system itself. A machine can play the game, and not just one particular kind of machine. It does not matter, from this point of view, that the basic design of a computer is utterly different from the basic design of a brain. They both manipulate symbols, so that the machine can be programmed to be a general intelligence, like our own. Many researchers saw no limits to this generality. If they were dealing with universal principles like heuristic search and serial symbol systems, then there was no reason, so they supposed, why systems that could solve theorems in mathematical logic and play board games should not go on to match and even surpass the human mind in generality, as well as in powers of intuition, imagination, and insight.

These high hopes were not borne out. General Problem Solver turned out to be quite nongeneral in the range of its intelligence, and it was extraordinarily difficult to find universal principles of thought that would broaden the system's scope.

True, it found solutions to a variety of puzzles, but it behaved like a perpetual beginner, coming fresh and innocent to each task, never acquiring the human expert's ability to simply recognize the answer to a problem. Patrick Winston, head of the Artificial Intelligence Laboratory at MIT, refers to the ten years or so which followed Newell and Simon's groundbreaking work as the "Dark Period," a barren decade when little of interest happened, largely because the effervescent optimism of the early days had seduced researchers into supposing it was simple to make an intelligent machine. "Everyone searched for a kind of philosopher's stone, a mechanism that when placed in a computer would require only data to become truly intelligent," Winston has said. The philosopher's stone did not exist. The Dark Period was followed by a renaissance, but many of the intelligent machines built during the renaissance were not general at all; they were narrowly specialized in a single domain of knowledge. They were not attempts to test theories about natural intelligence or discover universal principles of thought, but were aimed at the marketplace.

Today, David Waltz, professor of computer science at Brandeis University, believes the early "thinking" machines were based on false ideas about the nature of intelligence itself. "Building intelligent machines has turned out to be a very hard problem," Waltz says. "Traditional artificial intelligence has not shown that it can model thought very well. In fact, I think its methods are woefully inadequate for the task. It is doomed, to the extent that it presents itself only as the study of heuristic search and of problem spaces. That is absolutely not going to work for modeling intelligence, no matter what kind of computers you have. Intelligence is more than computation in the sense of taking all the data and combining it together or altering it, or crunching on it. That is what many researchers have assumed intelligence is. I assumed it myself for a long time."

Newell and Simon were right to emphasize the limitations of mere deductive reasoning. General Problem Solver made heavy weather of fairly simple logic, limping along like an amateur. The two scientists did, however, regard intelligence as the ability to solve problems in a serial fashion, using heuristics as a guide to finding the correct answer in a haystack of possible answers. Their mistake was to suppose that, at bottom, all problems are roughly alike, so that the same set of techniques can be used to solve them, provided information is available in a certain form. Pure generality, which is the essence of symbolic logic, and the secret of its power, became a dead end in the enterprise of modeling and understanding human thought.

Another questionable assumption arose out of the fact that Newell and Simon were intent on creating systems that were not just calculators, but were able to "think" about the puzzles they were set. They regarded the likenesses between human thinking and the way their programs solved problems as being far more interesting and significant than the *differences* between the computer as logic engine, the actual hardware on which General Problem Solver's software was run, and the human brain.

This made it possible to study intelligence on its own, without considering the extent to which it is the result of a real brain evolving in a real world. The brain and the world could be ignored, because the symbol-system hypothesis was a theory for all seasons, a universal doctrine making no distinction between the natural and the artificial. It mattered not at all whether the machine that manipulates symbols is a computer or a cortex. Little heed was paid to the fact that the human mind has certain peculiar strengths and weaknesses, and that these are a product of the brain's history, or evolution. Intelligent machines, Logic Theorist and its descendants, tended to amplify the *weaknesses* of natural intelligence and to neglect its assets. They did so because the sort of things the mind does well, without thinking consciously about how to proceed—understanding a sentence even when it is spoken in a thick foreign accent, recognizing the face of a friend, being able to conjure up an image of a cat just by hearing a faint meow—are very difficult to program on a serial computer. By contrast, the sort of things the mind does unreliably or badly, such as dividing 47,623 by 41, pursuing a logical chain of reasoning, thinking hard every step of the way, are easy to program. It is reasonable to suppose that the sort of cognition at which the brain is good had a high priority in evolution, and the sort at which it is bad had a low priority, so that the strengths and weaknesses are related to the basic design of the brain.

Some computer scientists are now beginning to look at the history of the brain as a guide to making machines that do not simply exaggerate those special types of thinking that are difficult for human beings. Rodney Brooks, a robotics researcher at MIT, bases a theory of intelligence on how evolution has "spent its time" over the last 4.6 billion years. Brooks points out that single-cell forms of life arose out of the primordial soup about 3.5 billion years ago, after which a billion years went by until the appearance of photosynthetic plants. Roughly 550 million years ago the first fish arrived, then, at intervals of tens of millions of years, the insects, the reptiles, the dinosaurs, and the mammals. Man came on the scene in his present form 2.5 million years ago, invented agriculture 19,000 years ago, writing in about 3000 BC, and expert knowledge only over the last few hundred years.

What this means, Brooks and others believe, is that it is hopeless to try to build a machine that has general intelligence by starting at the wrong end of evolution, with types of thinking that emerged right at the end point of human development. That leads to delusion, because such a machine may give the appearance of thinking with some of the sophistication and scope of the mind, but it is apt to break down because its knowledge of the real world is actually painfully restricted and shallow. Better to emulate evolution and start with the kind of intelligence needed simply to get by in a real world, to concentrate on the basic skills of seeing and hearing, moving around, understanding space and time, dealing with the noisy information that comes into the brain by way of the senses. If this reading of history is correct, what seems the easiest part of cognition, negotiating our actual environment, is relatively hard to implement in a brain or a machine, whereas what seems difficult, our ability to reason logically and solve abstract problems, is much easier to implement. What is more, the way in which the brain manages the hard, "worldly" parts of intelligence places interesting constraints on the manner in which the higher modes of reasoning operate. The mistake made by the makers of standard thinking machines, in this view, was to model a mind that was disembodied, deprived of the sort of knowledge that comes from perception and action, and therefore a complete stranger to the everyday world.

Some of the thinking strategies devised by Simon and Newell's programs, such as reasoning backward, using rules of thumb, and the rest, were intended to deal with a world that is messy, using mental resources that are limited, and in that sense they were realistic. Yet to the great disappointment of researchers, the attempt to extend these techniques to create machines with general intelligence that could cope with the real world met with setback after setback. A computer program that could play a decent game of chess could not perform the simple perceptual act of picking out chess pieces from a box and arranging them on the board so as to start a game, and a program that diagnosed exotic diseases in live patients, had not the slightest inkling of what a human being was.

Galileo's telescope, by providing artificial vision, showed how easy it is to be deceived by looking at the world with the unaided eye. The computer, the basis of artificial intelligence, has unmasked as comfortable delusions our longstanding ideas about the nature of human reason. In part these delusions arose, and lasted so long, because the worldly aspects of intelligence, the ones that evolution spent so much time on, are buried so deep, are so much a part of our everyday being, we do not realize they exist. That is why the people who were interviewed by Newell and Simon, and who thought aloud about the ways in which they solved problems, cannot be regarded as reliable witnesses because our access to the processes of thinking, as opposed to its products, is severely limited. Often a verbal "explanation" of how we think is nothing but a plausible story. That is an important *scientific* discovery. David Waltz thinks that the reason artificial intelligence embraced the doctrines of the physical symbol system and heuristic search for so many years is that it took these plausible stories too seriously, and decided that the main human strategy for solving problems is trial and error, a behaviorist approach to learning. Programs were written using the technique of trial and error, going step by step, manipulating symbols with rules, backtracking if a particular series of steps turned out to be fruitless. But that may not be the way the mind really works, especially when it is displaying common sense, a shorthand term for the vast quantity of knowledge and expertise that we absorb effortlessly and push beneath the surface of awareness. In fact, in the past decade a radical theoretical shift has taken place in artificial intelligence, that questions whether the "strength" of the human mind, its fundamental worldliness, is based on symbol systems. "It is no accident that the creatures that preceded the human race for the past billion years have had no symbol processing; they have not needed it," Hans Berliner of Carnegie-Mellon University has said. "That humans were able to build on top of simpler functions a formidable hypothesizing and reasoning facility is very impressive, and certainly appears necessary to achieve the highest levels of the intellect. But, as the workers in robotics have now been made thoroughly aware, it is impossible to produce behavior from sensors by symbolic means alone." The nonsymbolic heresy is the single most powerful new idea that has appeared in artificial intelligence since the 1950s, and it is driving the science of thinking machines in directions barely imagined only a few years ago.

One result of these upheavals has been to shatter established ideas about the nature of human intelligence. A venerable tradition, going back to Plato, regarded knowledge of abstract rules, and the ability to apply the same rules to many different kinds of information, as the hallmark of intelligence, enabling the mind to cope with novelty and change. Plato had unlimited faith in the power of the principles of mathematics to tame a disorderly world. In *The Republic*, he made clear his belief that arithmetical calculation, involving the use of "pure intelligence," has a remarkable effect in leading the mind toward truth. If a person has a natural talent for calculation, he or she is "generally quick at every other kind of knowledge, and even the dull, if they have had an arithmetical training, although they may derive no other advantage from it, always become much quicker than they would otherwise have been."

It is hardly an exaggeration to say that the story of the thinking machine, and of cognitive psychology over the past decade, is the story of a retreat from this Platonic creed of pure intelligence as the essence of human rationality, and of formal rules as the road to general understanding. The mind has been radically de-Platonized. The emphasis has shifted away from rule-using, logical ways of thinking and toward the importance of worldly knowledge. Early on, programmers had assumed that if a machine needed to be fed large quantities of specific knowledge, it could not be very intelligent. Carried to extremes, this would amount to telling the computer the answer to a question ahead of time, which seemed somehow dishonest, like a student cribbing in an exam, and a mark of a low IQ. Today, that notion has been turned upside down. It is an axiom of the trade that a machine cannot be intelligent unless it knows a great deal. A conventional computer program that learns must begin by being provided with many more facts than it will ever acquire.

This is much more than just a change of emphasis. Putting knowledge at the top of the agenda implies a different theory of the mind. If there is no knowledge-independent theory of human rationality, if logic is, as some of today's computer scientists believe, simply a result of the way knowledge about the world is organized in memory, then the brain must be built on principles very different from those of a digital computer.

That may sound odd, since standard digital computers are famous for their very fast and reliable memories. But human memory, which is a key to the marvelous generality of our intelligence that Newell and Simon's programs could not hope to match, has properties that are quite unlike those of a computer memory. It is much less reliable than a computer, but it is vast, and associative by its very nature. Human memory cannot help but connect one thing it knows with another thing it knows. It puts the world together in such a way that, given just a small fragment of information, it can amplify that fragment instantly, into a sizable parcel of knowledge, a process that often masquerades as logical reasoning. Memories of this kind do not seem to run "naturally" on serial digital computers, but they can be imitated on special kinds of hardware that have certain resemblances to the hardware of the brain. They seem to arise from the very way in which the brain is designed.

Today scientists are talking, half-playfully, about the "brain metaphor of mind." By that they mean that the brain's design, the way it is put together, its odd mixture of weaknesses and strengths, dictated by the need to get around and get by in the real world in which it evolved, is a way of gaining insight into the nature of human rationality. In some respects, the mind is a bundle of paradoxes. It has insight, but at the cost of more-or-less frequent errors. It harnesses the "vice" of prejudice in order to make new discoveries about the world. The mind is so good at making sense of poor-quality information that it often neglects information that is of superior quality, and its capacity to absorb surprises, to tame the unruliness of chance, makes human intelligence stable, but impairs its ability to learn from experience. And whereas it might be thought that having a perfectly open mind is an asset, a wholly desirable and attainable goal, it turns out that such a mind does not exist, and if it did, it would be a liability, unable to understand the world and therefore doomed to extinction. A completely open mind would be unintelligent.

A paradox of the worldly brain is that it needs to be as bad as it sometimes is in order to be as good as it usually is. This is not perversity on the part of nature, but the inevitable result of the compromises which are forced upon an intelligence that must make sense of imperfect information with limited resources. Evolution solved this dilemma by fashioning a brain that resolves the ambiguities and contradictions with which it is constantly faced, not by applying the rules of logic, or a small set of all-purpose principles, but in large part by the way knowledge is organized in memory.

Building a worldly machine is an immensely difficult undertaking, because it involves understanding the worldly brain. If the brain were a logic engine, or a simple information processor, the task would be a great deal easier. That is because logic and information are not at all mysterious, but brightly lit and well-paved landscapes where it is safe to walk and all the streets have names. Deductive logic is well understood, and the fact that it is understood is one of the intellectual triumphs of the twentieth century. As for information, it became a full-blown science soon after World War II, emerging almost complete, an adult without an adolescence. But knowledge is another matter altogether. Today, a science of knowledge barely exists. There are profound and important differences between information and knowledge, but the nature of those differences is still obscure. The relation between knowledge and experience is just beginning to be explored.

Out of the present turmoil in artificial intelligence—and consequently, in psychology—such a science may appear. It will require an approach that is radically different from much of the Western philosophical tradition, which emphasizes logic and treats the mind as a universal instrument that can be understood without taking into account the history of the brain. It will mean breaking down some of the bogus distinctions between the humbler kinds of knowing, such as seeing, hearing, and remembering, which we share with other animals, and the loftier sort, like reasoning and solving problems. Such mundane concerns go against the grain of centuries of theorizing about the nature of knowledge. As Stuart and Hubert Dreyfus have pointed out, we are in the thick of a revolution, a revolution of worldliness and the decline of the physical symbol–system hypothesis. "It was not just Descartes and his descendants who stood behind symbolic information processing, but all of Western philosophy," the Dreyfus brothers write. "Traditional philosophy is defined from the start by its focusing on facts in the world while 'passing over' the world as such. This means that philosophy has from the start systematically ignored or distorted the everyday context of human activity." It is thanks to the imperatives of artificial intelligence, where brains must be built, not simply speculated upon, that this bias is just beginning to be corrected.

2: ROTTEN
WITH
PSYCHOLOGY

The computer is the only form of intelligence in the world to be born logical. If we talk in metaphor about "generations" of computers, as if they were a living species, *Machina sapiens*, then we must recognize that the species has evolved in a curious way. In some respects it is the story of human intelligence in reverse. The computer was the child of modern logic, an offspring of the marriage that took place between logic and algebra in the nineteenth century. It was one of the very few instances of a useful application of modern logic to the real world. In general, modern logic, like modern art, is not "about" anything but itself. A painting ceased to portray nature and life, and became part of a theory of painting. In much the same way, logic turned inward and explored its own foundations. Ironically, it was out of this very inward turning that the new infor-

mation machines sprang, making a huge impact on everyday
life.

The computer was born in a Cambridgeshire meadow, in the
mind of Alan Turing, as a way of proving a theorem that dealt
with the very nature of logic: whether there are logical problems
that cannot be solved in a finite number of steps. It was the
culmination of the "big bang" of modern logic, the era of spectacular discoveries about what logic can do and what it cannot
do. As soon as the big bang was over, scientists started building
the machine that had existed only in Turing's imagination.

The brain evolved in a very different way. Its physical con-
struction is such that its logical properties are irrelevant to understanding what sort of instrument the brain actually is, and
what it can tell us about the mind. If we want to get to know the
mind, logic is the wrong place to start. There is no innate device
in the head for doing logic, although there may be one for doing
syntax, and for understanding the sounds of speech. This puts
language and logic in very different evolutionary categories. "In
philosophy, there is a concept we call 'natural kinds,' " says
University of Maryland philosopher Christopher Cherniak.
"Certain things fall together because of the way the world is
made; fish are a natural kind, but whales are not. So the question is, is logic a natural kind of the mind? Some psychologists
act as if it were, as if there is an engine in the brain that does the
logic process. I do not think logic is a natural kind. I think we
are about as wrong to look for such an engine as a Martian
would be if he visited Earth and decided it's the shine on the
bumpers that makes an automobile go."

It is interesting that psychology and artificial intelligence
should be deemphasizing logic as the key to human intelligence
at this late date in the twentieth century. Modern logic was
born, more than a century ago, out of something like a contempt
for the idea that the laws of truth are also the laws of the natural
workings of human reason. Almost the first move the new logic
made was to break off relations with psychology. In 1879, a slim
and almost unreadable book was published in Germany which
presented the first complete system of formal logic, ending the

two-thousand-year tradition founded by Aristotle. The name of the book was *Begriffsschrift,* usually translated in English as *A Notation for Concepts,* and the author was Gottlob Frege. A peppery man with a sarcastic edge to his tongue and a touch of fanaticism in his makeup, living a quiet life as a teacher of mathematics at the University of Jena, Frege was adamant in his insistence that logic has nothing interesting to tell us about how we think. Logic is not a "peep-show," providing insights into the workings of the mind. Frege saw psychology as a harmful virus which had somehow infected the body of logic and must be driven out, ruthlessly. In fact, "infected" may be putting it too mildly. The German word Frege used, *verseucht,* has been translated as meaning that the logic of his day was actually "rotten," or diseased, due to its association with the "mental."

Existing books on logic, Frege complained, were "bloated with unhealthy psychological fat." Psychology may appear to make the science of logic more profound, but in reality it only falsifies it. The notion that logic is naturalistic, that it is biologically given, was anathema to Frege. If we try to maintain that logic is an inborn engine of the mind, he argued, then the laws of logic must evolve as the human species evolves, according to the theory, then newly fashionable, of Charles Darwin. If logic is just the way we make sense of the world in order to survive, it might just as well be studied by anthropologists observing a primitive tribe, or by a surgeon poking at a piece of cortex, as by a mathematician, which Frege was. He refused most adamantly to consider that the history of the brain gives us any insight at all into the nature of logic. It was Frege's belief that natural reason is a mixture of the logical and psychological that led him to reject the idea that anyone would ever succeed in building a "thinking machine." An attempt to mimic formal deduction had already been made by an older contemporary of Frege's, the British economist and logician Stanley Jevons, who invented and showed to the Royal Society in 1870 a "logical piano," which drew all possible inferences from a set of premises mechanically.

A basic, unshakable principle for Frege was that logic is concerned with truth, and the laws of truth do not evolve, but stay the same forever, no matter how the mind may change under the impact of biological forces or new environments. He was as concerned with truth as some present-day artificial-intelligence researchers are unconcerned with it as an element of natural reasoning. The word *true*, Frege insisted, is the goal of logic, in the sense that *good* is the goal of ethics and *beautiful* of aesthetics. True thoughts are not invented by the mind, but discovered. They are nobody's personal property. Like a desolate, uninhabited island in the Arctic Ocean which is there whether anyone visits it or not, a truth exists whether anyone thinks it or not. It is good for all times and all places.

What all this comes down to, Frege decided, is that logic is unnatural, and we ought to accept it as such wholeheartedly, without any qualms or reservations. As a formal system like logic advances, as it ripens and deepens, it becomes less and less natural, and its distance from naturalness is almost a mark of the progress it has made since the early stages of its development. "There is no reproach the logician need fear less than the reproach that his way of formulating things is unnatural," Frege said. "If we were to heed those who object that logic is unnatural, we would run the risk of becoming embroiled in interminable disputes about what is natural, disputes which are quite incapable of being resolved within the province of logic."

Rejecting naturalism, Frege made logic artificial, and it remains artificial through and through to this day. This meant making a clean break, right from the start, with the naturalness of ordinary language. Frege began with the aim of simply putting mathematics on a firmer foundation, but the logical imperfections of ordinary language stood in his way. He invented an artificial language of his own, his "concept notation," a device designed to free the mind from the dominion of words and bring it to a perspective so new and fresh, that "we shall have, so to speak, our very noses rubbed into the false analogies in language."

Classical logic, which was founded by Aristotle in the fourth century BC, was strongly influenced by the grammar of ordinary language, even though Aristotle did introduce certain "unnatu-ral" symbols, using letters which did not exist in the languages of his day. Aristotle has been called the philosopher of common sense, the worldly philosopher, in part because his syllogisms show us how to use language in the most rational way. He took it for granted that all basic truths can be expressed in the form of a sentence, a subject followed by a predicate. The predicate is a way of describing what the subject is, or why it is. "Aristote-lian logic," Henry Veatch has said, "is simply a device for knowing what things are and why they are." Frege himself, try-ing to prove the laws of arithmetic by means of logic, began by using ordinary German words, but he quickly realized that they were unreliable. Beyond a certain level of complexity, the Ger-man language let him down. In particular, Frege decided to have no truck with the terms *subject* and *predicate*, because they make it more difficult to recognize the same truth as the same, and also conceal differences that are hard to detect. A logician, he said, must be as concerned with the purity of a thought, with its truth as opposed to the spurious overlay of psychology, as a chemist is concerned with the purity of the substances he ana-lyzes. So Frege invented a symbolism of his own, a code for reasoning that would make his chains of deductions firm and tight.

This new notation, described as "a formula language of pure thought modelled upon the formula language of arithmetic," was a sort of amplifier. It exaggerated certain features of lan-guage, the logical parts, and eliminated others. Frege's symbol-ism was like the telescope of Galileo, showing up the deceptiveness of our natural faculties. In fact, Frege compared it to a microscope, a specialized instrument that is more restricted than the eye in some respects but vastly more powerful in others. Logic is a microscope, he said, an artificial device that is useless for guiding us around the real world, because it is less adaptable and versatile than the naked human eye; but in the limited world it is designed to study, logic is much more accu-rate.

Frege's notation was forbiddingly complex, almost to the

point of unintelligibility, even for experts. The brand-new microscope of modern logic was available, but few people could see anything through its lenses. It had no Galileo to trumpet its virtues and proclaim its revolutionary import in vivid, accessible form until several years later, when a young logician at Cambridge, England, named Bertrand Russell, gave full and generous credit to Frege for making an original contribution to a new science.

Russell read the *Begriffsschrift* as an undergraduate, but for years he could not make out what the author was saying. Independently, he was advancing his own ideas along similar lines, and was just as adamant as Frege that logic must be ruthlessly uncoupled from psychology and from natural language if it was to make any headway. In what was to become the bible of the new logic, *Principia Mathematica*, Russell and his collaborator, Alfred North Whitehead, deliberately used a notation that was artificial, both in its extreme simplicity and also in its strangeness. They borrowed a system of symbols invented by the Italian mathematician Giuseppe Peano.

The authors of the *Principia* realized—and it was an important discovery—that underneath the seeming simplicity of ordinary language there lies the immense wealth of our implicit knowledge about the world in which we live. The words themselves are just the tip of an immense iceberg: the huge body of what we know, often without being aware that we know it, which the words evoke. There is a vast disproportion between the bare sentences on a page and the almost unlimited complexity and bulk of our worldly knowledge. Our knowledge of whales, for example, is endless, and ranges from molecular biology to *Moby Dick*. A scholar could write hundreds of books about whales and still not exhaust all the information needed to understand the creatures completely, and all this knowledge, encoded in millions of words, could in principle be evoked by the terse sentence "A whale is big." That puts a logician in a pickle, because if he tried to analyze in ordinary language the sentence "One is a number," seemingly so innocent and trivial, he would drown in an avalanche of words.

The notation devised for the *Principia* was as far removed from conventional scripts as the authors could make it. This had the added virtue of making even familiar ideas look strange when encoded in the new symbolism, forcing readers to look at those ideas askance, as if they had never seen them before. An English sentence that seems so manifestly and self-evidently true that we would never dream of doubting it, may turn out to be false when scrutinized under the microscope of an exotic artificial code. As a result, the *Principia* is not light reading, by any means. Russell once said he knew only six people who had read the book all the way through, and of those three were Poles later shot by the Nazis, and the other three were Texans. Yet the complexity of the work rests on a carefully contrived simplicity.

Russell made no apologies for the unworldliness of modern logic. In fact, he rejoiced in it, at least in his early days. Of his state of mind when he was writing the *Principia*, he said: "I disliked the real world." Much of the appeal of logic, he thought, is exactly that it is foreign to the natural universe of human experience. It exists outside ourselves and in spite of ourselves, free of human nature's many flaws and failings. "What do you particularly like?" Russell was once asked by his brother-in-law, Logan Pearsall Smith. "Mathematics and the sea, and theology and heraldry," Russell replied. "The two former because they are inhuman, the two latter because they are absurd." Logic was most inhuman of all, because it was even more abstract than mathematics.

Later, during the turmoil of the First World War, Russell was to change his mind about the sublime status of reason. The sight of young soldiers embarking in troop trains for France, to be slaughtered in battle on the Somme "because generals are stupid," made his previous views seem to him thin and trivial. All the same, his most important work in logic was carried out in the belief that logic exists in some high, austere empyrean, where human things are left far behind. It was such a strain on him that Russell said his intellect never fully recovered, and he did not attempt work of such great abstraction again.

One crisis in particular during the writing of *Principia*

brought home to Russell the critical difference between logic, which must create its own system of perfect information, and the worldly brain, which can live with the devil of imperfection because it is a knowledge medium. The crisis was the discovery of an inconsistency. The crisis pushed Russell to the brink of a breakdown (he had other, more personal troubles at the time), and sent Frege into a funk from which he never recovered.

Consistency becomes increasingly important as a system of thought becomes increasingly "unworldly." It is paramount in those sciences, like logic and mathematics, that reach a high degree of abstractness. And the converse is also true. The more strict the requirement of consistency, the more limited is a system's ability to express truths about reality. The system of Euclidean geometry, for example, is essentially worldly. It describes physical reality, the actual three-dimensional space of our everyday experience. In the nineteenth century, however, mathematicians began to invent non-Euclidean geometries that violated common sense. They found that they could prove theorems about a possible space in which there are no parallel lines. This was a tremendous intellectual liberation. It meant that logic, which has no intrinsic meaning in terms of how the world behaves or what it contains, could be used to deduce all kinds of exotic new spaces from axioms that were not the same as Euclid's. The fly in the ointment, however, was that since the new geometries were artificial and at odds with experience, the world itself could not be used as a check on the correctness of their theorems. If we assume that the physical world does not contradict itself, correspondence to actual space is a safe guarantee that a given geometry is valid. If there is no such correspondence, the only way of certifying the non-Euclidean geometries is to prove that they are internally consistent. For this reason the question of consistency in deductive logical systems, such as geometry and logic itself, became of overriding concern in the late nineteenth century. Frege wrote in 1884 that until the consistency of axioms was proved, the idea that logic is rigorous "is so much moonshine."

It was shown that non-Euclidean geometries are consistent

only if Euclidean geometry is consistent, which it is if ordinary arithmetic is consistent. But how can we guarantee the consistency of arithmetic? Modern elementary arithmetic is based on the theory of sets. The axioms of set theory, only about six in all, seemed eminently "natural" and straightforward, a case where we might suppose that ordinary intuition is a sure guide to truth. Yet it was exactly here that Russell, as he was developing his ideas for the *Principia,* discovered an inconsistency. Frege had used a commonsense idea about sets, namely that two sets are equivalent if and only if they contain the same objects. From that innocent-looking assumption, Russell found a paradox so simple it could be written down on the back of a postcard, yet so deadly it threatened to kill his own system. He broke the bad news in a letter to Frege, who had just sent to press a book that attempted to stand all of mathematics on the supposedly safe terra firma of the theory of sets. Instead, solid ground started to look like quicksand. Frege replied in a letter that began with the forlorn declaration, "Alas, arithmetic totters." Russell, after many sleepless nights, decided that common sense had led him into this trap, and he resolved the paradox by throwing common sense overboard.

Formal deductive logic, unlike natural reason, cannot tolerate a single contradiction, because it has chosen to sever its connections with the real world. Modern logic does not always need to assume that the world contains anything at all. It is not seriously inconvenienced by a universe that is entirely empty of all objects or facts. Logic provides a notation for stating as an explicit premise that the world is not empty: "E x," or "There exists an x."

Jacob Bronowski, the physicist, tells a story of Bertrand Russell at a dinner party. "Oh, it is useless to talk about inconsistent things," Russell remarked at one stage of the conversation. "From an inconsistent proposition you can prove anything you like." Another person at the table objected. "Oh, come on," he remonstrated. Russell stood his ground. He asked the other guest to name an inconsistent assertion. "Well," the man replied, "shall we say, 'two equals one'?" Russell accepted the challenge, and asked what he should prove. "Prove that you are the Pope," he was instructed. Russell did not hesitate. "Why," he said. "The Pope and I are two, but two equals one, therefore the Pope and I are one."

There is no better test of the contrast between the brittleness of logic, which is defenseless in the face of even a single contradiction, and the robustness of the worldly brain, which can tolerate inconsistency, than the fact that we find that story funny. One of the important and interesting differences between deductive logic and natural reason is that the first is a *local* process, going one short step at a time, using only a tiny fraction of all the information known to the system at each step. It behaves like the "microscope" Frege declared logic to be. This means that very long chains of argument are usually needed in logic in order to prove anything really interesting, and the chains are at liberty to be long, provided consistency can be guaranteed. Natural reason operates in quite a different fashion, holistically, using as much as possible of all the information available in one or two giant leaps. If there is a small amount of bad information, it is "put in its place" by an overwhelming quantity of good information. In the case of Bertrand Russell's dinner party, natural reason, drawing on its world knowledge, would conclude that a pope is not usually an atheistic English mathematician with a reputation for romantic adventures.

In fact, the word *paradox* once meant simply a statement that goes against generally accepted opinion, something at odds with the way people typically believe the world works. Only later did the word acquire its logical sense of a seemingly valid argument leading, calamitously, to two contradictory propositions. In the plays of Oscar Wilde, paradoxes are rampant, and are used as vehicles to thwart and disrupt the audience's normal expectations of what life is like. They explode stale ways of thinking by showing that truth is many-sided; by mobilizing a greater quantity of knowledge, we can see that the contrary of an accepted fact may be more accurate than the fact itself. As Algernon Moncrieff remarks in Wilde's comedy *The Importance of Being Earnest,* "The truth is rarely pure and never simple. Modern life would be very tedious if it were either, and modern literature a complete impossibility!"

The founders of modern logic recognized what is now becoming a central issue in artificial intelligence, namely the importance of the distinction between information and knowledge. They realized that memory is organized in the brain in such a way that large amounts of relevant world knowledge are triggered almost instantly by a very small quantity of incoming data. Ordinary language takes advantage of this state of affairs to say much less than it means, to imply and hint and suggest, to avoid the obvious, to omit steps in an argument, to be inconsistent or ambiguous. Even when it is being relatively straightforward and literal, when it seems to be spelling out exactly the message it intends to convey, no more and no less, language still uses words as cues to conjure up preexisting knowledge in the mind of the reader or listener. The statements

> Dumbo is an elephant.
> Dumbo is a mammal.

which might appear to leave no gaps nor omit a single logical step, are in fact deficient. From a strictly logical point of view, there is a sentence missing. A complete syllogism would need to say

> All elephants are mammals.
> Dumbo is an elephant.
> Therefore Dumbo is a mammal.

Without thinking consciously about it, the reader supplies from his or her own store of knowledge the fact that all elephants are mammals. In order for us to be aware of all or even most of the gaps that ordinary language contains, we would have to adopt a completely literal frame of mind, which is a difficult if not impossible feat, because it is profoundly unnatural. Human intelligence is not designed to be literal-minded. In ordinary language, we leave gaps and expect the reader or listener to fill in the gaps. That is why language is such an unsuitable vehicle for logic. It is imperfect information, but our brains are so constituted that we find it extraordinarily hard to realize the extent of its imperfection, because our intelligence is at home with defective data as a fish is at home in the sea. It took the deliberate efforts of logicians like Frege, Russell, and Whitehead to frame an artificial language that was so "literal" it required no contribution whatever from the reader in the form of preexisting worldly knowledge.

The old idea that logic is the language of thought, the psychologist George Miller points out, collapses once we understand just how short are the steps that logic can negotiate. Deductive logic leaves no gaps, makes no leaps, but the mind thrives and flourishes on gaps; it tolerates great gaping holes in what it hears and reads, because it is so adept at filling in the holes with what it knows. This peculiar gift, which is universal in humans because it arises from the architecture of the brain, and is therefore part of our biology, is what modern logic had to struggle against to become a true science.

The whole purpose of Frege's concept notation was to close up all the gaps, seal up the crevices, plug the holes, so that knowledge could not squirm in unawares. It was a device to keep logic local, and protect it from the globalness of natural reason. "My initial step," Frege wrote, "was to attempt to reduce the concept of ordering in a sequence to that of logical consequence, so as to proceed from there to the concept of number. To prevent anything intuitive from penetrating here unnoticed, I had to bend every effort to keep the chain of inference free of gaps. In attempting to comply with this requirement in the strictest possible way, I found the inadequacy of language to be an obstacle."

Frege knew that without the microscope of a new logical notation, the "naked mind" cannot tell the difference between a tight chain of reasoning with short steps and no chinks, no missing links, and one in which certain links are missing. In his system, no step may be taken that does not obey one of a small number of rules of inference selected because they are purely logical.

The battle between the localism of deductive logic and the globalism of the mind's operations waged by the founders of modern logic is being fought out afresh today by rival schools of artificial-intelligence researchers. Allen and Newell's "core doctrine" of computer science, that all intelligence involves the use and manipulation of various symbol systems, has its roots in the seminal ideas of Frege, Russell, and Whitehead. It is based on the view of logic as a "symbol game," played with meaningless tokens according to purely formal rules. "Progress was first made by walking away from all that seemed relevant to meaning and human symbols," Newell and Simon have written. "Thought was still wholly intangible and ineffable until modern formal logic interpreted it as the manipulation of formal tokens. And it still seemed to inhabit mainly the heaven of Platonic ideals, or the equally obscure spaces of the human mind, until computers taught us how symbols could be processed by machines."

The champions of the symbol-system doctrine, with its moorings in formal logic and the serial nature of the digital computer, are arrayed against the representatives of a new breed of computer theorists, who have designed and are building machines based on an entirely different tradition, not anchored in symbolic logic, and operating in a way that is more global than local. These scientists, many of whom believe they are making a revolution in their discipline, have much in common with neurologists earlier in this century, men like Pierre Marie, Kurt Goldstein, and Henry Head, who regarded the brain as a single, highly integrated organ, and extremely robust, since an intellectual activity was distributed across a wide area of the whole brain and therefore could tolerate damage in one part of the brain. They were antilocalists, believing that the brain works not by dealing with one separate signal at a time, but by responding to patterns, surrounding information with a context, and that it is organized not in digital fashion, but as a complex of neural fields, sending waves of activity across broad expanses of the cortex. The new intelligent machines are designed along some-what similar lines. Their robustness is part and parcel of their globalness, and this in turn gives rise to that most characteristic property of the worldly brain, its ability to make sense of in-complete, ambiguous, or contradictory information. The new machines operate on statistical, rather than logical principles.

The localist point of view in artificial intelligence was once so powerful it crushed the globalist enterprise in the 1960s with a stinging artillery of criticism, scornful of the "flourish of roman-ticism" that surrounded the globalist research program and warning of a "holistic" or "Gestalt" misconception in the field of computer science as dangerous as the theory of vitalism in biol-ogy. Now the globalists have come back stronger than ever. Their resurgence coincides with clear signs of disenchantment among the localists with the notion that commonsense knowl-edge can be written down in the language of predicate logic, an enterprise once bright with hope. There is a new concern with understanding how people use knowledge, as opposed to how they merely possess knowledge; a sense that logic works well only in worlds that are clearly defined, of which our own world is certainly not one; and a suspicion that the mind may not be one universal computer, but many different computers, perhaps operating on principles so various that the localists and the glob-alists ultimately one day may be able to settle down to an uneasy peace.

3 : NO MACHINE
WE WOULD WANT
AS A FRIEND?

t is the supreme generality of logic that makes it seem a plausible language for imitating human thought in a machine. The mind's extraordinary capacity to make sense of novel information surely suggests that it uses a system of universal rules that apply quite generally to all kinds of material, no matter what the content, and what could be more general than logic? That speculation sounds very reasonable, but we should beware of it.

In logic, an argument can be valid even if it is completely meaningless, which ensures a very wide range of application. Logic is indifferent to the content of particular statements; what is important is the quality of the connections that link one statement to another. It does not even matter whether a statement is factually true or false on its own. What does matter are the possible combinations of truth and falsehood, as statements are linked together in a chain of reasoning. The syllogism

Edwina is a mermaid.
All mermaids are swimmers.
Therefore Edwina is a swimmer.

can be expressed in a more abstract way as

A is a B.
All Bs are C.
Therefore A is a C.

Because content has vanished, and only the connectives, "all" and "is" have meaning, the argument can be applied to all kinds of things apart from mermaids. It produces valid conclusions about waiters who like big tips, taxi drivers who scorn short rides, politicians who make boring speeches. Even utter nonsense is legitimate: Radishout is a cormander, all cormanders are gistwicks, therefore Radishout is a gistwick.

As logic became increasingly formal, it also grew increasingly general. But the effect of such generality was to transform logic into a different cultural entity. It lost any pretensions to be an aid to successful reasoning in the everyday world. Most of the great modern philosophical systems from the seventeenth to the twentieth centuries neglected formal logic, which in the Middle Ages had played a central role in the work of the Scholastics, who used it to resolve conceptual puzzles, often theological in nature. The Scholastics were essentially Aristotelians who talked syllogistically about why things are as they are in terms of what classes of things they belong to. They did not want to see the commonsense view of the world made obsolete by theories, and while some of them recognized that the surface form of ordinary language is a poor medium for logical argument, they went only halfway in their efforts to denature it, producing a "semiartificial" language that was extremely clumsy.

In the time of Aristotle, logic was not just an intellectual exercise, but a practical discipline aimed at separating good arguments from bad ones, and it played a part in the education of men of affairs, the politicians and lawyers of the day. Early ideas about logic probably originated in the Athenian law courts, where the rules of public dispute were already well established. Experts were paid to instruct others in the art of disputation, and Sophists, men who made a living by inventing plausible but fallacious arguments and proving paradoxical propositions, paraded their skills in public. That was the climate in which Aristotle developed the laws of reasoning. The *Topics* is really a guidebook for debaters.

Aristotle created the science of logic virtually from scratch. He let his readers know that if they had an inkling of how difficult the task had been, they would refrain from grumbling and complaining about the results. As a rebel against the doctrine of other worldly ideas championed by Plato, Aristotle was a this-worldly philosopher whose logic increased knowledge of the natural universe, of things as they really exist. He approached universals by studying particulars, finding out what sorts of things there are in the material world, which is why he is called the philosopher of common sense, of everyday realities. In the great era of Scholastic philosophy, which lasted for three centuries, up to the Renaissance, Aristotle was referred to simply as "the Philosopher." During the Renaissance, however, while Aristotelian logic remained just about the only game in town, his effect on mainstream philosophy, outside the church, went into a decline. Some humanists regarded the semiartificial language of medieval logic, with which Aristotle was associated, as aesthetically repellent, preferring to spend their time studying the graceful and elegant Latin writers like Cicero and Ovid, who were being rediscovered. The philosopher and brash polymath Petrus Ramus, a professor at the University of Paris, a popular author with hosts of admirers, made a frontal attack on Aristotle, calling him disorganized and obscure. According to popular legend, Ramus's thesis for his master's degree was entitled *Whatever Aristotle Has Said Is a Fabrication*. The influence of Ramus was artificially inflated and the numbers of his readers considerably swollen after he became a martyr in the wars of religion. A convert to Protestantism, Ramus was stabbed to death on the third day of the Massacre of St. Bartholomew's Day, 1572, and his body was thrown out of a fifth-floor window, perhaps at the instigation of an academic rival, Jacques Charpentier.

Another reason for the crumbling prestige of logic in the Renaissance was that mathematics and science began to strike out in new directions, where logic was not the all-powerful guide to discovery it once had been. By the nineteenth century, when the philosophical system builders were in full flower, logic had fallen into an almost scandalous neglect. Only Leibniz among the leading philosophers was a logician of high caliber. When the revival of logic occurred in midcentury, however, the long supremacy of Aristotle was overthrown, and the beginning of the war between modern logic and common sense could be discerned. The first blow for greater generality, and less worldliness, was struck in 1847, when an English schoolteacher named George Boole, the largely self-taught son of a shoemaker, invented an algebra of reasoning that carried logic far beyond Aristotle's syllogisms. Boolean algebra made logic more general, and in doing so, began the revolution in which logic "denatured" ordinary language, as scientists denature living stuff in the laboratory—not in a halfhearted fashion, as the commonsensical Scholastics had done—but by making the vocabulary of natural language, as well as its rules, entirely artificial. Boole is said to have had "a genius for generalization," which led him to realize that the xs and ys of algebra need not refer to quantities, but could be used to symbolize classes of ideas, and that the rules of algebra, which had always been used to manipulate numbers, could manipulate those ideas. Boolean algebra, being so general, was powerful enough to handle all the forms of inference of Aristotle's syllogisms and an immense number of other ones besides. The syllogism, once the supreme method of logic, the very model and foundation of correct reasoning, the ultimate test of a good argument, fell on hard times.

Yet as Boole's system gained the ascendancy, breaking the lock that Aristotelian techniques had held for so long, logic still

retained something of its usefulness as a guide to practical argument, a training for the mind, a sharpener of wits. The divorce
between logic and the actual processes of everyday thinking was
not yet final. Boole himself was interested in psychology, and
believed that symbolic logic, his invention, was a means of in-
vestigating the fundamental principles that govern thought.
After he died of pneumonia, brought on by giving a lecture
soaking wet after being out in a Scottish rainstorm, his widow
Mary disclosed that at the age of seventeen he had had a sudden
insight that there is in the human mind a mysterious source of
knowledge that is not logical, and which she called "the unconscious."

There is abundant evidence that Boolean logic, for all its
generality, did not abandon the role of instructor in the art of
reasoning in the vastly entertaining work of Lewis Carroll, alias
Charles Lutwidge Dodgson, a geometer and don at Christ
Church College, Oxford. Dodgson was the creator of the im-
mortal *Alice in Wonderland,* and was also a Boolean logician. He
wrote his book *Symbolic Logic* for a general readership and in
particular for children, his favorite audience, using the pseudo-
nym of Lewis Carroll to attract readers of *Alice* to a much more
challenging subject, yet one he considered could be understood
by anyone of moderate intelligence. Dodgson's career fell neatly
into the Boolean period, and he attempted to develop a logical
algebra with a simpler notation than that of Boole.

New light has recently been shed on Lewis Carroll as a logician rather than as just a spinner of delightful nonsense, by
William Warren Bartley, of the Hoover Institution, who discovered some of Carroll's lost writings on logic, as well as an old
workbook consisting of some sixty pages of previously indeci-
pherable jottings owned by Princeton University. Bartley believes that Boolean logic, which replaced the Aristotelian variety
and lasted from the middle to the end of the nineteenth century,
is really quite distinct from modern logic, which began with
Frege's *Begriffsschrift* and extends up to the present day. For
logicians in the tradition of Aristotle, the main problem had
been to reduce all forms of reasoning to the syllogism. After

Boole, however, the task changed, and became one of extracting all the information possible from a given set of propositions, not unlike a detective who solves a crime by milking all the available evidence. Consider, for example, the Lewis Carroll problem of the grocers and bicyclists, where the idea is to deduce a conclusion from five "universal" statements:

1. All honest industrious men are healthy.
2. No grocers are healthy.
3. All industrious grocers are honest.
4. All cyclists are industrious.
5. All unhealthy cyclists are dishonest.

The correct deduction, which a good detective could extract, is that grocers never ride bicycles, but the puzzle is best approached back to front, by supposing a false conclusion, that grocers do ride bicycles, and then showing that the conclusion cannot be correct because it contradicts one of the premises. The Boolean method is to replace all the terms with symbols: H = honest, I = industrious, X = healthy, G = grocer, and C = cyclist. We can deduce that since C is I, CG is I, and so CG is GI. Therefore, since IG is H, CG is HI, and since HI is X, CG is also X. But that conclusion, "cycling grocers are healthy," contradicts premise 2, "No grocers are healthy." Therefore, it is impossible that C is G. So we arrive at the solution: G is not C. Grocers do not ride bicycles.

Such puzzles, Bartley points out, are completely foreign to the spirit of modern logic, which does not concern itself at all with helping people to think more effectively, or to extract information from premises. The whole nature and aim of logic has undergone a complete transformation. Even in textbook problems, students today are not taught to deduce conclusions, but are usually given the conclusion and then asked to test the argument for soundness. Every day, logicians prove new theorems, but the theorems are usually proofs about logic itself, such as whether some exceedingly complex form of implication does or does not hold, or questions dealing with the foundations of mathematics. Bartley asked a number of logicians of high distinction, at universities in the United States and Britain, to solve one of Carroll's trickier puzzles, the famous Schoolboy Problem. This concerns some English, Scots, Welsh, Irish, and German schoolboys and prefects sitting together in a large room. A prefect, an avid reader of the mystery novels of Wilkie Collins, takes notes on their activities, just in case a sensational murder is committed and he is required as a witness. The prefect's notes are in the form of twelve premises ("Whenever some of the Scotch are dancing reels, and some of the Irish fighting, some of the Welsh are eating toasted cheese"), and the puzzle is to complete the final premise, "Whenever some of the English are singing 'Rule, Britannia,' and some of the Scotch are *not* dancing reels..."

For several years, Bartley tried to find a logician willing and able to solve the Schoolboy Problem. Even when he supplied Carroll's own solution ("None of the prefects is asleep"), which he found on the back cover of one of Carroll's own copies of the second edition of his *Symbolic Logic,* and asked logicians to test the argument for correctness, a task for which they had been trained, "they still tended to scamper off like white rabbits." Only at the end of ten years of searching, just as his book on Carroll was going to press, did Bartley find two friendly logicians who came up with correct, but different, proofs.

Even in Carroll's witty, exuberant puzzles, however, there is an unspoken assumption that, where rational thought is concerned, content is of no real importance. That is why he can indulge in fantasy and nonsense, writing premises that are absurd and arbitrary, because what matters is not meaning, but the manipulation of symbols that do not mean anything at all. In the Carroll universe, all rabbits that are not greedy are black, some oysters are silent, no lobsters are unreasonable, and all teetotalers like sugar. It is possible, but difficult, to solve the problem of the grocers on bicycles by thinking about a world in which grocers behave in certain universal ways. The reasoning would go something like this: Since cyclists are industrious, cycling grocers are industrious grocers. Therefore, since all industrious grocers are honest, and all honest industrious men are healthy, cycling grocers are also healthy. But that contradicts the second premise which states that no grocers are healthy. Therefore, the conclusion must be that grocers do not ride bicycles. It is easier, however, to manipulate nonsense by means of symbols that can mean anything and everything, using rules that apply quite generally to any subject matter whatever.

In the work of Boole's successors logic became even more general. Modern logic came to deal with nothing more specific than the rules by which propositions of any kind can be legitimately connected. In the *Principia,* logic is licensed to make connections between assertions that to our everyday way of thinking have no connection whatever. Such a logic can say that *"A* implies *B"* without requiring any link of sense or meaning between *A* and *B.* As far as common sense and ordinary experience are concerned, the two propositions can be completely unrelated, having nothing whatever to do with each other. Content imposes no restrictions at all on the way propositions are linked. All that matters is the combination of truth and falsehood, and even that constraint is extremely permissive. As far as the logic of the *Principia* is concerned, all three of the following implications are valid:

1. If Beethoven was a horse thief, then a dime is worth ten cents.
2. If the sea is wet, then the Marx brothers are funny.
3. If Cleopatra was ugly, then love is a five-letter word.

These sentences, examples of the logical relation known as material implication, may seem as outlandish as anything in *Alice in Wonderland.* They tie together statements that are not related in the world we know. Yet material implication is one of the basic building blocks of Russell and Whitehead's logic. It is useful because of its extreme generality, permitting one assertion to imply another with only one limitation: a chain of reasoning must never be allowed to proceed from truth to falsehood. One can even proceed from falsehood to truth. An implication is forbidden only when the first statement is true and the second is false. Such permissiveness enables arguments of great complexity to be constructed, resulting in assertions which are true in logic, but are counterintuitive, and may seem patently false to the untrained eye of the layperson. Logic aims for a high level of generality because that is where it is most powerful, and it does not care whether or not the facts are connected as we would normally connect them in everyday experience.

Because logic is so general, and because part of the mind's genius is the generality of its intelligence, it is tempting to suppose that human reasoning is based on rules that operate, like logic, independent of the content of the information they are manipulating. It turns out, however, that this view is so wide of the mark that going to the opposite extreme—arguing that content is of such importance that it actually determines how we reason in a given circumstance—is likely to lead to a truer understanding of the nature of human intelligence.

The search for generality, beset by the most unexpected and formidable difficulties, is a thread that runs strongly through the short but turbulent history of artificial intelligence. The first true intelligent machine, the General Problem Solver of Newell and Simon, was, as its name implies, based on the idea that there are broad, universal laws of thinking as well as highly specific, local, makeshift rules that apply to particular problems and allow for a certain amount of muddling through. There were "general" rules of thumb, such as the ingenious logical device of means-ends analysis, which searched forward and backward at the same time. As a result, there was a certain amount of misplaced euphoria about the prospects for putting general intelligence into a machine. Yet, paradoxically, General Problem Solver was abandoned because it was less general than its inventors had hoped. It could operate only in a world of perfect information. Its programs had to specify explicitly all the situations it was to encounter and exactly what would happen if a given action was taken. That restricted the machine to very simple, well-defined problems. In order to make artificial intelligence systems solve many different kinds of problems, the programs needed to be highly general, but this turned out to be a limitation rather than a strength.

As the 1960s came to an end, a crisis developed, partly because of trenchant criticisms by scientists outside of artificial intelligence, in particular the British mathematician Sir James Lighthill, who claimed that the new thinking machines were little more than laboratory curiosities that could not be scaled up in such a way as to operate in the real world of the factory floor, in fighting wars, or in outer space. Under such withering fire, and facing a severe financial pinch, artificial-intelligence researchers began to talk much less about universal laws of thought, and buckled down instead to building machines that were of practical use, as experts in a special domain of knowledge.

Expert systems, as these are known, are able to reason, make tentative recommendations, and advise on courses of action in such fields as medicine, chemistry, business, and engineering. Creating them seemed to be a good way for artificial intelligence to go at the time, because, unlike the mysterious and horrifyingly diffuse knowledge known as "common sense," what an expert knows was presumed to be already nice and tidy, already logical, and easy to convert into the formal language of a computer program. Deductive logic would be just the vehicle for the neat thought processes of a human expert. Or so it was thought. Essentially, an expert system reasons by means of a set of production, or "if-then" rules, which prescribe a course of action in a given situation: "If the patient has a headache, then give her two aspirin." There are rules to supervise the execution of rules, and rules that decide which of two competing rules takes precedence. In this respect expert-system programs, though they are single-purpose and use a great deal of special knowledge, are similar to the programs of Newell and Simon's general-purpose machines, which also used production rules. The double attraction of if-then rules for encoding the knowledge of a human expert in a machine is, first, that it is easy to encode what a human expert says he knows about a given domain in the form of such rules, and, second, that the rules are particularly well suited for manipulating symbols, which is what mainstream artificial intelligence is all about.

Psychologists, however, have always been somewhat suspicious of production systems. They regard them as being too brittle, either working or not working, never giving a "sort of" correct response which may not be exactly right but is not exactly wrong either, as human beings do. What is worse, production rules tend to break down when it comes to doing exactly what the brain does with such spontaneous ease, namely, to generalize. It is not that production systems cannot be used to generalize, but rather that they generalize too much, and do not know when to stop. Human beings see a poodle and know at once, without using logic, that the poodle is also a dog and, at a more general level still, an animal. Such an ability is central to our ability to learn, by taking novel information and placing it in a context of familiar knowledge. That makes the world much more predictable, much more manageable, than it would be otherwise. But we know, without thinking about it consciously, that if generalizing is carried too far, it loses its usefulness.

"Generalizing is a matter of throwing away information," as Denise Cummins, a psychologist at the University of Arizona, puts it. "A poodle has curly hair and its face has a pointed shape, but you can discard that information if you want to generalize and classify it as a dog. Dogs have four legs and two eyes and they bark and chase cats. It doesn't matter whether they are black or white, big or small, cuddly or ferocious. If you throw away some more information by regarding a poodle simply as an animal, it doesn't need to be able to bark or chase cats. In fact, it can even have no legs and no eyes and still be an animal. But this process must go only so far and no farther. There comes a stage when you have to call a halt. You have to say 'Look, you can't lose any more information because now you're talking about rocks.' With computer models of thinking that are based on rules, this is a very serious problem, because you don't know when to tell the machine to stop generalizing. It's very hard to write a rule into your production system that says 'Stop dropping information.' It's difficult to draw a boundary."

This is closely related to the curious prodigality of logic in generating an unlimited number of truths from a given set of premises, most of them silly or useless. From the statement "The president is in the rose garden," logic can deduce that

1. The president is in the rose garden.
2. The president is in the rose garden and the president is in the rose garden.
3. Either the president is in the rose garden or today is Tuesday.
4. It is not true that the president is not in the rose garden.
5. If the president is not in the rose garden, the stock market will crash.
6. If it is April Fool's Day, the president is in the rose garden.

And so forth and so on.

The hope in artificial intelligence was that eventually single-purpose machines that are limited to little isolated domains of special knowledge, and which manipulate facts with rules, could develop into general-purpose ones by combining the domains, but progress in this work has been disappointing. One stumbling block is the fact that how we think cannot be separated from what we are thinking about, and is closely connected with what we know and how we use our knowledge. The nature of reasoning changes, sometimes drastically, when domains of knowledge change. So it may be impossible to program universal rules of thought into a machine and expect it to be a general reasoner. "If you are going to ask about reasoning, you're going to have to ask about the domain that the reasoning is taking place in," Dr. Cummins says. "Altering the content can change the entire ball game. That is why logic is a bad model for the brain, because logic is blind to content. If you take a purely logical view of the brain, one that assumes we are using formal rules that apply to every domain, you end up finding what appear to be inconsistencies in its knowledge base. Those are really a result of the way the brain makes sense of the world, and it doesn't do that by using general rules."

Being able to throw away just the right amount and type of information is the essence of a general intelligence, in the view of many. Yet expert systems and other thinking machines are given simple assertions by human operators who have already thrown away most of the details, so that the machines are fed very bare, stripped-down knowledge. MYCIN, an expert system which diagnoses human bacterial infections, has no idea what human beings are or the likely things that happen to them. If MYCIN is told that the aorta is ruptured and the patient is losing blood at the rate of a pint a minute, it will blindly try to trace the disaster to a bacterial infection.

Today some researchers believe that the way to build a general reasoning machine is not to make it "intelligent" in the sense of having powerful techniques in narrow domains, but to endow it with vast amounts of commonsense knowledge. Douglas Lenat, at the Microelectronics and Computer Technology Corporation in Austin, Texas, is working on an immense project called Cyc, that may take ten years to complete, to encode all the information in the *Concise Columbia Encyclopedia* and put it into a machine. Lenat decided to undertake this mammoth enterprise after creating Eurisko, a program that was intended to learn how to learn, by the use of heuristic rules, which it would modify and improve as it went along. Eurisko entered and won a naval war-game contest in which the object was to build a fleet of ships that could defeat all attackers, and won again even when the rules of the contest were changed in an attempt to prevent computer programs from taking part. But Eurisko, though it made discoveries of a kind, inferring new rules for naval warfare, was not as independent a thinker as it might appear. Many of the heuristics needed to be spelled out to the computer, and Lenat had to help the system decide which lines of inquiry to follow. The program could not reason in a commonsense way, because its knowledge of the world was not general enough. Eurisko "stumbled" onto some of its discoveries, Lenat says, by using low-level analogical reasoning, not by finding new analogies on its own. It decided that fleets of ships used in the war games should be symmetrical, because it had previously worked on the design of integrated computer circuits and at that time happened upon the fact that being symmetrical is a desirable property for these chips, without understanding why it is desirable. Eurisko's decision to make fleets symmetrical was made simply by referring to its earlier experience in designing chips.

"Compared with human capabilities," Lenat said, "this is extraordinarily meager. The poor performance of computer programs in finding and using analogies may be attributable more to the narrowness of their knowledge than to the inability of programmers to come up with suitable algorithms. People have an enormous store of concepts to draw on as possible analogues; perhaps a million distinct memories of objects, actions, emotions, situations and so on." Eurisko, even though it was run for weeks at a time and restarted with most of its records intact, had experiences which were not nearly as rich and diverse as those of a human infant.

Expert systems are not only hopelessly brittle, in Lenat's view, but they do not cope well with novelty, and they do not communicate well with each other. They give only the illusion of being clever, not the reality, because as they perform their narrow symbol manipulations, a human observer interprets what the machine does as meaningful. The machine itself is too ignorant to have anything like an understanding of what it is talking about, and brittleness arises from such a lack of understanding.

No compact, powerful, elegant methods exist that form a set of first principles for commonsense reasoning, Lenat believes. They are no more than a dream. So he is trying to make his Cyc program intelligent by giving it a vast knowledge base, consisting of tens of millions of facts, beliefs, categories, relations, and problem-solving methods that span what we call our worldliness, our common sense. Lenat stresses that Cyc is intended to be intelligent in "this world, not in all worlds that might have been." The knowledge is so immense it would take one person two centuries to install. It is as if a child absorbed a new item of information every ten seconds of his waking life up to the age of eight. Cyc has about twenty special-purpose inference schemes instead of one general-purpose scheme, and it generalizes chiefly by means of analogy to other parts of its huge store of knowledge. The sheer breadth of the domains in which the program operates will force it—Lenat hopes—to be much broader and more sophisticated in its techniques for manipulating symbols. Lenat predicts he will see "isolated flashes of useful commonsense reasoning" as Cyc's knowledge base grows from ten percent to fifty percent of its total size, and then, as the knowledge reaches a critical mass, an explosion of intelligence. At the moment, with only about a million pieces of data installed, Cyc has less than one percent of the knowledge needed to understand a typical article in the *National Enquirer*.

Since no one has ever attempted such a colossal effort to dump knowledge into a machine without a detailed understanding of how that knowledge will be used, there is no telling how intelligent Cyc may become. The idea is that if a machine is worldly enough, then the world will provide natural constraints on the machine's reasoning. If the world were highly volatile and chaotic, Lenat points out, our gift for making analogies would lead us astray. The same would happen if we had a terribly wrong view of the world. We might think that comets and thunderstorms were sentient beings and try to placate them with offerings. It is only because the world is quite stable, and our knowledge of it is quite accurate, that generalizing by analogy is a reliable and useful way to reason. The world itself, and our knowledge of it, puts a brake on runaway generalization. That is why formal logic, for all its generality, cannot simulate general intelligence. It is not "this-worldly" enough. It does not take advantage of the myriad regularities that the real world is forced to live by, because it is not designed to deal with them. About the simple, basic constraints of space and time, cause and effect, movement and rest, logic has little to say.

The hopes for a general-reasoning machine based on commonsense knowledge are not likely to be fulfilled anytime soon, however. Even admirers of Lenat's encyclopedia venture such as Daniel Bobrow, of Xerox Palo Alto Research Center, are cautious. "I think we are a long way from making a general-intelligence machine," Bobrow says. "I certainly don't think we'll get close in this century. In the year 2001 there will be lots of machines that can help us in many ways in specific domains. But I don't think there will be any machine we would want to have as a friend. Such a machine would need, at the very least, a tremendous amount of knowledge, and that knowledge has to be gained, not just by a few people programming a few things, but through interaction in a world. And that might take as much time as it takes a human being to grow up and become a mature adult."

Artificial-intelligence research, in a thirty-year effort, has won a victory of a sort; it has learned what a general intelligence is not. It is not based on rules, whether universal or makeshift, it is not blind to content, as logic is, and it cannot be attained by trying to integrate little isolated domains of knowledge into a grand synthesis. The road to generality may lie through common sense, but that road is likely to be a long and thorny one. The result is a new respect for natural intelligence, a recognition that what were once seen as weaknesses must now be regarded as strengths so formidable it may be impossible to imitate them on existing machines; and the emergence of a new school of researchers and theorists who believe that the design of the brain is so fundamentally, so drastically unlike that of the standard computer that a completely different kind of machine needs to be built if anything approaching natural intelligence is to be embodied in silicon and steel. Even the central tenet of artificial intelligence, that cognition is a matter of symbols and the manipulation of symbols, is under challenge.

The optimists hold to the belief that a general-intelligence machine is possible because the brain is a machine, not an impenetrable mystery, and it is nonsensical to suppose that anything in nature can evade the conquest of science indefinitely. Perhaps that will mean looking at the brain in an entirely new way. David Waltz has suggested that mainstream models of human reason are wrong, and until better ones are found there is little chance of creating machines that will display even a highly simplified version of common sense. The greatest successes in artificial intelligence have been programs that dwell in tiny, intense microworlds of knowledge, tightly restricted islands of special competence, cut off from each other. Yet attempts to build bridges between the islands is probably a hopeless enterprise. These microworlds cannot be enlarged and generalized into commonsense knowledge using existing techniques. Nothing short of a theoretical revolution, an entirely new view of human cognition, will do the trick. What Waltz is calling for is breathtaking, because it entails not only a new kind of machine, but a brand-new science of the mind.

"We have no suitable science of cognition," Waltz has written. "We have only fragments of the conception, and some of those are certainly incorrect. We know very little about how a machine would have to be organized to solve the problems of intelligence. Virtually all aspects of intelligence—including perception, memory, reasoning, intention, generation of action, and attention—are still mysterious. Even if we understood how to structure an intelligent system, we would not be able to complete it, because we also lack an appropriate science of knowledge."

It may be, however, that the new kind of machine and the new conception of the mind are already converging to produce the first glimmerings of an answer to the question of what human intelligence is all about.

4: THE KNOWLEDGE MEDIUM

One of the central insights of modern psychology is that we cannot even begin to say what an intelligence is until we first ascertain what kinds of knowledge are available to it. That statement sounds so simple and transparent it is easy to overlook its dire implications for the enterprise of building a machine that thinks like a human being. On the other hand, it opens up some brilliant prospects for understanding the mind.

If rational thought depends on what a thinker knows, then depriving him or her of certain types of knowledge will introduce serious distortions into the very heart of the thinking process. An intelligence that knows only a few special things about the world is likely to *reason* in quite a different fashion from an intelligence that is familiar with a larger and more catholic body of facts. How we solve the puzzles of everyday life, whether or not we work them out according to the canons of sound logic, depends on how the content of the puzzle interacts with the worldly knowledge in our heads. When what we know coincides with the logical structure of the problem we are trying to solve, we can be as brilliant as Aristotle. When those two conflict, we become irrational.

Some cognitive scientists speculate that the great divide separating the intelligence of a machine, no matter how sophisticated, from that of a person, is the nature of the knowledge that comes into play in each case. What we are is what we know, by virtue of being the product of millions of years of evolution in a particular kind of environment, and of the learning that goes on over a lifetime. When Aristotle said that man is a rational animal, he may not have realized how intimate is the connection between our reason and our creaturehood, so that it is impossible to talk of one without taking the other into account. There is more than one way to be rational, and the ways that we use are closely linked to the kind of animal that we are, and to the intense drama of our history as a species, because knowledge is the crux of the matter. The fact that a computer program cannot cry, or laugh, or pray, or fly into a rage, is not an issue here, because we are talking about *intelligence*.

Bernard Meltzer, in a presidential address to an international conference of computer scientists, criticized many of the present artificial-intelligence programs on precisely this score, that they neglect the very types of knowledge that are the hallmarks of a natural intelligence. Until quite recently, Meltzer says, concepts basic to ordinary common sense, such as space and time, were either ignored or dealt with in a fragmentary, unsystematic fashion. Programs for thinking machines "seem to model a ghostly, ethereal world in which there is not only no space and time, but not even any physical objects—a solipsistic world insomnia, as we say in Italy."

Perhaps, Meltzer suggested, science can progress toward the goal of a general, commonsense intelligence if it gives its computer models experiences of the real world. A rudimentary project of this kind was undertaken several years ago at **SRI**

International, in which a robot on wheels named Shakey was given the wherewithal to plan simple actions, like pushing objects in and between rooms, moving out of the way of obstacles, and changing its plans when things went awry. Shakey was given some knowledge of space, and a means of storing and generalizing plans, so that it could react to the unexpected and even be serendipitous in a modest sort of way. It was able to learn. As the robot roamed its little world, it was not flummoxed when it came across odd or novel objects, but sometimes made use of them to improve its own performance.

"These remarkable results stemmed from studying the problems of direct experience of the physical world," Meltzer declared. "So, for example, learning became an issue not because a bright student wanted to do a PhD thesis on learning, but because Shakey was laboriously having to work out anew time and again rather similar sequences of actions." What made Shakey unique was the fact that its inventors at first intended to create a simulated model of the world to use as Shakey's habitat, but later decided to put the robot in the actual world, because they were convinced that the essence of intelligence is to be able to cope with the new and unexpected, and that it is almost impossible to create such an ability by simulation. Alas, the project was killed by the government agency that was funding it. But Meltzer is sure that the underlying idea, that a general intelligence is possible only if it has a relationship with a real world, and the knowledge afforded by being in the world, holds tremendous promise.

Rodney Brooks, who makes robots at MIT that move around his laboratory and show a remarkable amount of independence, has decided that creating little symbolic models of the world for a robot is not the way to make such a creature intelligent. It is much better to turn the robot loose in the real world, so that it acquires the knowledge on which true intelligence is based. It is disastrous to succumb to the temptation of testing a robot in a highly simplified world, Brooks believes, even with the best intention of moving it later to an unsimplified world, because the robot may have to be rebuilt in its entirety, every single piece of it, if it is to be intelligent in its new, complex environment. Worse than that, its creators may have to rethink the whole design.

One of the shocks that jolted artificial-intelligence workers in the 1970s was the discovery that making little cleverly crafted symbolic worlds as an environment for thinking machines did not enable them to put a lot of those miniature "fairylands" together to form a big, complex whole that has some resemblance to the real world. It turned out to be prohibitively difficult to combine and extend the tiny domains because they were artifacts bereft of that essential background of human knowledge and common sense, of meaning, that would have served as the glue cementing them together. Trying to put worlds together as if they were tinker toys is a hopeless enterprise. It was a sharp lesson, and it led to some radical new thinking about how mind should be embodied in a physical system.

The idea that worldliness is basic, and that "intelligence" grows out of it, is not a new one by any means. Novelists have explored its implications. It appears with particular vividness in the work of that magical maker of fictional worlds, Leo Tolstoy. Realism was all-important for Tolstoy. In his novels the characters change and develop, but always in a natural, believable way, through their everyday small encounters with life and their active experiences. Whereas Dostoyevsky builds an artificial, even grotesque, model of the world for his characters to strive and suffer in, Tolstoy uses the world as a model of itself, and lets his creatures explore it. He did not believe that an author can make a personality from scratch, in a vacuum. "You can invent anything you please, but it is impossible to invent psychology," he once remarked, of Gorky's fiction. A critic has said that *War and Peace* demands "eyes, ears, voice and all other organs of sense and perception that are responsive to a total human world."

Tolstoy was a holist, not a localist. He recognized that logic is a brittle, artificial system. At the end of *War and Peace,* Natasha and Pierre, together as man and wife, much altered by their adventures from how they were at the beginning of the story, talk at their fireside by "apprehending one another's thoughts and exchanging ideas with extraordinary swiftness and perspicuity, contrary to all the rules of logic, without the aid of premises, deductions, or conclusions." In fact, for Natasha "it was a sure sign of something wrong between them if Pierre followed a logical train of thought. When he began proving something, coolly reasoning, she knew they were on the verge of a quarrel." Tolstoy spoke of the "endless labyrinth of links" by which everything in life is connected to everything else. Every thought, he said, "expressed by itself through words loses its meaning, is terribly diminished when taken out of the interconnection in which it lies."

Isaiah Berlin, in his magnificent commentary on Tolstoy, *The Hedgehog and the Fox*, asserts that the "worldliness" that is so much an attribute of the heroes and heroines of Tolstoy's novels is not a matter of deliberate reason, ordering facts by means of rules, analyzing data, but of being immersed, submerged, in a knowledge medium that we take for granted because it is part of the universal texture of human life. Since we are inside this medium, surrounded by it, we cannot observe it from the outside, or manipulate it with logic. We are almost unaware that it exists. It has no "outside." This medium in which we are, as a result of being alive, is an immense totality that includes the basic concepts and presuppositions by which we think. It provides us with a natural understanding of what human reason can do, and what it cannot do. Worldliness means that how we think is influenced by the unalterable medium in which we act, as it is influenced by the pervasiveness of time and space. It is the ever-present sense of this medium that is the basis for Tolstoy's determinism, realism, pessimism, and contempt for the faith people place in science, Berlin thinks, because the knowledge medium "does what no science can claim to do; it distinguishes the real from the sham, the worthwhile from the worthless, that which can be done or borne from what cannot be; and does so without giving rational grounds for its pronouncements, if only because 'rational' and 'irrational' are terms that themselves acquire their meanings and uses in relation to—by 'growing out of'—it, and not *vice versa*."

The search for a general-intelligence machine that displays common sense has failed, in the view of some critics, because of a belief that thinking is the manipulation of symbols uncoupled from the everyday context of human experience, divorced from the Tolstoyan "medium" in which natural intelligence is bathed.

It so happened that during this period of setbacks for computer scientists, psychologists were making very rich, compelling discoveries about the everyday irrationality of the human mind. In a paradox that turned previous ideas about reasoning on their head, these investigations showed that what is universal in human thinking is not "logic" but certain nonlogical and illogical biases that are so systematic, so predictable and characteristic, that they can be collected and classified, as if they were various species of butterflies. A major cause of such biases is the deep human tendency to reason in terms of what we know, or think we know, about the world, so that it is easy to distort reasoning—to make the mind rational or irrational—simply by manipulating the availability of certain types of knowledge.

As early as the 1940s, before artificial intelligence was properly born, some ingenious studies revealed that if a syllogism triggers an opinion in the mind of the person trying to solve it, that person immediately becomes about half as logical as he or she would have been had no opinion been aroused. One of the syllogisms went like this:

1. All Russians are Bolsheviks.
2. Some Bolsheviks are undemocratic people.
3. Which of the following conclusions are true: (a) All undemocratic people are Russian. (b) No undemocratic people are Russian. (c) Some undemocratic people are Russian. (d) Some undemocratic people are not Russian. (e) None of these conclusions is proven.

The correct, *logical* answer is (e), but because people have an opinion that Russians are undemocratic, they choose (c), letting what they think they know about the world override rational argument.

During the early days of artificial intelligence, and perhaps influenced by the prevailing computer metaphor of the mind, some psychologists speculated that if they could strip a problem of its everyday meaning, peeling away layers of worldliness like the leaves of an artichoke, they would find at the core of cognition a pristine and naked logic engine that is the universal motor of rational thinking. They could not have been more wrong. Eliminating worldly content often results in the disappearance of logical reason altogether. Philip Johnson-Laird and Peter Wason, who set out in a careful series of studies to discover the elusive logical component of thought, found that the ordinary mortal "passes into a looking-glass world" when faced with a puzzle that does not connect with his mundane concerns. In such circumstances he is doubly forlorn; he often loses not only his rational thought, but also his intuitions about the real world, which might guide him to a correct answer.

What happens is that basic, powerful concepts that are rooted in the sort of primitive level of intelligence that robots or babies display—concepts of space and time, of cause and effect—are imposed on problems willy-nilly. It is just a matter of luck whether reasoning in terms of these deeply implanted, ancient patterns of thought will produce a logical answer or whether they will not. People usually have no trouble solving this puzzle:

1. If Susan goes to her aerobics class then she skips lunch.
2. Either Susan eats lunch or else she slows down in the afternoon.

They arrive at the correct answer, "If Susan goes to her class, she slows down in the afternoon." This looks like a logical deduction, but it may be only an inference based on the idea of cause and effect, that Susan does skip lunch as a result of going to class. It can be exposed as a fake by changing the wording of the puzzle:

1. Susan goes to her aerobics class only if she skips lunch.
2. Either Susan eats lunch or else she slows down in the afternoon.

This version of the puzzle is logically equivalent to the first version, but it turns out to be much more difficult to solve, because the effect and the cause in the first premise are reversed. People conclude from the first premise that Susan goes to her class, but that is useless for deciding on the answer to the second premise. It is a loose end dangling instead of being the logical key to the puzzle. So being "rational" is easy when the pattern of cause and effect matches the logical form of the argument, but when they collide, being rational is a good deal more difficult. The two psychologists who devised this puzzle report that they caught only a glimpse of the "deductive component" as an "intermittent groundswell on which are imposed the perturbations of causal thought."

This curious tug-of-war between logic and real-world knowledge is not confined to bright, well-educated Western adults. It has been observed in the Kpelle, a rice-farming tribal people in Liberia, in the neighboring Vai, and in villagers in the Yucatán, Mexico. The notion that primitive peoples cannot reason in a logical fashion is quite wrong. It depends what they are reasoning about. The single most salient feature of how villagers solved such problems as

All Kpelle men are rice farmers.
Mr. Smith is not a rice farmer.
Is he a Kpelle man?

was the extent to which the problem connected with real-world knowledge and experience. One Kpelle farmer sensibly replied: "I have not laid eyes on the man." These studies, as reported by Sylvia Scribner, suggest that logical thought may be a special learned idiom, like narrative, arising when societies acquire the special kind of talk needed for trade, contracts, treaties, and legal agreements.

One of the most ambitious attempts in this century to tackle the question, central to artificial intelligence, of whether the sort of mind we would recognize as human can exist in a universe which is abstract and totally empty of material things, was made by the Swiss psychologist Jean Piaget. The son of a medieval-history scholar, from whom he inherited an almost superhuman patience and a meticulous appetite for detail, Piaget was trained as a biologist whose special field was mollusks. As a boy, he was introduced by his godfather to the philosophy of Henri Bergson, and was swept away by the idea that God is identified with life and evolution. "It stirred me almost to ecstasy," Piaget said, "because it enabled me to see in biology the explanation for all things and of the mind itself." He devoted his life to explaining the mind, and how and why we know what we know, in terms of biological development and the evolution of the species. Piaget's approach to logic would have appalled Frege.

Most philosophers had missed the boat in trying to create a satisfactory theory of knowledge, in Piaget's opinion, mainly because they failed to understand that knowledge is not passive, a mere copy of experience, but active, and the kind of knowledge we can have is not the same from one period of growing up to the next. The fact that the mind is in a body, and the body is in the world, is of critical importance in his theory. Piaget saw the mind as a dynamic, self-regulating system making sense of the world by means of certain internal organizing principles that are not innate, but are constructed by interaction with the environment. Rational thought is profoundly natural, not because it is given to us at birth, but because it develops in a series of stages out of much simpler bodily mechanisms for mastering and getting to know our physical surroundings. Piaget talked about the environment as *aliment*, food for the mind; the more nutritious the food, the more quickly a child will succeed in building new mental structures out of earlier ones.

In Piaget's theory, the mind progresses through four stages, each stage organizing experience in a different way. The order in which this sequence unfolds is the same for everyone, but it is not programmed as a computer is programmed, and some people move from one stage to another more rapidly than others. At stage one, from birth to about the age of two, a child learns how to act, but lacks a mental image of the world, so that when an object is out of sight, it ceases to exist. Representation of that kind comes at stage two, when children understand how objects can be classified and grouped. At stage three, from age seven to about twelve, a child acquires a set of skills called operations, no longer accepting appearances as true reality, but going beyond them to discover underlying principles and devise basic theories of how the world works and how objects relate to one another. This is a cognitive revolution in the child's life, but the child is still largely a prisoner of concrete reality, able to classify objects in complex ways but only if the objects are physically present. It is at the final, fourth stage, which begins at about eleven, that the mind is able to escape the actual and live in a world of abstract possibility, in which symbols are manipulated according to formal rules. Reality, as Piaget put it, "is now secondary to possibility." This is the age group at which Lewis Carroll aimed his popular books on logic. A third-stage child might balk at the Carroll premise, "a fish, that cannot dance a minuet, is contemptible," declaring it nonsensical, but a child at the fourth stage of formal operations is likely to accept the premise and try to reason out an answer to the puzzle. He or she is capable of using the "if-then" rules of deductive reasoning.

Piaget writes as if a teenager at the fourth stage is a logician, actually "intoxicated" with logic, reveling in the ability to manipulate abstract symbols with rules and search possibilities. He even suggests that this subordination of what is actual to what is possible may explain adolescent idealism, which does not yet accept the practical limits on what is possible. What is more, Piaget maintains that the formal operations at the fourth stage are quite general. A single set of rules can be applied to all kinds of different problems, so that knowledge acquired as a result of dealing with one problem can be used immediately to solve another. What matters is not the kind of knowledge available to the teenager, or the specific content of the problem, but the power of abstract reason, based on logic. Ironically, an intelligence that has grown out of bodily actions and a need to adapt to the world, becomes independent of both; as Piaget portrays him, the fourth-stage person develops into something resembling Newell and Simon's General Problem Solver. (Piaget himself may have arrived at his belief that logic is the engine that generates knowledge in his own late adolescence. At the University of Neuchâtel, his teacher, Arnold Raymond, a philosopher and logician, made clear to Piaget the relationship between Aristotle's logic and biology, which in the writings of Bergson, Piaget's childhood hero, are kept quite separate and distinct.)

Lately, however, studies inspired by Piaget's work suggest that he went wrong in severely underestimating the effect of what we know on how we reason. In fact, it is possible to throw Piaget's orderly sequence of stages of intelligence into confusion simply by altering the content of a test, just changing the wording so as to elicit a different kind of knowledge. This contradicts certain basic tenets of Piaget's theory, which states that while the four stages of intelligence are not programmed into the brain in the sense that all children inevitably go through them, and at the same rate, the order of the stages is universal. A child goes forward from a lower stage to a higher one, but not backward, from a higher to a lower. Also, such results throw serious doubt on the extent to which the adolescent, and even the adult, is unworldly, at home in a universe of possibilities.

If a child as young as three years, supposedly at stage two and therefore prelogical, is presented with a problem in such a way that it evokes her implicit knowledge of the world, she may give a correct answer, as if displaying logical thought. On the other hand, a mature, intelligent adult is apt to throw logic to the winds if given a problem specially constructed so as to have no connection with her worldly knowledge. It is as if an infant jumped ahead two Piagetian stages in a moment of time, to another type of intelligence entirely, a different way of organizing the world, and the adult slipped back two stages, just because a clever experimenter manipulated the content of the test and the type of knowledge that would be used to answer it. Piaget's theory prohibits such frisky leaps forward up the ladder of stages, or slippings back. Each stage is supposed to be a brand-new way of organizing the world. The child of seven lives in a mental universe that is different from the universe of his previous stage, which is why it is difficult for the child even to remember what the world was like before he organized it in this particular way.

A celebrated puzzle illustrates this curious phenomenon. It suggests that the way a person reasons may have less to do with the Piagetian stage he is at than with what the puzzle is all about, whether it does or does not elicit certain kinds of knowledge. The beauty of the puzzle is the ease with which it can be manipulated so that when presented in one form, university professors with tenure are flummoxed, and when it is presented in another form, the average dunderhead can solve it easily. Try it for yourself. Suppose you are shown four cards, laid out facedown in a row. On the visible side of the cards are printed these symbols:

F   4   7   E

You are told that each card has a letter on one side and a number on the other. You are then given a rule: "If there is a vowel on one side of a card, then there is an even number on the other side." You must decide whether this rule is true or false by turning over those cards, and only those cards, that show the rule to be true or false.

The puzzle, invented by the British psychologist Peter Wason, looks so innocent, so simpleminded, that, when it was given to some French military recruits, more than a third of them refused to attempt it, scribbling such rude comments on their test papers as, *"C'est pourri, idiot, débile; c'est gaspi"*— "This is rotten, feebleminded, it's a waste of time." One recruit wrote, *"Ça c'est Belge une fois"*—"Now this is even Belgian," the

French equivalent of an American joke about the mental ability of Poles. As a trial of wits, however, as a test of logic, as a bomb thrown at the stately edifice of the Piagetian theory of knowledge, the puzzle is formidable, wicked in its power to debunk and demolish. It is a test of logic, yet even career logicians have been known to make a hash of it.

Most people, including university teachers with lofty IQs, MENSA near-geniuses, and bright college students, turn over card E alone, or cards E and 4. By doing so, they fail the test. They are not logical enough. The correct answer is to turn over E and 7. Card F is irrelevant, because the rule applies only to vowels. So too is card 4, since the rule does not state that a card with an even number on one side must have a vowel on the other. Only E and 7 together can establish whether or not the rule is true, but usually less than ten percent of university students make this selection.

The four-card game embodies one of the most elementary principles of standard logic, the proof of the falsity of a proposition. The rule is of the form "If p, then q," which is exactly where the fourth stage Piagetian child is supposed to exercise mastery. Here p stands for the vowel card E and q stands for the even-number card 4. The existence of a "not-q," that is, the discovery of a symbol that is not a 4 on the reverse side of an E, would render the proposition false. So the right decision is to select p and not-q, in other words, an E and 7, the odd-number card. An extremely common mistake is to ignore the 7, which in logic is exactly the one that ought to be turned, since it may prove the rule false immediately and conclusively. A general statement cannot be proved true by any number of confirming instances, but it can be proved false by just one disconfirming instance.

Something startling happens, however, when the content of the puzzle is changed so as to make it more worldly. People who behave illogically when the cards are given letters and numbers suddenly become "logical" when they attempt the test in its new form. They jump ahead a couple of Piagetian stages, which according to Piaget means organizing the world in an entirely different way. Suppose the rule to be tested were changed from "If there is a vowel on one side of the card, then it has an even number on the other side," to "Every time I go to Miami, I take a plane." The four cards now read

Miami   Baltimore   Plane   Train

Each card represents a journey. On one side is the destination and on the other side is the means of travel. To test the truth or falsity of the proposition, the correct, logical answer is to turn over "Miami" and "Train," corresponding to E and 7 in the abstract version. Here "Baltimore" is equivalent to card F and "Plane" to card 4. Now, the irrelevance of "Baltimore" and "Plane" is much more apparent than in the case of the numbers and letters. I can go to Baltimore by train or plane, or travel by plane to anywhere in the world, and in neither case do I disprove the rule that every time I go to Miami I take a plane.

When the game is played in this version, the success rate soars. In one test, ten out of sixteen people made the correct choices, compared with only two out of sixteen in the abstract version. The explanation is that by altering the form of the puzzle so that commonsense knowledge of the world could be used to solve it, a different type of reasoning appeared, one that conforms to the rules of logic. When the knowledge changes, so does the reasoning. A rule that is less worldly, less commonsensical, will elicit fewer correct answers. Given the rule "If I eat haddock, then I drink gin"—which seems to belong to Lewis Carroll's world, where logicians are apt to have a passion for pork chops and men with dreamy eyes are fond of barley sugar, rather than to the actual world—the success rate falls, though not to levels as low as those produced by the abstract rule involving letters and numbers.

A standard digital computer would solve all versions of the puzzle with equal ease, because the machine's thinking is more independent of the knowledge stored in its memory than is the thinking of a human being. A digital computer is more Piagetian in this respect than we are. The results of Peter Wason's four-card game show with striking simplicity that humans are not general-purpose logicians, that what they know has a powerful effect on how they think. Something as seemingly serene and detached as reason turns out to be intimately entangled with the business of being and acting in the world. Interestingly, people who solve the puzzle in its storylike version do not become better at solving it in its abstract version, even though the logical form is exactly the same in each case. They fail in exactly the same way as people who come completely fresh to the game, so that reasoning in terms of content, even when we arrive at the right answers, does not provide us with the general rules that apply to all kinds of content. It is the type of knowledge, and the way such knowledge is organized in memory, that determines whether we reason validly or invalidly. What gives logic its tremendous power—its indifference to content—is not what gives natural intelligence its power.

Children aged four, who according to Piaget do not even have the ability to grasp the truth that lies behind appearances, can reason "deductively" when listening to stories. Margaret Donaldson describes a study in which a stage-two child looks at a picture of a wedding where the groom seems a little feminine and exclaims, "But how can it be that they are getting married? You have to have a man, too." The reasoning underlying this statement can be expressed in the form of an Aristotelian syllogism:

1. All weddings require a man and a woman.
2. This one has no man.
3. Therefore it can't be a wedding.

When presented in terms of what the child knew about weddings, the problem elicited a "rational" answer. That would not be the case, however, if it were rewritten in the language of propositional logic:

1. If p, then q.
2. Not q.
3. Therefore not p.

Preschoolers, it appears, can reason well about events in stories because the stories are "sustained by human sense," and the conclusion does not conflict with what the children know and believe. It is only when meaning is eliminated, and the use of such knowledge is ruled out, that the minds of children, as well as those of adults, begin to boggle.

5: BAKER STREET REASONING

rom the standpoint of logic, Sherlock Holmes is something of a fraud. According to his faithful companion and chronicler, Dr. John Watson, MD, Holmes reasons with an unwavering formality. The doctor is emphatic on this point. He calls his friend "the logician of Baker Street," a man who argues his way to the solution of a crime like a Greek mathematician proving a theorem in geometry, proceeding step by step along a flawless chain of inferences. More than once, Holmes himself refers to his craft as "the science of deduction." It offends him that Watson's literary style veers toward the sensational and romantic, obscuring the austere mathematical elegance of his reasoning. Indulging in such embellishments, Holmes warns his admiring Boswell, is like inserting "an elopement into the fifth proposition of Euclid."

If Watson were writing today, he might say that his friend had a mind like a computer (let us say an expert system, since the great detective is a walking encyclopedia on such special topics as poisons and sensational literature, and has a good practical knowledge of British law, but is so bereft of basic commonsense knowledge he has never heard of the Copernican theory). Yet very often Holmes does not think at all like Euclid or an IBM PC. Instead of arguing from premises to conclusion, using the rules of logic, he arrives at an answer in a flash of what seems to be magical intuition. Nowhere is this more true than when he dazzles the impressionable Watson by giving an instant biography of a total stranger after a momentary glance. In *A Study in Scarlet,* for example, Holmes spies a "stalwart, plainly dressed individual" walking along the street outside their Baker Street lodgings and immediately pronounces him to be a retired sergeant of marines. "Brag and bounce!" mutters Watson. "He knows that I cannot verify his guess." When the stranger enters their room unexpectedly with a message, Watson inquires with a malicious smile what his former profession might be. "A sergeant, sir," the man replies. "Royal Marine Light Infantry." Watson is suitably deflated.

How did Holmes reach his astute conclusion? By "deductive science"? Not exactly. "Even across the street I could see a great blue anchor tattooed on the back of the fellow's hand," he explains. "That smacked of the sea. He had a military carriage, however, and regulation side whiskers. There we have the marine. He was a man with some amount of self-importance and a certain air of command. You must have observed the way in which he held his head and swung his cane. A steady, respectable, middle-aged man, too, on the face of him—all facts which led me to believe that he had been a sergeant." Watson is thunderstruck. "Wonderful!" he exclaims.

Holmes himself is not consistent in his accounts of how this thought process works. At one moment he insists that he follows a train of reasoning step by step, though without being aware of some of the intermediate steps. At another, he declares that it is more like being sure that two and two make four, without being able to prove it. "It was easier to know it than to explain why I know it," he remarks to Watson.

Clearly, Holmes did not prove a "theorem" about the stranger's military career by deriving propositions from axioms using general rules of inference, or searching all conceivable possibilities by brute force. Instead, he summoned up, at lightning speed, relevant knowledge about the world that was evoked by a few fragments of information. He generalized from the clues he observed in the stranger's manner and bearing to the concept, fully formed in his mind, of a typical sergeant of marines. The finished product masqueraded as deduction, just as players of Peter Wason's four-card game appear to think by the rules of logic, whereas they are really bringing to bear their knowledge of the world.

What Holmes is actually doing is thinking by means of what modern cognitive scientists call knowledge structures. He is using patterns of worldly knowledge to process information. Baker Street reasoning is logic without logic, which is what natural intelligence is all about.

Knowledge structures of this kind go by the general name of "schemas," and they are so important they have been called the building blocks of thought, as fundamental to a theory of human reason as cell biology is to an understanding of the living system. In fact, schemas tend to explain too much rather than too little, which is why some psychologists distrust them. It is their mysterious power that makes them suspect. There is no way of proving that schemas exist, and in their present form they are probably crude simplifications of the actual structures of thought. Yet even if they are only a metaphor, they are the best metaphor around. They are the basis of Baker Street reasoning.

When Immanuel Kant created a revolution in the theory of knowledge in the eighteenth century, he introduced the notion of a schema as part of the process by which the human mind takes the information that the senses deliver and turns it into knowledge. The mind, in Kant's theory, is not designed to give us uninterpreted knowledge of the world, but must always approach it with a certain bias, from a special point of view. We can never hope to know the world as it "really" is, because we see it as if through a pair of mental spectacles we can never take off. The spectacles are built into the mind at birth. Even if we could remove them, there would be no world to see, just a meaningless blur, because looking through the lenses of the spectacles is a prerequisite of having an experience of the world of any sort. We know the world as it appears to us bespectacled or we do not know it at all.

Space and time, under these conditions, are not actual, out there in the world, independent of the mind's design. They are a product of innate organizing activities in the brain. Tables and chairs are spread out in space, and one moment follows another moment in time, not because space and time exist in the physical universe, but because of the way our mental apparatus works. We are simply unable to experience a spaceless or timeless universe. Kant also proposed that we understand and interpret the world by means of twelve inborn concepts, among them the categories of substance, cause and effect, unity and totality, negation, and limitation. He called the rules by which such categories are imposed on what the senses perceive, "schemas."

For Kant, schemas enable us to have knowledge of the world that is sure to be correct, even though it is based neither on the certainty that deductive logic offers, nor on the eyes and ears of direct experience. The statement "All actresses are female" is a logical truth, guaranteed for all times and in all places, because actresses are female by definition. The second part of the sentence merely makes explicit what is already implicit in the first part. A statement such as "All effects have causes" is also certified to be correct, but in a totally different way. Here, the predicate is not implicit in the subject and the sentence is not a logical truth; but it is true for us always and everywhere, because the rules of organization built into our minds do not permit us to interpret the world in any other fashion.

One striking feature of the Kantian categories is that they are not specifically logical modes of thinking. Logic, for Kant, is not a necessary precondition for having an experience and it is not built into the mind. Effects without causes are not a logical impossibility. They may occur in heaven perhaps, who knows. The important point is that they do not occur in the sort of world our minds enable us to know.

In this respect the laws of logic are quite different from the laws of physics or of Euclidean geometry, because they hold good not just in the world that we inhabit, but also in many fictional worlds, including Shakespeare's Forest of Arden, Sherlock Holmes's London, and the court of King Arthur, to name only a few. As a matter of fact, the laws of logic are more general even than that. A modern definition of a logical truth is one that is true in all possible worlds. A possible world is one in which anything may happen as long as falsehood cannot be derived from truth in a chain of reasoning. That includes worlds so fantastic that they can be described but not imagined, such as a world of ten dimensions. That is why modern logic is an unsuitable vehicle for everyday reasoning, because there is nothing in the laws of logic to distinguish our actual world from some other possible one.

In a logically possible world, a man can grow as tall as a skyscraper, then shrink to the size of a bee, become a swarm of bees which descend on thirteenth-century Paris, and proceed to write the *Encyclopaedia Britannica*. Logic licenses all such bizarre goings-on. That is part of its peculiar permissiveness. Such a world becomes impossible, however, as soon as we assert that it contains a table that is both perfectly round and perfectly square at the same time. In a logically possible world all manner of incredible things may happen as long as that world can be described without a contradiction. If a single contradiction arises, a world becomes impossible and is wiped out. (The modern mystery writer Loren Estleman has pointed out a contradiction in the world of Sherlock Holmes that, strictly speaking, disqualifies it as a logically possible world: in one place we are told that Dr. Watson was wounded in the leg by a jezail bullet while serving with the Berkshire regiment in Afghanistan, while in another the same bullet is said to have penetrated his shoulder.)

So the Kantian categories of the understanding, and the schemas that mediate them, are more mundane than the organizing principles of deductive logic. They restrict the range of possible worlds we can know, and they give us true information about the actual world in advance of our experience of it. The schemas are a sort of bias inherent in the mind; we know what is out there through the medium of the categories, so that either we understand the world from that perspective or we do not understand it at all.

Schemas in the modern sense of the word are also a means of explaining how the mind knows what it knows and why we cannot have uninterpreted knowledge of reality. One difference is that today's schemas are even less logical than the categories of Kant. The statement "All actresses are female" can be made while sitting in an armchair, in the comfort of one's room, without bothering to observe so much as a single actress to confirm the fact that she is female. The same applies to a statement like "All causes have effects," which is also an armchair truth that does not need to be checked by observation, because it is true by virtue of the way the mind is made. A third kind of statement, "All actresses have press agents," is not an armchair truth, however. It is a generalization based on our experience of a world in which the overwhelming majority of actresses have press agents, but some may not. Such a generalization can be called a schema, which is a structure of existing knowledge that is used to process and interpret new information. That means we understand and "reason" about the world through the lens of schemas that are not guaranteed to deliver infallible truths about what we see and hear. Since the mind is by nature a knowledge medium rather than a logic machine, it tends to use schemas which tell us what is typically the case, how the world usually goes, and not what is necessarily true. Yet we place considerable trust in such schemas as guides to an understanding of reality. This has a powerful effect on the way we think and reason. To meet an actress is to predict that somewhere in her entourage there is a press agent, perhaps to falsely remember that a press agent was present when that was not the case, and even to resist or ignore evidence that suggests the actress does her own publicity.

Schemas in their modern incarnation were introduced into psychology by Henry Head, the English neurologist who championed the doctrine of holism in the brain. But they became really interesting when applied to the theory of memory. In 1932, Sir Frederic Bartlett, an English psychologist, made the intriguing proposal that memory is not a clear window through which we view the past, exactly as it happened. Remembering, Bartlett suggested, is more Kantian than that. Memory is like a lens, organizing the stored data in our heads, so that we do not have uninterpreted knowledge of the past as it "really" was. When the mind remembers, it reconstructs a kind of story, fitting together bits and pieces of information about the past, using networks of preexisting knowledge. The mind works with clues and connects them in terms of what it already knows. One of Bartlett's sources of inspiration was a party game called "Russian whispers," in which players sit in a circle and pass along a whispered message from person to person. When the message reaches the last person in the chain, it is transformed into something quite bizarre, though it often remains a grammatical sentence. A message might start out as "The Russians are coming," and end up as "The crushed Persians armed in the morning." Since whispering makes transmission noisy and unreliable, each player has to reconstruct a sentence out of a few ambiguous clues.

A particularly arresting feature of memory, Bartlett found, is the way it tends to conventionalize the past. If people try to remember exotic and strange material, they often make it more normal, more typical of their own view of the world than it really is, without being aware of what they are doing. Bartlett made his students read an Indian folktale, called "The War of the Ghosts," about a young man hunting seals by a river. The youth is taken in a canoe by five strangers to a town farther upstream, where a battle starts and many people are killed. The young man, hearing one of the strangers remark that he has been hit by an arrow, thinks to himself, "Oh, they are ghosts."

He does not feel sick, and yet the stranger says he has been shot.

The story seems odd and curiously disconnected to Western ears. English readers, when asked to remember the passage, tended to make it more connected than it actually was. They recalled it as being shorter and more consistent with their own ideas about how the world usually works. What seemed to be gaps in the narrative, sudden shifts of content, were filled in by using knowledge of what causes normally produce certain effects. Parts of the story that appeared incomplete were completed, some material was dropped altogether, and the plot was altered so as to resemble existing stories familiar to English readers. The more often people tried to recall the story as it really was, the more they conventionalized it, until it settled down into a more-or-less permanent form in their minds. They used schemas of boat trips they had taken and ghost stories and adventure tales from their childhood.

Schemas, Bartlett showed, are structures of connected knowledge, acquired through our special experiences of being in the world, which are used to make sense of information that may be seriously deficient, strange, fragmentary, ambiguous, contradictory, or full of holes. They provide plausible scenarios, into which bits and pieces of data can be made to fit. Sherlock Holmes astonished Watson with his "powers of deduction" by applying a schema for a typical marine to the scraps of information about the stranger's appearance, which was all he had to go on. What he saw was not much, but it matched a vastly richer and more complete pattern of knowledge in his head.

Unlike the if-then production rules in a computer program, which generalize too freely, and logic, where a set of premises and a few rules can produce hundreds of valid conclusions, most of them trivial, schemas are devices that extend and amplify information, but do so in a controlled way, abiding by rules of relevance and plausibility. They add to the data they are given, turning mere clues into elaborate, connected scenarios, but they do not run wild, tending to remain within the boundaries of what is appropriate and useful for making sense of the world.

Possessing schemas, we can glance at a newspaper headline, GILBERT WEAKENS IN MEXICO, and predict that the story underneath it will report that hurricane Gilbert, raging through the Caribbean at force five, is losing its power as it moves across Mexico and is wreaking proportionately less havoc. There are many other, logically sound conclusions to be drawn from those four words, but this one conforms best to what we know. Headlines are clues to stories, and the information they provide is so impoverished it is often open to more than one interpretation. Schemas are remarkably adept at supplying the most plausible interpretation, because they are at home with imperfect information and are able to process poor-quality data in a worldly fashion. They are guides to what is likely to be the case, based on our knowledge of how the world usually works.

Schemas are also guides to action, since they resolve uncertainty. The English philosopher Alasdair MacIntyre has argued that Hamlet is immobilized for most of Shakespeare's play, unable to decide on a clear course of action to avenge his murdered father, because he arrives at Elsinore from Wittenberg with too many different schemas in his head to guide him through the complexities of the intrigues at court: the revenge schema of the Norse sagas, the renaissance courtier's schema, the Machiavellian schema about competition for power. Until Hamlet has adopted a specific schema, he does not know what facts to treat as evidence, and until he knows that, he cannot tell which course of action to adopt. He has a crisis of interpretation. So do members of the audience, who can understand the play in any one of a number of different ways depending on which schema they adopt.

The psychologist R. C. Anderson and his colleagues showed that a reader's interpretation of a story can be manipulated in quite a dramatic way by altering the schema used to make sense of it, if the story is sufficiently ambiguous. One such story ran:

> Rocky slowly got up from the mat, planning his escape. He hesitated a moment and thought. Things were not going well. What bothered him the most was being held, especially since the

charge against him had been weak. He considered his present situation. The lock that held him was strong but he thought he could break it. He knew, however, that his timing would have to be perfect. Rocky was aware that it was because of his early roughness that he had been penalized so severely—much too severely from his point of view.

When this story is given the title "The Wrestler," it seems quite straightforward and easy to follow. Change the title to "The Prisoner," however, and it means something else entirely. People not only read it differently; they also remember it differently. What is more, most of those who read the story with one title are unaware that it can be interpreted in another way, while they are reading it. They are blind to even the most obvious ambiguities. Schemas resolve ambiguities, but they may exact a price, by pointing the mind toward a single interpretation, a particular way of making sense of the world, and making other interpretations much less accessible. They manipulate reason by restricting the kinds of knowledge available to the conscious mind. This is a very Kantian property of schemas, that they bias our understanding so that we know the world from a certain viewpoint, which excludes other viewpoints.

Schemas make "worldly" connections between facts even when the connections are not spelled out or seem to be missing altogether. For amusement, we can think of schemas to make sense of examples of material implication, the logical relation used to great effect in the *Principia,* in which statements are juxtaposed solely on the basis of whether they are true or false, and nothing else:

> If glass is a fragile material, then a ship can float.
> If the wings ice up, then the word is abbreviated.
> If pigs can fly, then breakfast is an evening meal.

These sentences appear to be completely disconnected as far as meaning and relevance are concerned. They seem fragmented, containing no link of cause and effect. A link emerges in the first sentence, however, as soon as the schema "launching a battle-ship with a bottle of champagne" is applied. The second sentence makes sense if it is fitted to a schema for skywriting. The third is more of a challenge, but imagine a scenario in which a remote Midwestern town is cut off by a blizzard. The inhabitants have eaten nothing all day, but in late afternoon a planeload of slaughtered pigs is flown in and by seven PM everyone is sitting down to bacon and eggs. Schemas seem to be able to manufacture relevance, to conjure connections out of thin air, with a genius for interpretation that transforms the possible worlds permitted by logic into a plausible world more like the one of our everyday experience. They turn defective data into information of fairly good quality.

Schemas are so good at finding links, filling gaps, removing ambiguity, and the mind, in consequence, is so at home with imperfect information, that it finds perfect information intolerably tedious. Perfect information is unnatural. A person who spelled out everything in excruciating detail—even if that were possible—would be ostracized as unfit for civilized society, and rightly so. He would be blackballed from every club in town. A good talker leaves much ambiguous and unspoken, scatters clues, invites interpretation. Stories and novels, as Jerome Bruner has emphasized, may be about events in a "real" world, but if they are to have literary merit and attract a readership, the author must create gaps in that world for the reader to fill in. This leads to the paradox that in modern fiction a writer cannot express explicitly what it is he really wants to say. The meaning is so thoroughly implicit it does not exist at all until a reader uses the clues buried in the text to construct an interpretation of his own. Annie Dillard, in her study of the modern novel, *Living by Fiction*, goes a step further and asserts that even the clues should be removed. To write fiction that anyone will read, an author must painstakingly conceal what to him is the whole point of the book, "like a good scout whose job it is to blaze a new trail, all traces of which he must carefully obliterate."

Schemas are about connections. They can put together whole tracts of knowledge out of a scattering of parts, amplify and extend impoverished data, and make sense of what seems to be nonsense. Schemas guide us through the thickets of complexity that confront us at every waking moment, and by their power to make much out of little, enable us to ignore most of the complexity and still represent reality to ourselves as a coherent whole. As aids to action, they are apt to anchor us in the mundane, the plausible, the familiar, and they are ruthless in the way they murder possibilities, cutting a path along which we can move in confidence without being diverted by alternative routes.

That is not the way logic proceeds. Logic, as the most general of the sciences, deals with the possible rather than with the merely plausible, or what seems to make sense in a real world. In the interests of generality, logic puts together assertions that need not be connected in experience. Schemas enable us to eliminate possibilities wholesale, but logic is more promiscuous in this way. It cannot be chained to the actual, or to what experience tells us the world ought to be like. It needs to investigate the consequences of statements that are false. Logic inhabits the kingdom of the possible. It is, as Morris Cohen said, "an exploration of the field of possibility just as truly as astronomy is an exploration of the field of stellar motions."

Human beings, in their everyday traffic with an actual world, cannot afford such luxury. Ironically, the computer, with its unique powers of dealing with complexity, has helped to show that exploring all possibilities, even in fairly simple systems of knowledge, is a pipe dream. The idea of mind as a magic medium, free of the limits of space and time, possessed of unbounded resources, cannot be sustained in the face of surprising and even shocking discoveries about the nature of complexity, some of which I shall outline in the next chapter. Making sense of the world need not and often cannot be a deductive science, even in Baker Street.

6: CAN CROCODILES RUN STEEPLECHASES?

Aristotle called man the rational animal because he regarded reason as the hallmark of the species; by exercising reason we develop and perfect those natural powers that make us distinctively human. In fact, reason offers even grander possibilities than that, changing the very status of the rational animal, lifting him above and beyond mere humanness, into the eternal realm of the gods.

In neoclassical economics, however, "rational man" is an altogether different creature from Aristotle's conception. He is godlike, but in a very special, restricted way. The cornerstone of economics is the idea of the man of perfect reason, who knows the things that he prefers, and is able to place them in order from most desired to least desired. Rational economic man is aware of all the alternatives open to him, and never fails to choose the ones that give him most satisfaction, no matter how many there may be, because he has unlimited powers of computation. He is able to cope with the real world in all its complexity, not shrinking from the most fearsome probability calculations, and doing those things for which the benefits exceed the costs. This paragon of reason keeps a cool head even in the bedroom, where, according to University of Chicago economist Gary Becker, he would read in bed only if the value of reading exceeded the value to him of the loss of sleep suffered by his wife.

Rational economic man, "preposterously omniscient," has been subjected to vigorous debunking by Herbert Simon in a series of polemical writings, and replaced by a more plausible and lifelike figure known as "administrative man," who is rational, but only up to a point and within certain limits. Administrative man, a species found in organizations of all kinds, commercial and bureaucratic alike, simply ignores most of the complexity that rational man rejoices in. He forms in his mind a drastically simplified model of the "buzzing, blooming confusion" of the world because he assumes the world is almost empty and that what things it does contain are mostly unrelated to one another. The few connections he does recognize between events and objects tend to be short and simple. Since he believes that nearly all the facts in the world have little to do with what he is doing at any given time, he cheerfully ignores all but a tiny part of reality. Simon calls administrative man a cousin of rational economic man, but he must be a very distant cousin. Unlike his scrupulous relative, who considers all alternatives when making a choice, he is not even aware that most alternatives exist. He brushes them aside. He makes decisions mainly by fairly simple rules of thumb.

The world, of course, is not largely empty, and the things it contains are linked by cause and effect in intricate and sometimes roundabout ways. To illustrate this truth, Simon tells the story of a statistician who was surprised to discover a high correlation between the number of old maids and the size of the clover crop in several different counties of England. How, he wondered, could these two facts be related? The statistician, who was extremely rational, puzzled over the riddle for a time and finally discovered the connection. It turned out that old maids kept cats, and cats ate mice. Field mice are natural enemies of bumblebees, and bumblebees are the chief agents in fertilizing the flowers of clover plants. This curious chain of consequences suggests that administrative man should not make laws increasing the marriage bonus without first taking into account the effect on the clover crop of a reduction in the number of spinsters.

Administrative man, who is most of us, assumes that the world is nearly empty and unconnected because his computational powers are so limited. Artificial-intelligence researchers realize that simply ignoring complexity is part of common sense, and it is one of the reasons why people are worldly while computer programs are not. Surprisingly, when people reason informally they seem not to make better choices just because they consider a large number of alternatives.

Economics, the science of allocating scarce resources, Simon thinks, ought to pay more heed to the way the mind uses its scarce resource, computation, in dealing with uncertainty and complexity. A theory of an ideal rational agent, producing optimum decisions under all circumstances, is not only incomplete, but can be seriously misleading because it provides "solutions" to economic questions that will not work in the real world. The need to use makeshift rules that give answers that are only approximately correct is an imperative of the human condition. Breeding smarter people will not remove it, because the world is more complex, and the mind simpler, than we might suppose.

An intriguing discovery of the last few years is that a physical system that solves problems must make compromises with rationality just by virtue of the fact that it is embodied, and dwells in a world of space and time. That is true whether the system is a sophisticated modern computer or a brain that has evolved over millions of years. The existence of a real world, in which space is not endless and time does not go on forever, has important consequences for the way such a system makes sense of that world. Put in the form of a slogan: reason is not an independent agent.

What is more interesting, the sort of problems that force such a system to be less than rational need not be extraordinarily complex or out of the way. During the 1970s, a computer scientist at Berkeley, William Kahan, achieved a wide celebrity for his remarkable ability to take any pocket electronic calculator and make it, in the words of a contemporary, "start spitting out the most terrifying gibberish that would make your skin crawl." Kahan was compared by his circle of admirers at Berkeley to the magician of Lublin, the hero of one of Isaac Bashevis Singer's stories, a burglar of some distinction who was able, even though blindfolded and in his cups, to pick the trickiest and most ingenious locks brought to him by his fellow break-in artists as part of the booty of their nocturnal expeditions. Kahan worked his magic, sober and with his eyes wide open, on pocket calculators, devices that do simple arithmetical problems, such as finding square roots, using very small pieces of software. They are among the least complicated computers that exist, and might be expected to crank out foolproof, safe, and accurate answers with complete reliability under any circumstances.

Like the locks of Lublin, however, these little machines could be teased into a state of breakdown almost regardless of how well they had been designed. The reason is that, simple as they are, and rational as they may seem, the calculators do not have unlimited space for their circuitry or endless time in which to come up with an answer to an arithmetical problem. In the world of pure, disembodied mathematics, the number system is in principle infinite. The square root of two is expressed as $1.4142135623\ldots$, a sequence that can be continued to any number of decimal places. Being a physical system, not an abstraction, however, a computer rounds off the string of numbers, usually after about eight places of decimals. This may seem a generous allowance, but because the machine carries out a vast quantity of operations in a matter of seconds, rounding off can lead to errors, especially when two numbers of almost equal size are subtracted. In such a case, most of the leading digits cancel out. Not being permitted the luxury of dealing with the infinite, the computer must make do with procedures that are quick rather than elegant, "dirty" rather than pure.

Under ordinary circumstances, errors caused by rounding off or truncating strings of digits occur in the computer as more or less random fluctuations. Algorithms, precise, step-by-step instructions for solving a given problem, programmed into the machine, are written so as to mitigate the effect of round-off errors, which usually cause no trouble and go unnoticed by the user. In the hands of the magician of Berkeley, however, the behavior of such errors became diabolical. Kahan manipulated the pocket calculators so that the fluctuations became an oscillation, and the oscillation was amplified. The machines produced square-root values that departed from the correct ones by as much as ten times.

"Before a conference, computer people would come to his hotel room with their latest calculators, some of them so new they didn't even have a tag on them yet, and he would have the things burping out the most horrible garbage in no time at all," recalls Christopher Cherniak, now a professor of philosophy at the University of Maryland. "On campus, his office was littered with hundreds of calculators that were selling for as much as a hundred dollars a pop, the newest and fanciest machines. You would think nothing could be simpler than these devices. They come with algorithms hard-wired into them, seemingly the cleanest and most straightforward that can be. Yet the fact that square-root values can be made to go haywire shows that the simplest procedures, when they are condemned to adapt to the finite space and time of a machine, can break down in unexpected and even scary sorts of ways. I mean, these calculators were being used to build bridges, and bridges can fall down."

What happens to rationality in the real world where thinking is embodied, whether in silicon or in flesh and blood, is a question that is being actively investigated as part of the flourishing and rapidly growing science of complexity, to which many highly gifted mathematicians are contributing. Surprisingly, it turns out that many seemingly easy problems in the real, everyday world, including some popular games like checkers, are extremely costly in terms of computing power. Computer chess-playing programs have achieved master ratings, and they exploit the brute-force abilities of modern computers to search millions of possible moves, but even they cannot search all possibilities, and one of their weaknesses is Eurisko's weakness, a lack of understanding of what it is they are doing. They are not, and may never be, infallible.

The "big bang" of modern logic, which culminated in the brilliant theorems of Kurt Gödel and others, among the most important discoveries in the whole history of ideas, showed that there are ineradicable limits to what a formal system can do. In 1931 Gödel proved that all deductive systems that are sufficiently complex are incomplete, and their consistency cannot be established without using principles of reasoning whose consistency is as dubious as that of the system itself. Later Alan Turing showed that there are some problems that cannot be decided in a finite number of steps; he imagined a computer that, once embarked on a proof, would never stop, but go on computing forever. These results were momentous, revealing as they did that formal systems like mathematics and logic are prevented from doing certain things in principle, by their very nature. There are no general-purpose rules that are guaranteed to produce the right answers to all problems, even in a system as clearly defined, as free from the messiness of the real world, as mathematics. It is not simply difficult or tedious or impractical to decide in advance whether a given assertion is computable, but forbidden, prohibited in principle, impossible. Less noticed at the time were results that showed there are reasonably short assertions in logic that, while not impossible to demonstrate, require proofs that are so long there are not enough years in a human lifetime to write them down. In some cases, even if generation after generation of workers attempted the task, the universe would cool down before they were able to finish.

Today it is recognized that certain problems in logic and mathematics require enormous amounts of computing time to solve. An ideal computer, a science-fiction machine as large as the universe itself, would take at least twenty billion years to determine the truth or falsity of certain logical statements only 675 symbols in length. In 1963, the proof of a conjecture in the theory of groups ran to two hundred fifty pages and took up an entire issue of the journal in which it was published; the final solution to the problem spread over some ten thousand pages, representing the combined work of hundreds of mathematicians.

One of the most celebrated long proofs of modern times is that of the four-color problem, which baffled mathematicians for nearly 125 years, since it was first described by Francis Guthrie, a young graduate student in Victorian London. Guthrie had wondered whether any map of counties can be drawn on a sheet of paper in such a way that only four or fewer colors are used, and no two counties sharing a common border have the same color. Repeated assaults were made on the four-color problem, resulting in failure after failure and severely bruising the self-esteem of many overconfident mathematicians. In the 1930s and after, when the famous theorems setting limits to the powers of formal systems were published, it began to seem as if a solution might be ruled out as impossible. It turned out, however, that a proof is possible, but immensely costly in terms of time and space. When, in 1976, the four-color problem was solved by Kenneth Appel and Wolfgang Haken at the University of Michigan, the answer was not exactly scribbled on the back of an envelope. It took four years of work, an analysis of about two thousand maps, and twelve hundred hours of computer time. The proof was highly unusual. Not only was it long, but its correctness could not be checked without the help of a computer. If the proof were to be written out in its entirety on paper, it would occupy so much space that a person would need more than a lifetime to read it. We may never know whether there is a proof of the four-color problem that is sufficiently brief and elegant for a human mind to take it all in.

Space and time are of no consequence in the world of pure mathematics. Turing's imaginary machine, the first computer, had tape of boundless length on which to print its symbols.

Theorems proving that something could *never* be done were therefore much more interesting than theorems proving that something could be done, but it would take an awfully long time. Today, however, there is intense interest in the effects of this second kind of limit on a computing system, and in the fact that space and time may force the system to act in less than fully rational ways. If the time taken to run an algorithm increases with the size of the problem as a fixed power, it is called a polynomial algorithm, and is generally good, that is to say efficient and of practical use. In computer science, a problem is regarded as well solved only if a polynomial algorithm has been written for it.

In the game of checkers, for example, the number of possible moves increases exponentially with the number of pieces on the board. If s is the number of pieces, then the number of possible moves grows, not as a fixed power, such as s^2, which would be manageable, but as 2^s, which is a fearsome rate of increase. Even for fairly small values of s, 2^s can be an enormously large number. So exploring alternative moves consumes an immense stretch of time. If $s = 70$, for example, and a million moves were checked every second, it would take more than three hundred thousand centuries to complete the task. This is known as combinatorial explosion, and it is one of the thorniest difficulties besetting scientists who make intelligent machines or try to explain how the human brain works. Just adding a few more pieces to a checkerboard results in an astronomical explosion in the number of moves to be tried.

If an algorithm is written to solve a given problem perfectly, and the time it takes to run such an algorithm on a computer explodes in an exponential fashion, then it is a "bad" algorithm and the problem is intractable, which means it cannot succeed in a world where space and time are not endless. Hundreds of problems are now believed to be inherently intractable, in the sense that all algorithms guaranteed to give a correct answer are bad and explode. The famous puzzle of the traveling salesman, who must find the shortest route between a number of cities, is in this class. These are not arcane philosophers' riddles, but arise in the ordinary affairs of life, such as economics and operations research. Something as mundane as trying to match college freshmen sharing dormitory rooms according to how congenial they are likely to find each other, turns out to be so complex that an ingenious "good" algorithm, devised by Jack Edmonds of the University of Waterloo, can solve it only if each room is occupied by just two students. If there are three students to a room, the algorithm explodes and the problem is believed to be intractable.

The brain avoids the perils of explosion, which is one of its remarkable assets, but standard computer programs that imitate the intelligence of the brain do not, as yet. Scientists who write the programs are keenly aware that whether an algorithm explodes or does not explode depends not on the information itself, but on the form the information takes. In one form algorithms are good, but in another form they are bad. Different forms have radically different computational properties.

"Suppose I ask you the question, 'Can crocodiles run steeplechases?' " said Hector Levesque, a computer scientist at the University of Toronto, who is trying to discover the forms of information that might enable a machine to think in a human-like way. "You can answer that question in a fraction of a second, and yet you've probably never thought about crocodiles and steeplechases before in your life. That ability, to take one piece of information from here, and another piece from there, and put them together in a novel way, and extract a whole lot of new information, like the legs of the crocodiles being too short to jump a fence, is something we just don't understand very well. How are we able to ignore certain things that we decide very quickly are irrelevant and still by and large find the right conclusions? You know at once that it doesn't matter whether crocodiles are brown or green, or how many teeth they have, but a machine does not know that. That is one of the central challenges for artificial intelligence, to discover how it is that the human mind can have all this information and somehow decide in an instant to discard large chunks of it as not being worth considering."

A standard computer can deal with an immense amount of information without getting sidetracked in a morass of otiose details, but only if the information is of a certain form. A data-base computer system, for example, is worldly in the sense that it holds large numbers of facts and can answer questions about them in a reasonable amount of time. It does not balk at something as immense as the US census, which contains some one trillion records about individual Americans, many more than would be found in a large encyclopedia. The system is quite unlike a human brain, however. It can accept information only if that information is encoded in a very special, limited form. Everything is fine as long as the machine is required merely to process specific facts about specific things, say, the name, address, and age of a particular person. It is useless to expect a data-base system to remember and behave reasonably toward such information as that Susan Smith's age is either fourteen or thirty-nine, however, or that most opera singers are taller than five feet five inches. The machine becomes an idiot; it simply does not know what to make of facts when they are expressed in such a form. With the brain, almost the reverse is true. If books contained information in the form in which it is stored in a data-base computer system, lists of specific facts—Washington, DC, is the capital of the United States, Ottawa is the capital of Canada, Paris is the capital of France—we would never read them for fear of going mad with boredom and disgust. We approach a subject in a much more general, much more flexible way.

The paradox is that, if a standard computer is to emulate human thinking, it must be given tremendous quantities of information, yet it seems to be able to handle such large amounts only if the information is in the narrow, limited form that a data-base system will accept. Small computer models have been built that behave intelligently, in the sense of being able to accept and think about unspecific facts and discard irrelevant material, but trouble starts when scientists try to "scale up," increasing the knowledge in such small models so as to make them more powerful, closer to the breadth of human intelligence. It is then that the nightmare of combinatorial explosion, intractability, bad algorithms, and solutions that take centuries to reach, begins. Adding extra facts to the machine's fund of knowledge is like placing a few more pieces on a checkerboard: the explosion in the number of possible moves to be explored is like a Fourth of July fireworks display.

"A lot of the properties of human reasoning and putting facts together to come up with interesting conclusions are very combinatoric," Levesque points out. "That means that the difficulty of making a machine reason in a mindlike way increases dramatically with the amount of information it deals with. Often it is the case that for small problems things work out fine and you can deal with slightly larger problems if you imagine a vastly improved computer architecture, like some of the new highly parallel computers. But if you want to make the system extremely large, then there is nothing in the physical universe that can do it. The numbers become so huge that even if you could apply every atom in the universe to the task you still would not have enough time to complete it before the heat death of the cosmos."

Whether explosion occurs or does not occur depends in large part on the form of the information in which a problem is encoded: Is it a bare fact that only a data-base system could love, such as "John is four years old"? Is it a general statement, like "All dogs bark"? Or is it a probability: "I think it will rain today." Crucial to an understanding of the brain, and to the challenge of imitating human reason with a machine, is the insight that these various types of expressions have profoundly different computational properties, some more desirable than others. Difficulties arise chiefly when the form of the information requires a thinking agent to consider alternatives.

"People, and machines as well, have a terrible time dealing with problems if it means juggling possibilities," Levesque says. "If I tell you that the person who smokes Camel cigarettes lives next door to the orange-juice drinker, and the person who drinks milk lives next door to the person who is older than the person who smokes Du Maurier cigarettes, and so on in that vein for six or seven statements, and then ask you a specific question such as, 'Who is the person who drinks coffee?' you are going to find it very difficult to give the right answer because I'm giving you not-very-specific information and you have to keep track of alternatives. You are faced with exploring a large number of individual possibilities. People by and large bend over backward to avoid doing that in their everyday thinking. If I tell you my daughter is five or six years old, and then later in the conversation ask you a question about her, you won't consider first what is implied by her being five, and then consider separately what follows if she is six. If you did, you'd never get off the ground. The cases would multiply too quickly. What you probably do is to think of her as a first-grade schoolchild and draw conclusions from that."

Knowing more about the nature of complexity means understanding better why the mind behaves as it does. In particular, it explains why the mind tends to reshape the information it is given into a form that is restricted in certain ways, less logical, more prone to error, wiping out fine distinctions. By doing this the mind can avoid the disaster of combinatorial explosion. Thinking with restricted information has been called irrational by many psychologists. In the light of what we know about intractability, however, such behavior may be more rational than it seems.

A failure to appreciate the implications of the boundedness of thought may be due in part to the unacknowledged influence of Descartes, who believed that the body and the mind are two entirely different things. The body is a machine and occupies a region of space, but the mind is a pure thinking entity, and cannot be located in space any more than the abstract structures of mathematics can be. Many modern cognitive scientists, Christopher Cherniak thinks, make the mistake of extending the Cartesian idea of the mind as spaceless to the brain, which led them to assume that the brain has unlimited resources. That is why they tend to envisage the mind as a collection of "impossibility engines," profoundly unfeasible mental mechanisms that are supposed to be able to perform any logical operation, no matter how complex.

Any computer superprogram that aims to represent the mind in its entirety would need to be very large, but finite in size. It would not be a neat and tidy affair, but branchy, radically inelegant, buying computational tractability by using quick and dirty rather than formally complete and correct procedures. Such properties seem to be essential to an intelligence that thinks as efficiently as ours, yet they are also the very properties that appear to rule out any reasonable possibility of ensuring that such a program is the correct one. The full mind's program may be unknowable in practice, as Kant believed reality to be unknowable. We might never be able to debug, verify, or evaluate it, much less establish that it maps the whole human mind. The program would be unmanageable, and the unmanageability would be inherent in the nature of the mind, in its messiness and enormous size.

Even if a fully intelligent program could be constructed, Cherniak suggests it might be a white elephant, a toy or laboratory curiosity, less reliable than, say, a human taxi driver. "Our stance toward it might end up a little like that of coral animals toward the vast reef they have built."

7: UNDER THE NET

A curious feature of a mind that uses Baker Street reasoning to create elaborate scenarios out of incomplete data is that its most deplorable biases often arise in a perfectly natural way out of the very same processes that produce the workmanlike, all-purpose, commonsense intelligence that is the Holy Grail of computer scientists who try to model human rationality.

No bias is more pernicious, more wrongheaded and irrational, it might seem, than to think in stereotypes. How unintelligent, how uninteresting, to assume that the French are rude, feminists shrill, journalists drunken and cynical, cabdrivers loquacious, politicians slippery. When members of a society mobilize to improve their status, they usually begin by trying to break down the stereotypes that bolster and preserve oppression and injustice.

Yet it could be argued that stereotypes are not ignorance structures at all, but knowledge structures. They are members of the schema family, and as a species of schema they are used to process information, to interpret and make sense of the world. From this point of view, stereotypes cannot be understood solely or even chiefly in terms of attitudes and motives, or emotions like fear and jealousy. They are a device for predicting other people's behavior, for deciding, on the briefest acquaintance, what sort of person the stranger we have just met will turn out to be. Stereotypes are an example of the way natural intelligence avoids the paralysis of combinatorial explosion by selecting a tiny fraction of the new information in a problem and then adding to that fraction from its own organized knowledge of the world.

One of the earliest thinkers to talk about stereotypes as knowledge structures that mediate between the mind and the social world was not a psychologist, but a writer on politics, Walter Lippmann. In his book, *Public Opinion,* published in 1922 and now a classic, Lippmann saw stereotypes as devices for coping with complexity and making judgments under the real-world constraints of limited space and time. Opinions, he said, are a way of making our minds cover a larger space, and a longer span of time, than they can possibly experience directly. They embrace a larger number of events and people than a single individual could possibly encounter in the course of an entire lifetime. Our opinions cannot be based on exhaustive acquaintance with all the facts about a given topic or about this or that person. They are cognitive devices for making a little experience go a long way, which is exactly what schemas and theories do. Everyone needs opinions, from the merest skimmer of a daily newspaper to eminent political insiders who draft treaties and make laws. We observe only a tiny part of what is going on around us, know only a few people intimately, see just one aspect of a public event. Each person's intelligence catches what it can of life "in a coarse net of ideas," Lippmann said. No one can hope to understand the social world, with its immense complexity, fact by fact, item by item. Opinions, therefore, are webs of connected thoughts, constructed by the mind, that interpret a world we can never know as it "really" is, because there is so much of it, and so little time for us to observe. They are amplifiers, enlarging the meager input of the moment.

Stereotypes, like opinions, are generalizations, Lippmann maintained. They put people into categories: agitators and intellectuals, plutocrats and foreigners. Because the world is partly uniform, our generalizations are often accurate and useful; they make sense of a universe that otherwise would be totally unpredictable. Opinions stabilize the world, make it manageable, reduce the number of surprises it is apt to spring on us. They are part of the brain's propensity to tame the novelty of life, to relate something new to something we already know. That means the mind need not search for a great deal of information in order to make a judgment. We usually notice a trait which marks a well-known type, Lippmann said, and "fill in the rest of the picture by means of the stereotypes we carry around in our heads."

The brain, in Lippmann's view, is something of an economist. It takes advantage of the fact that the world, for all its variety, contains certain regularities and samenesses. Nothing we encounter is ever entirely new and unpredictable, because the new can always be placed in a known category whose other members are familiar. However bizarre the design of a chair, we know it is a member of the category of things meant for sitting in, and however exotic a breed of dog seen for the first time, we expect it to bark and chase cats. It is just a short step from classifying dogs according to what they typically do to putting our fellow human beings into categories whose members behave in similar ways. The brain, with its limited resources, economizes by making a little new information go a long way. It is exhausting to try to see each chair, dog, person, freshly and in detail, and easier to sort them into types and generalities, so that the knowledge stored in a generalization can be used to make inferences about a stranger. We substitute foresight for sight, because relying on sight alone is expensive and spendthrift. "Were there no practical uniformities in the environment," Lippmann said, "there would be no economy and only error in the human habit of accepting foresight for sight. But there are uniformities sufficiently accurate, and the need of economizing attention so inevitable, that the abandonment of all stereotypes for a wholly innocent approach to experience would impoverish human life."

Even when the information arriving from the world is severely restricted, the brain is able to amplify it by means of stereotypes that are surprisingly elaborate. American voters, for example, can often form opinions of a political candidate on the basis of a television commercial that lasts no longer than thirty seconds. The clues and hints that a viewer picks up from a political advertisement are mostly about a candidate's appearance: the cut of a suit, the color of the eyes, the shape of the face. About ninety percent of the information retained is visual. But the clues have remarkable power to evoke stereotypes and other schemas that provide a complete profile of the candidate in the viewer's mind. Such profiles are opinions, plausible versions of a reality the viewer has no hope of observing in any detail because of the grotesquely brief time span of the commercial. Stereotypes make it possible to behave as if time were stretched out, and viewers had been able to study the personality of the politicians at their leisure.

Robert Teeter, formerly head of Market Opinion Research, and an advisor to George Bush in the 1988 presidential election campaign, has made a study of how people create these schematic portraits out of wisps of data. He shows short videotapes and still photographs of politicians, plays recordings of snatches of speech, and asks people to make dozens of judgments on the basis of what they see and hear. He finds that viewers and listeners conjure up intricate life histories, ambitious interpretations, which seem coherent and smooth, almost seamless, as if they had been woven from the genuine cloth of experience instead of the man-made fabric of opinion. No obvious gaps appear in these creations, which are strikingly consistent and replete with plausible embellishments and confident strokes of portraiture. "You would be amazed at how deep and rich in detail the judgments are," said Mr. Teeter's research specialist, William Feltus. "You show them a man wearing a knit shirt with a little football helmet embroidered on the front and they'll say he's a football coach, that he bowls, drinks beer, the whole picture." These creations form the basis for inferences and predictions about character, intelligence, trustworthiness, and they are remarkably stable.

Out of starvation rations of data, rich interpretations are made. That is not so surprising, because the brain is adept at throwing away large amounts of information without discarding so much that the world becomes hopelessly unpredictable. This is something that is difficult to imitate on standard computers. Robert Teeter and his colleagues had already deprived viewers of all but a tiny remnant of what they would need to observe if they were to judge the politicians in question without generalizing at all, seeing them with a perfectly "innocent" eye.

The mind throws away information in peculiar ways. One of its strategies is to generalize about things and people by sorting them into categories. We do not need to scrutinize a tall, leafy object in elaborate detail to know that it belongs to a class of life forms called trees. This process sounds neat and logical, but it is really much less tidy, and much more interesting, than that. The classical view of categories treats them as logical devices, having precise and clearly marked boundaries, with each category being separate and distinct from other categories and containing members which all share equally the defining properties of the category in question. Boolean logic is based on this notion of what categories are, which makes it ideal for the digital computer, because an item either belongs to a class or it does not belong, just as in logic a proposition is either true or false, with no third option. In a logical category, each member has full and equal status. The Lewis Carroll premises "Opium eaters never wear white kid gloves" and "All well-fed canaries are cheerful," are generalizations that apply to the categories of opium eaters and well-fed canaries without exception, and do not apply outside the categories. Notice, too, that these categories are completely arbitrary. They do not describe the real world and its connections, but only the nonsense world of Carroll's imagination. The digital computer, which grew out of Boolean logic, can deal just as easily with an arbitrary category that makes no sense in terms of human experience—"All elephants are parking meters"—as with a more natural category such as "All Irish wolfhounds are dogs."

In the 1970s, Eleanor Rosch did much to undermine the classical view by showing that most of the categories we form in everyday thinking have little to do with Aristotelian or Boolean logic. Her early work was concerned with how people form categories of colors. Since the color spectrum is continuous, each hue merging into the next, it can be divided up in any one of thousands of different ways. Some human societies have only two or three names for colors, while others have dozens, so it seemed likely that people classify colors according to culture and personal preferences. Rosch had made a study of the Dani, a Stone Age people in New Guinea, who have only two basic color categories, *mola* for bright ones such as white, red, and yellow, and *mili* for dark ones, like black, green, and blue. When shown a wide range of different colors, the Dani, as expected, divided up the spectrum into *mili* and *mola* idiosyncratically, often disagreeing among themselves as to which hue belonged to which category. When it came to recognizing and remembering the best examples of a color, however, the cultural difference vanished and the Dani behaved much like any sophisticated American. They agreed on what is a typical hue, just as Americans may have trouble defining the boundaries of a given color, but easily pick out the shade of a typical eating orange from an array of other colors. Good instances of a color are remembered by people of all cultures even if a particular culture has no name for them, and poor instances are remembered less well. That seems to be a universal trait, built into the human nervous system.

When Eleanor Rosch arrived home in America, she looked at other kinds of mental categories, and found they are constructed in much the same way. People find it easier to remember items that are close to the best example, or prototype, of the category, and more difficult to remember ones that are distant from it. A robin or canary is a typical member of the category of birds (just as a tomato is a typical shade of red), but a penguin or an ostrich is not. A barstool is a less good example of its category than a dining chair. The pope is a highly untypical member of the category of bachelors.

A prototype, as a kind of schema, is a memory structure that can amplify information. A Hilton is a prototype of hotels, Lord Byron is a prototype of romantic poets, a martini is a prototype of cocktails. These typical members of their various categories provide us with certain expectations when we come across a new example of the category in question. Remembering how a Hilton works tells us what to do when checking into a strange hotel, and the poetry of Byron is a sort of road map for finding our way around the literary world of other romantic writers. One way of describing a prototype is to say that it shares, or seems to share, more relevant properties with less typical examples of a category than those examples share with the prototype. A Hilton offers everything a small wayside inn offers and more besides, including a drugstore, twenty-four-hour room service, a swimming pool, and same-day laundry. A robin is a prototype bird and a kiwi is not, because, while a kiwi has feathers and two feet like a robin, it does not fly or perch in trees. A prototype is remembered more easily than other category members, and is recognized more quickly. It is often allowed to stand for the category as a whole, being a reference point for inferences, judgments, and decisions. Thinking in terms of typical members simplifies reasoning. Instead of moving step by step through the syllogism

Most dogs bite.
This animal that has me backed up against the wall is a dog.
Therefore this animal will probably bite me.

the mind simply matches the beast in question with a member of the dog category close to the prototype, perhaps a German shepherd, which does everything lesser members of the category do, including biting people.

Curiously, the mind tends to encode in terms of prototypes even classes of things that belong to something as abstract and logical as the system of whole numbers. It turns out that people treat certain numbers, such as 100, as typical examples, the Lord Byrons of the number system, and regard others that are close to the prototype, like 97 and 102, as being "essentially" 100. They do not, on the other hand, think of 100 as being essentially 97 or 102. Prototypes guide thinking, but they are not logical. They may even be at odds with logic. They can lead the mind into a trap. Christopher Cherniak points out that we are more ready or less ready to accept a conclusion as valid depending on whether or not the premise refers to a typical member of a category. People are quicker to agree with an argument when it is worded in this way

> All the drinks on this table are martinis.
> Therefore all the drinks are cocktails.

than when the wording is changed:

> All the drinks on this table are blue bombshells.
> Therefore all the drinks are cocktails.

They even tend to mistake an invalid conclusion for a valid one when the premise contains a prototype:

> Some of these drinks are cocktails.
> Therefore some of the drinks are martinis.

Is this a sound argument? No, because the cocktails may all be blue bombshells. Most people's immediate inclination, however, is to agree with the conclusion, even though it is wrong, because a martini is a typical example of its category.

Eleanor Rosch realized that the categories people use in everyday reasoning are not logical but psychological, and her insights sprang from that basic assumption. What a psychological category is, and how it is used for inference and prediction, are questions that can only be answered in the light of the human brain itself; what sort of computer it is and what kind of Faustian bargain it must make with the devil of imperfection in order to find its way around the world.

An important part of that bargain is that the brain practices economy. The theme of mental economy is not a new one. It goes back at least to Freud, who was influenced by the then-fashionable theory of scarcity economics, and regarded pleasure as a limited resource which is spent sparingly and must be saved in order to be spent. Pleasure, to Freud, was like money in a bank account, where credits must balance debits. The psyche ekes out its meager allowance of sexual excitement, and such frugality is reflected in the one-man, one-wife arrangement found in civilized societies.

Cognitive economy is something quite different. It is a matter of stretching limited resources, such as attention, and squeezing as much information as possible about the world out of the categories the mind uses to organize its experience. The more properties of an object or a person we can predict as a result of knowing just one property, the better, but that would mean creating a large number of categories, all finely discriminated from one another, which puts a strain on mental resources. At the same time, it is economical to treat different things as being the same as much as possible if the differences are unimportant to the mental task at hand.

One answer to this dilemma in the economical brain, Rosch found, is that we tend to think and talk about things at a certain level of abstraction that she called the basic level. A table is a table. At a higher level of abstraction in its category it is furniture, while at a lower level, it may be a Queen Anne gate-legged table in walnut with rosewood inlay and brass lion's-paw feet. Under normal circumstances, it seems more natural to talk about a table, because to call it furniture does not convey enough information and to call it a Queene Anne gate-legged table with all the trimmings conveys too much. The lower the level, the more we can infer about an object or event, but in everyday conversation we do not need to be encyclopedic.

When life is categorized in sub-basic level terms, the effect can be unnatural, sarcastic, pretentious, or extravagantly ostentatious. The reviewer of *Decades*, a novel which drastically reduced its level of abstraction in order to create an impression of high sophistication, satirized the author's style by ending the review: "And so, after putting away my 10-year-old Royal 470 manual and lining up my Mongol number 3 pencils on my Goldsmith Brothers Formica imitation-wood desk, I slide into my oversize squirrel-skin L. L. Bean slippers and shuffle off to the kitchen. There, holding *Decades* in my trembling right hand, I drop it, plunk, into my new Sears 20-gallon, celadon-green Permanex trash can." Reading that sort of stuff for any length of time would be exhausting, because it is wildly uneconomical.

Basic levels reduce the complexity of the world and wipe out differences between things, but not too drastically. They throw away just about the right amount of information. This is efficient, because it enables the brain to obtain a large amount of data without straining its resources. So basic levels are the most important when it comes to learning and remembering.

Thinking about people in stereotypes is a form of cognitive economy, as Lippmann emphasized. It is a way of obtaining the most information about the world with the least mental effort, and it is a natural type of "reasoning" for us, because our knowledge is organized in memory, not according to the principles of logic, but in such a way as to reduce the complexity of the world, while still being able to make sense of it. The need to be economical is set against the need to be completely rational. So, just as the typical member of the category of birds is one that flies and nests in trees, so the typical member of the category of feminists is likely to be strident and ambitious, and a typical member of the category of accountants is pedantic, wears spectacles, and smokes a pipe. Gentle and polite feminists, boisterous and amusing accountants, are likely to be written off as weaker members of their categories, distant from the prototype, just as a kiwi, which does not fly or nest in trees, is distant from a typical member of the bird category such as a robin, which does both. There is some evidence that we tend to stereotype people, and make inferences about them based on those stereotypes, at the basic level, in terms of the roles they play rather than of the specific traits they possess.

Understanding how psychological categories work is a step in the direction of understanding how natural intelligence works, and why it avoids the peril of combinatorial explosion. Best examples and basic levels are devices that bypass the need to explore immense numbers of possibilities. If a question is framed in such a way that logic and the rules of probability theory conflict with the mind's tendency to think with categories, logic is likely to lose. Consider the following problem (from a study by Amos Tversky and Daniel Kahneman):

> Linda is thirty-one, single, outspoken and very bright. She majored in philosophy in college. As a student, she was deeply concerned with discrimination and other social issues and took part in anti-nuclear protests. Which of these two statements is more likely?
>
> (a) Linda is a bank teller.
> (b) Linda is a bank teller and is active in the feminist movement.

Most people, even highly intelligent ones, think Linda is a bank teller and a feminist, since she seems to match the prototype of a feminist more than that of bank teller. Logic decrees otherwise, however. It rules that the likelihood of any two uncertain events happening together is always less than the likelihood of either event happening alone. So the odds that Linda is both teller and feminist are less than the odds that she is a teller, even though she seems unsuited to that career. The evidence that she is a feminist ought to be discarded, but the mind finds it almost impossible to discard, because the prototype fits.

Generalizing, throwing away information, reducing complexity, is essential to the success of natural intelligence. It is one way in which we are superior to standard artificial-intelligence programs. The social world is perhaps the most complex the mind encounters, and the need to organize knowledge so as to amplify the small amount of information we are able to observe is all the more imperative. Yet the more we generalize, the more unreal that world becomes. Iris Murdoch, a philosopher as well as a writer of fiction, has given much thought to this dilemma. In her first novel, *Under the Net*, she puts the question: can a human being be anything other than a generalizer, a maker of concepts and categories and theories? A central character of the story, Hugo Belfounder, embodies the daring speculation that we can be something else. Belfounder despises the ease with which the mind generalizes and he struggles to avoid generalizing. He walks among flowers and tries to see each one as unique, stripped of its connections with the rest of nature. He wants to throw away none of the information a particular flower conveys, to notice details with the clarity of a botanist, but resist the botanist's urge to classify. "All theorizing is flight," Belfounder believes. Generalizing is an escape from the truth.

The title of the book suggests that human beings, in their everyday lives, are trapped in a web of generalizations, which separate them from the real world. Such generalizations let us down, Iris Murdoch argues, because no two individuals are alike: all are different and peculiar, "more randomly made, more full of rough contingent rubble, than art or vulgar psychoanalysis leads us to imagine." In her novels, characters often build up elaborate and plausible theories about why other people behave as they do, only to have such scenarios collapse in ruins when the true state of affairs is made plain. Mistaken generalizations of this kind are the cause of many hilarious twists and turns of a Murdochian plot. Yet the brave attempt to see each person in terms of the differences between him or her and the rest of the world, cannot succeed. Social life is too complex for that, too varied and opaque, too ambiguous and full of gaps. We are forced to generalize about it whether we like it or not, and therein lie rich possibilities for comedy.

8 : FAREWELL THE OPEN MIND

Can an intelligence that is perfectly open make sense of the world? In a limited organ such as the brain, working under the constraints of space and time in a real world, reason cannot explore all possibilities, but needs to be guided by organized structures of knowledge stored in memory. And the essence of organized knowledge is that it tilts the mind toward a particular interpretation of reality and tilts it away from other interpretations. Our mental categories, with their best examples and basic levels, enable us to anticipate that things and people will behave in certain ways, and that is good, because it amplifies the restricted data of experience. At the same time, it suggests that common sense and a certain bias go hand in hand. We may not have one without the other. Unless the mind is partly blinkered, it cannot know the world at all.

Psychologists have noticed lately that the mind's natural tendency to approach everyday problems from a certain point of view, from a definite perspective, can result in the sort of thinking that is irrational according to the norms of logic. People may give different answers to the same question, depending on its form, because the way in which the question is worded determines the point of view they take. In a celebrated puzzle devised by Daniel Kahneman and Amos Tversky, some students were asked which of two programs they would choose to prepare for the outbreak of a rare Asian disease which is expected to kill six hundred people. The programs were identical, but they were described in two different ways to two different groups of students: "If program A is adopted, two hundred people will be saved," or "If program A is adopted, four hundred people will die." Three out of four students chose this program when it was worded in terms of lives saved, and four out of five rejected it when it was worded in terms of lives lost. Evidently, how people reason about a problem can be influenced by manipulating their point of view. The "dirty little secret" of opinion polling is that error is more likely to arise from the way a question is worded than from faulty methods of sampling.

No mind could be more open, more free from points of view, presuppositions, and biases, it might be thought, than the mind of a scientist. Francis Bacon, who is regarded as the prophet of modern science and the shaper of the modern skeptical intellect, insisted that a scientist must first clear his head of all inherent biases. It was foolish of the logicians, Bacon declared, to hold the operations of the mind in such high respect, because the mind looks at the world through the lens of its own knowledge, beliefs, opinions, and prejudices. In fact, Bacon said, the intellect is more prone to error than the senses are. "For let men please themselves as they will in admiring and almost adoring the human mind, this is certain: that as an uneven mirror distorts the rays of objects according to its own figure and section, so the mind, when it receives impressions of objects through the sense, cannot be trusted to report them truly, but in forming its notions mixes up its own nature with the nature of things."

The understanding, in Bacon's view, imposes on the external world an order and pattern that are in the mind but not in reality. Each person is inclined to interpret what he learns in the light of his own peculiar and singular disposition. Philosophy itself is one of the chief obstacles to the truly open mind, because philosophies are really fictions, phantoms, theatrical shows, stage plays, that have a false relationship to experience and lead us to see the universe as if it were an invention, not as it really is.

Much of Bacon's scorn for the amateurish methods prevalent in his day was aimed at their faulty logical underpinnings. The Baconian tradition, which modern science has inherited, took logic as the foundation of its thought and practice.

Lately, however, the idea that science is an exclusively logical, perfectly open-minded process has been seriously undermined. Scholars who have taken a closer look at what actually happens when the Baconian program of stripping away nature's secrets bears important fruit in the form of new theories, have discovered that the methods used, the cast of mind of the investigator, is not as Baconian as we might imagine.

In economics, for example, the concept of "rational man," who always chooses in such a way that the expected benefits of his choice will exceed the expected costs, is not a logical deduction, or a fact derived from observation. It is an assumption, a point of view, which can be neither proved nor disproved, and yet it is a cornerstone of economic theorizing. Rational man is a sort of automaton, acting in a perfectly consistent fashion. He is a stereotype. No such creature ever drew breath in the real world; he represents a highly restricted and even warped view of human life. All the same, economists find the concept useful for the very reason that it rules out other, less rational kinds of behavior, and thus directs their thinking. They do not claim that the concept can explain all of human experience, and in fact it places sweeping limits on economics as a science. Yet economists need rational man, because without a point of view, without partly closing the mind, it would be impossible to organize the information they collect, and thus impossible to understand any of it.

Even in the hard sciences, such as physics and chemistry, the minds of the great investigators have not been wholly free from the phantoms Bacon deplored. In a splendid study of the roads by which scientists such as Kepler, Newton, and Einstein journeyed to their discoveries, Gerald Holton, a Harvard historian of science, maintains that presuppositions, themes, and points of view may actually play a central role in penetrating nature's mysteries. These mental biases do so, Holton argues, because in the process of closing a scientist's mind to certain possibilities, they also open it up to other more daring and original avenues of inquiry. Einstein, for example, was influenced in his thinking by a whole collection of concepts that were more aesthetic than logical. He began with certain built-in nonlogical assumptions about the physical world; that nature is not unreasonably complex, that the universe is essentially harmonious and intelligible to human beings. Ideas about symmetry and simplicity were powerful considerations in his work, and they created a set of expectations about nature, not unlike the expectations that are generated by knowledge structures in commonsense thinking about the everyday world, though very different in some ways.

Einstein did not bring an "open" mind to the riddles of space and time. He was able to resist the allure of prevailing notions by adhering unswervingly to the preconceptions implicit in the equations of Clerk Maxwell, and these led to ideas that were startlingly different from those of nearly all his contemporaries. It was a bias, of a highly rarefied and very special kind, that brought Einstein to new knowledge about the universe which, like Galileo's, seemed absurd in the light of ordinary observation and flew in the face of common sense. They were at odds with the established beliefs of the naked mind. As he became increasingly persuaded of the importance of preexisting concepts in making his discoveries, Einstein joked about his transformation from a physicist into a "metaphysicist." At the same time, he freely acknowledged his debt to Kant, whose "Copernican revolution" in the theory of the mind was founded on the insight that we cannot observe the world as it really is, but can only interpret it by means of implicit mental structures that are not in themselves logical.

In scientific investigation, Gerald Holton finds, men and women of genius are especially apt to bring themes and other forms of subtle bias to their work. "Themes force upon people notions that are usually regarded as paradoxical, ridiculous or outrageous," he writes. They enable bold adventurers in the scientific enterprise to disregard fashion and the firmly entrenched beliefs that seem so rational, so self-evident, and so right at the time when they are widely held. In physics, unlike logic, "paradox" can be a road to hidden truths.

Thus a form of prejudice, a certain point of view, creates a blindness that blocks a scientist's mental vision in certain directions, while extending it in other, perhaps more interesting, directions. The implicit themes that influenced Einstein were not so much descriptions of the universe itself, of its objective properties, as they were constraints on the ways in which he thought about the universe. In Holton's view, such themes have little to do with logic or with direct observation of the facts. A scientist engages in logical reasoning while developing an explicit, formal theory, but in the early stages of discovery, nonlogical or even illogical elements may be present in his thinking, and behind these are preconceptions that can neither be proved true nor disconfirmed.

An especially dramatic example of a bias of this sort was Newton's premise, which he tried to avoid stating openly, that God is the cause of all natural forces, including gravity. This theme, which could not possibly be demonstrated, logically or in any other way, was a means of filling in the gaps in the impoverished data at Newton's disposal. It enabled him to think and reason in an efficient way in the presence of information that was incomplete and of poor quality. In a similar way, the success of Kepler's astronomy depended on the introduction of unashamedly metaphysical presuppositions when his physical suppositions had carried him as far as they could. Kepler's theme of the universe as a machine led him to new knowledge only when it was bolstered by two added preconceptions, that of the universe as a mathematical harmony, and as a theological order.

Einstein maintained that new scientific theories are "free creations of thought," but, as Holton points out, if that were really the case, there would be an infinite number of different axioms from which to choose, most of them useless, and success would come only by a lucky accident or fluke, as the scientist in his boundless freedom happened to make a leap to exactly the right axioms. In fact, this freedom is narrowly restricted by the set of themes that tilt the imagination in one direction or another, often without the scientist being aware of the power they exert. This is a highly personal process. A scientist's themes, Holton says, identify him as surely as his fingerprints.

A theory acts as a guide to the discovery of new knowledge, because it tells researchers what to look for, what information may be relevant and interesting, and what is not worth pursuing. A theory is a very sophisticated way of making the mind less open than it might otherwise have been, leading a researcher through a maze of possible interpretations to the unique, correct one. A case in point is the curious story of the detection, in 1965, by two astronomers, Arno Penzias and Robert Wilson, of the diffuse background radio static left over from the big bang with which the universe supposedly started fifteen billion years ago. Penzias and Wilson were studying the intensity of radio waves coming from our own galaxy. They were surprised to notice a large amount of microwave noise which scarcely varied in strength no matter where they pointed their antenna, and regardless of the time of day or season of the year. This odd observation suggested that the static did not emanate from the Milky Way, but from the universe in general.

Penzias and Wilson were baffled. They assumed at first that something was wrong with their equipment. A couple of pigeons had been nesting in the long horn of the antenna and became major suspects in the mystery, but when the pigeons were shooed away and the horn cleaned out, the noise remained. The two astronomers cast about for all kinds of other explanations, and only after a chance telephone conversation with another radio astronomer, Bernard Burke of MIT, did they surmise that the puzzling activity was a remnant of the birth pangs of the cosmos. Steven Weinberg, a Harvard astronomer who tells this story, points out that the momentous discovery of background radiation could have been made at least ten years earlier. Theories predicting it had been around for nearly twenty years, but they were unknown to astrophysicists in general. Nobody set out to look for the telltale cosmic static, and when Penzias and Wilson stumbled upon it by accident, they had no idea what they had found. Even the few astronomers who knew about the predictions dating back to the 1940s had not taken them very seriously.

Weinberg thinks the reason for this strange neglect was partly a breakdown in communication between people who make theories and people who make observations. The theorists did not think radiation with such a low temperature could be detected with the instruments available at the time. Partly, too, the big bang theory did not lead to a search for radiation because physicists found it hard to take seriously any theory of the early universe, seeing that the circumstances of the cosmic birth are so remote and unfamiliar. The result was that new knowledge about the universe was lying around for years but could not be picked up for want of a theory to produce expectancies, to provide a point of view, and rule out other possibilities. "This is often the way it is in physics—our mistake is not that we take our theories too seriously, but that we do not take them seriously enough," Weinberg says. "I do not think it is possible really to understand the successes of science without understanding how *hard* it is—how easy it is to be led astray, how difficult it is to know at any time what is the next thing to be done."

Scientific theories, like schemas and even stereotypes, make sense of the world by excluding certain ways of interpreting ambiguous or incomplete information. This is a form of cognitive economy. A theory is a summary, a device that stores and organizes knowledge, putting together the bits and pieces of data that have been observed into a coherent whole, and also providing a pattern of connections into which future observations can be fitted. It reduces the amount of new information about the world that is needed for understanding, and amplifies that small amount by means of the knowledge it stores.

In his landmark book, *The Structure of Scientific Revolutions*, Thomas Kuhn describes the almost random gathering of facts that goes on in the absence of a theory. Pliny's encyclopedic writings, for instance, or works on natural history in the seventeenth century, consist of a morass of unconnected observations, some of which later proved to be highly illuminating when connected by a new theory, and some of which were too complex to fit into any theory for years to come. No natural history can be interpreted without an implicit body of organized knowledge or belief that makes it possible to select, evaluate, and criticize the facts. If such a pattern is not implicit in the collection of facts, Kuhn argues, it must be supplied from outside, perhaps from metaphysics, or by accident. That being the case, it is not surprising that in the early stages of any science, different investigators who look at the same facts describe and interpret them in different ways.

Kuhn's book, which was highly controversial, and remains so, strongly challenged the traditional view that science is a perfectly rational enterprise, governed by logical rules of procedure that never change as time goes on. Scientific knowledge comes rather from seeing the world from a particular point of view. Kuhn makes a distinction between "normal" science, which goes on within a context of accepted ideas he calls a paradigm, and periods of revolution, when scientists break through to a new and different paradigm. Normal science simply extends our knowledge of those facts that a given context of ideas shows to be particularly revealing. During such periods, researchers not only refrain from seeking new theories, but actually resist them when they appear. This is both good and bad for the advancement of understanding. It is good because scientists are able to investigate an aspect of nature more deeply than would be possible if the context of ideas did not exist, and bad because of an intolerance that arises toward novel ways of thinking. During regimes of normal science, the prevailing context of ideas does more than determine what problems are to be solved; it also selects the sort of puzzles that are assumed to have solutions, which is one reason why a hallmark of normal science is that it proceeds at a rapid pace. Preconceptions, points of view, implicit in a particular regime, are the "rules of the game" for these puzzles, constraining the kind of answers that are acceptable and the steps by which they are reached. Only by changing the rules of the game are new sorts of answers possible, and it is a side-effect of the intolerance often bred during periods of normal science that a regime is eventually shattered.

The network of prior commitments to concepts, theories, and methods may have long-lasting influences on a science. After about 1630, for example, due mainly to the writings of Descartes, most scientists assumed the universe was made of tiny particles, and everything that happened in the universe could be explained in terms of the shape, size, motion, and interaction of the particles. Such a prejudice drastically limited both the problems and the theories that scientists worked on, in domains as diverse as chemistry, mechanics, optics, and heat.

Paradoxically, it is during normal regimes, when science is least open-minded, that it advances with greatest assurance and verve, penetrating nature's mysteries deeply within the limits set by the rules. Only a crisis, Kuhn thinks, enables new theories to emerge, and these are usually produced by workers who are very young or very new to their field. In all the history of science, Kuhn found no instance in which a theory has been falsified by direct comparison with nature. Usually it is overthrown by a new theory, but even the creation of such a theory is not the rational, open-minded process it might seem. When the rules are in force, scientific choices are rational, within narrowly defined constraints, but when the rules are put aside, during a period of revolution, the choice of a new worldview is in part arbitrary and nonrational, an accident.

Kuhn uses the word *stereotypes* to describe the commitment to certain theories, beliefs and methods that enable science to move so fast and confidently in normal periods, suggesting a link between the knowledge structures of everyday common sense and the mental operations of the scientist; both leave the mind unfree, so that it can thread its way through the complexity of the world without drowning in irrelevant detail.

So a kind of bias underlies all our efforts to make sense of the world, from the Olympian level of theory-making in physics to the down-to-earth task of reading the ambiguous clues that other people send us in the most routine social encounters. Karl Popper, a modern philosopher who has written with great insight about the open mind, believes that we do not learn by observation, but by creating anticipations, sending up mental trial balloons. Such anticipations, guiding discovery, tilting the mind in a certain direction, amount to a kind of prejudice. What we expect to see influences what we actually do see, and what we find relevant or irrelevant. The process of discovery, as opposed to the testing and criticism of a particular discovery, is never pure, never unbiased.

Popper insists that the criticism of a theory must be all the more severe because its creation is the product of a mind that cannot be fully open. As a young man living in Vienna, Popper became a Marxist, only to suffer a sharp disillusionment at the age of seventeen, when he watched several unarmed young socialists being shot to death by police while demonstrating to obtain the release of some agitators. The protest had been instigated by the communists. Popper was shocked by the brutality of the police, but the experience also jolted him into realizing that he had accepted a complex doctrine like Marxism uncritically. He had assumed it was on the side of the proletariat, the majority, and yet even among workers in the factories of Vienna the communists were a minority. Popper came to the conclusion that Marxism, like Freudian psychoanalysis, is full of presuppositions that are nonrational in the sense that any new fact can always be made to confirm the theory, but no fact can ever disprove it.

Most philosophers, at least until Frege, had taken it for granted that there is only one kind of knowledge, the interior kind that is either innate or a result of experience. Popper, in a more venturesome spirit, proposes not one, but three varieties of knowledge. They are so different from one another that he assigns them to three distinct "worlds." World 1 is the domain of physical objects, things. World 2 is the realm of our subjective thoughts, ideas, expectations, presuppositions, which limit the openness of the mind. World 3 is knowledge that is out in the public arena for all to see, where trial balloons float but can also be pricked and deflated, where theories are exposed to the bracing and perhaps destructive winds of criticism, doubt, and debate. In World 3, knowledge is stated in an explicit, and usually a written or printed form. It is the world of books, art, science, computers, and logic.

Only in World 3 can the mind be described as truly open. Here the products of thought can be examined under the magnifying glass of logic, ideas checked against reality. One of the surprising features of World 3 is that although the systems of knowledge it contains are human inventions, they often take on a life of their own. They turn out to have unexpected properties and regularities never intended or foreseen by their authors. We make discoveries about them in much the same way that explorers make discoveries about such objects of World 1 as continents and oceans. The natural number system, for example, may be a pure creation of the mind, but that does not mean it is fully under the control of its creators. Seemingly simple questions about the nature of numbers may present nightmarish difficulties. The innocent-looking conjecture that every even number can be written as the sum of two prime numbers is in fact so opaque that it has yet to be proved. Logic, too, which was regarded by eighteenth-century minds as a tamed and settled continent, suddenly revealed itself to be inhabited by monsters, in the form of strange and deadly paradoxes.

World 2, by contrast, can be talked about in psychological terms only, and is not inherently rational. It is the headquarters of common sense, but common sense is a type of knowledge we cannot fully trust. World 2 knowledge is conjectural only, never certain, and it can lead us astray. It tends to harbor bias and prejudice, and may embrace contradictory beliefs and expectations. In World 2, the mind tends to look for evidence that will confirm its conjectures, rather than for facts that will disprove them.

Our conjectures and opinions, expectations and beliefs, are, in Popper's words, "nets in which we try to catch the real world." They are not mirrors of reality, but patterns of connections that help us to construct a fabric of interpretation out of the scattered clues we pick up from the environment. What the mind catches in these knowledge nets is an imperfect and sometimes seriously biased version of reality, but the alternative, the fully open mind of World 3, would not be able to catch reality at all; it would not even know where to start.

What better evidence can there be of the inadequacy of the open mind, than the fact that after nearly four decades of trying to model human intelligence in its World 3 manifestation, artificial-intelligence researchers are at last beginning to talk about new computer architectures that have some of the hallmarks, the shortcomings and strengths, the enabling biases and efficient prejudices, of the World 2 mind?

9: THE
SILKEN
WEB

In an essay that seems to reflect the influence of his psychologist brother William, Henry James once speculated on one of the most puzzling yet absolutely basic properties of the human mind, its ability to act as if it knows much more about the world than it can possibly experience.

His answer, which is strikingly modern, and might almost stand as a headline for the story of today's investigations into intelligence, natural and artificial, is that we find such a capacity for world-making mysterious only because we misunderstand the nature of experience, perhaps because we also mistake the nature of the mind.

Consider, said Henry James, the case of the artist, especially the storyteller, who must create a whole universe on paper out of mere scraps of building materials that can be gleaned from the observation of everyday life. How is it possible to make so much out of so little? It happens because a writer possesses the power of being worldly far beyond the amount of his actual contact with the world, to an extraordinary degree. James called it "the faculty which, when you give it an inch, takes an ell." (An ell is an old English unit of measurement, about forty-five inches.)

The novelist cannot simply transcribe what he sees and hears onto the page. He must work with clues and tokens. He must be able to guess the unseen from the seen, and judge the whole piece by the pattern. To illustrate, James told an anecdote about an English woman novelist he knew, who won the applause of the critics for a story about the life of young Protestants in France. So lifelike was her portrayal of this scarce breed, that her readers assumed she had spent years studying her subjects, immersing herself in their world. In fact, the entire extent of her investigations was this: once, in a house in Paris, she was walking up a staircase and passed an open door where some young Protestants sat around a table after finishing a meal. She glimpsed the scene for no more than a moment. Still, the mind being what it is, and the woman being a genius, a moment sufficed. From this inch of observation the ell of her story, in all its realism, was built.

Was this a matter of "writing from experience"? In a sense it was, but not in the usually accepted sense. Experience is not just a matter of observing the world. It is also an activity of the mind. It is internal as well as external. Experience, James proposed, is a mental structure, "an immense sensibility, a kind of huge spider-web of the finest silken threads suspended in the chamber of consciousness, and catching every airborne particle in its tissue. It is the very atmosphere of the mind, and when the mind is imaginative—much more when it happens to be that of a man of genius—it takes to itself the faintest hints of life, it converts the very pulses of the air into revelations."

The Jamesian view says that experience is not so much a matter of what the eye observes, as of what the mind does, of how its weblike connections trap little motes of data and enlarge them into full-blown scenarios, lifelike personalities, sweeping narratives. Because the mind is organized in the way it is, experience is something vastly more subtle, more profound, and more interesting than its ordinary dictionary definition: "conscious perception of reality." If it was a shock for artificial-intelligence researchers to discover the enormous difficulties involved in building a machine that is worldly in the sense that human beings are worldly, one reason for the setback was that they had failed to understand the nature of experience.

What is more basic, more straightforward, it might be thought, than to create a computer program that can understand English prose, and translate texts from one language into another? If the words on the page contribute nearly all of the reader's "experience" of them, then all that is needed to translate the text into French, or German or Italian, is a dictionary and the rules of grammar and word order, along with a list of idiomatic expressions. There is no reason why a computer should not perform such a simple task. That is why millions of dollars were spent on research into machine translation over a ten-year period in the late 1950s and early 1960s, with high hopes of success. The project was funded generously by the US Department of Defense, which wanted a quick and painless way of reading Russian scientific journals. These hopes were dashed, however, because the scientists who worked on the project at Harvard and a number of other universities had neglected to consider one very important fact: a sentence which looks transparently clear to a human reader, literal to the point of banality, and which appears to be doing all the work in carrying meaning, simply transferring information to the reader's mind, may be highly, even hopelessly, ambiguous to a machine programmed simply to look up words in a dictionary and use rules of grammar. One of these dense machines insisted on translating the technical term "hydraulic ram" as "water goat."

Yehoshua Bar-Hillel, in a celebrated review of machine translation efforts, at a time when euphoria still lingered, pointed out that the computer programs of the time were so far from human powers of comprehension they could not even deal with a passage as simple as

> Little John was looking for his toy box. Finally he found it.
> The box was in the pen. John was very happy.

Assuming that *pen* has only two possible meanings, a writing device and an enclosure where small children play, Bar-Hillel claimed that no "existing or imaginable" program could tell a computer that the second meaning is the correct one, whereas we know it so naturally and easily we are not even aware of any ambiguity. Being unaware, we take it for granted that the meaning must be clear to a machine. It is difficult, almost unnatural, to force ourselves to be literal-minded, but only if we are literal-minded can we appreciate how much preexisting knowledge of the world we must bring to words in order to make sense of them. We know that the typical writing instrument is smaller than the typical box, so that if a box is in a pen, it must be a playpen, and we know it immediately, without needing to work it out by logic. In the early days of machine translation research, it was thought that if enough words on either side of the ambiguous word could be taken into account, the correct meaning could be extracted, but this is a fantasy. Text can be translated only by an intelligence that already knows an immense number of facts about the world.

This discovery, a very expensive one, led to new theories about how the mind experiences the world. It dawned on researchers that in order to disentangle the sense of even the most innocent and guileless-looking sentence, we must go to work on it with our knowledge. Words began to be seen, not as neatly wrapped parcels of meaning waiting to be picked up, but as triggers, symbols that evoke structures of knowledge in the mind, little charges that set off grand explosions of thought, slight hints that give rise to revelations when they meet the Jamesian spiderweb in the brain.

One person who pursued the implications of this point of

view with particular intensity was Terry Winograd, now at Stanford University, who between 1968 and 1970 devised a computer program called SHRDLU, which was given knowledge about a small domain—a "microworld" consisting of an empty box, a tabletop, and a few colored cubes and pyramids—and a robot arm to handle the blocks by stacking them up or putting them into the box. The program could answer questions and carry out commands typed in English such as "Pick up the red block next to the green pyramid." SHRDLU could also respond to queries of a general nature, like "Can the table pick up blocks?" Asked why it had put a block in a certain place, the program might reply, "Because you asked me to." It could sort out the reference of a pronoun and answer the one-word question "Why?" The world of SHRDLU was claustrophobic in its narrowness, however. The program could comprehend certain sentences that were too complicated for humans to grasp at first hearing, but it could understand nothing outside its little tabletop domain of blocks and balked at commands that were less than utterly explicit, even ones that are immediately clear to humans, like "How many blocks go on top of each other?" which, if taken literally, but only if literally, makes no sense.

One important feature of Winograd's invention was the emphasis on language as a trigger of action. The meaning of a sentence was not represented as a fact about the world, but as a command for the machine to do something, say, stack a block or answer a question. Winograd came to realize, however, that one of the program's shortcomings was that a direct correspondence existed between the form of a sentence typed into the system and the kinds of processes the machine carried out. SHRDLU simply obeyed a command or stored away a fact. When human beings converse, no such correspondence exists; something much more interesting is going on. In real life, there is no way for us to predict in detail what response the words we speak will evoke in the mind of the person we are talking to, because the knowledge structures triggered by words are different in different people. "There is an important germ of truth in saying that the meaning of a sentence 'is' the process it evokes," Winograd said.

Winograd decided that in natural language understanding, as opposed to the highly artificial world of SHRDLU, a sentence is not a description of something in the world, nor a command that specifies an action to be carried out. It is a "perturbation" to an active cognitive system that is engaged in a continual effort to make sense of what is said or written, and of the world it inhabits. The most important question to ask about a sentence, therefore, whether spoken or written, is not what it refers to in the world, but rather what changes it causes in the activity of the mind. Reason, memory, perception, and many other mental processes are part of the activity that words perturb.

Winograd was influenced in his thinking by a series of informal discussions about the nature of language and mind that took place at Berkeley in the 1970s, attended by linguists, computer scientists, and philosophers. Among the topics that caught his fancy was hermeneutics, the study of the principles of interpretation, originally the interpretation of sacred texts. Hermeneutics investigates the competence that was beyond the powers of the Defense Department's machine translators but comes easily and naturally to human beings: the understanding of natural language.

In its modern incarnation, hermeneutics challenges the standard approach to texts, which is to regard them as objects "out there," to be dissected and manipulated as something quite separate from the mind of the reader and the intentions of the author. Such an approach is too logical, and too technological, for hermeneutics, which asserts as a central belief that interpretation can only arise out of a personal experience of the work to be interpreted, where the mind of the author meets the mind of the reader, who "risks his personal world" in entering the world of the text. And we never simply read a text, just as we never simply look at the world; the mind is endlessly engaged, at every moment, in the work of interpretation. In order to understand, we must interpret, and that means bringing everything we know and are to the task. It also means that a reader should not simply "bombard the text with questions," in Richard Palmer's words, but listen to the questions the text puts to the reader. Hermeneutics is not concerned with artificial languages like symbolic logic, in which each symbol has one and only one designated meaning, but with natural language, where words have multiple meanings, which must be teased out and disentangled from one another.

Terry Winograd emphasized the hermeneutic notion of "pre-understanding" in his search for computer programs that go beyond SHRDLU. Hermeneutics asserts that meaning is a matter of context, but not just the external context of the words that surround an ambiguous word in the text, as the early researchers into machine translation believed. There is also the internal context of the beliefs, opinions, and knowledge that exist in the reader's or listener's mind. Interpretation is "horizontal," as Richard Palmer puts it, and must be made within a horizon of already granted meanings and intentions. Whenever we read or hear language, we bring to it certain kinds of knowledge organized in certain ways, and these knowledge structures themselves arise from our previous experience of the world. This circular process, where understanding is necessary for interpretation, which in turn begets understanding, is called the hermeneutic circle. The set of schemas stored in memory is the system's "pre-understanding," Winograd thinks, and the use of the schemas affects the interpretation of what is said or written. A word in a sentence can trigger a hypothesis that an instance of some particular schema is being conveyed, and if other parts of the sentence fit the schema it is likely that the hypothesis is correct. Given the sentences

A man wearing a ski mask walked into the bank.
One of the tellers screamed.

a computer might have difficulty in deciding why the teller screamed, but a brain at once applies a bankrobber schema, which is part of its preexisting understanding, its worldliness.

Without that inner context of knowledge, which guesses "the unseen from the seen," in James's words, the text is radically incomplete. Only when scientists tried to create machines that read prose did the full extent of language's incompleteness become apparent. Before, it was concealed by the hermeneutic operations of the mind, which is designed to be an interpreter, not a mere receiver of information, and is so adept at filling in gaps that it does not even notice that the gaps exist. Of course, the interpretation may be wrong, because it is based on what is typical, rather than on logical deduction. The bank in question could have been in Aspen, Colorado, and the teller might have screamed because she saw a mouse run across the floor.

Winograd came to appreciate the crucial role played in human thinking by the limited nature of the brain's processing resources. For example, people sometimes reason on the basis of what kind of world knowledge they do *not* possess. Asked, "Is the Mekong River longer than the Amazon?" a person might conclude, "I don't know how long it is, but if the Mekong were longer than the Amazon, I would have heard of it, and since I haven't heard of it, it can't be longer." This is cognitive economy in its most barefaced form, where incompleteness of knowledge actually makes it possible to jump to a correct conclusion. Sometimes it works and sometimes it does not. Absence of knowledge enables us to answer the question, "Were any US presidents women?" but perhaps not the question, "Were any US presidents natives of Indiana?"

The mind's ability to make sense of poor-quality information is intimately linked to the fact that its processing resources are limited. It comes to conclusions based on partial evidence, makes assumptions about what is to be expected in typical cases, and is not immune to mistakes and contradictions. This somewhat surprising mixture of weakness and strength arises because the brain reasons not only on the basis of statements about the world, but is also influenced by the form of its own knowledge structures. It may decide that something is false because it is usually false, or true because it is normally true, and the evidence for what is normal and usual is often the availability of stereotypical knowledge in memory. Schemas are economy devices for making a little knowledge go a long way, for saving scarce resources like attention and memory, and they are cavalier in their regard for the principles of logic. They are not generators of universal truths. And because words "evoke" schemas, information embedded in a schema that is highly accessible may supersede information that is logically equivalent, but is not so available. The organization of knowledge in memory is not primarily a logical organization, but reflects the way the world is put together in our experience. Memory, as often as not, is a plausible reconstruction of reality rather than a copy of it, with an emphasis on what typically happens. When we read a text, what we remember is not so much the bare information in the text, the propositions it contains, as the inferences, expectations, and presuppositions we apply to the text while we are reading it. The sentence

Miss America was prevented from playing the tuba.

carries the *logical* implication that she did not play the tuba. But the sentence

Miss America was not prevented from playing the tuba.

does not have the same logical force. There is a strong invitation to infer that Miss America did play her instrument, but it is not a watertight logical deduction. The invited inference does not have a truth value; it cannot be labeled true or false. When people recall the second sentence as opposed to reading it, however, that logical distinction is wiped out. Asked later to say whether the proposition "Miss America played the tuba" is true or false, most people reply that it is definitely true. A mere conjecture is stored in memory in such a way as to be indistinguishable from a logical truth. In logic, assertions are quite distinct from presuppositions, and implications are not the same as inferences, but in memory they are all coded in much the same form.

You might think that if a computer were given literal, and only literal sentences to read, it could extract the intended meaning without needing vast amounts of worldly knowledge to resolve ambiguities. That is the case with deductive logic, where one can determine the truth of a statement without having to consider any information outside the system itself. The trouble with this idea however, is that it fails to understand the nature of language, and since language is a mirror of the mind, it also fails to understand the character of human thought.

A fairly recent discovery in the theory of how people understand language is that the same kind of cognitive processes are used whether the language itself is figurative or whether it is literal. Stanford University psychologist David Rumelhart, who devoted much ingenuity to the creation of plausible models of ordinary language understanding, found that comprehending "literal" text requires mechanisms of thought that are sufficiently powerful to understand metaphor. As far as psychology is concerned, there is no clear distinction between the two kinds of language, and an artificial device that is unable to deal with metaphor is likely to be too weak to cope with the plainest prose. The mind seems to be metaphorical to its foundations.

The surprise is that even for sentences that seem fully literal, as well as for those that are clearly metaphorical, meaning cannot be found by simply looking up each word in a mental dictionary. The mind can understand a text only by resorting to knowledge that extends well beyond the definitions of the words themselves. No rules exist that enable us to combine dictionary meanings in such a way as to produce the intended meaning of the sentence. "I believe that the processes involved in the comprehension of nonfigurative language are no less dependent on knowledge of the world than those involved in figurative language," Rumelhart decided. A theory that is not rich enough to deal with the second kind is not rich enough to deal with the first kind.

Interpreting a sentence may call upon any knowledge the reader possesses, a vast totality. What is more, Rumelhart suspects, such knowledge is not used in an ad hoc way, to filter out all readings of the sentence except the correct one, but instead plays a central role in determining what interpretations are possible.

Consider this fragment of information:

> Business had been slow since the oil crisis. Nobody seemed to want anything really elegant anymore. Suddenly the door opened and a well-dressed man entered the showroom. John put on his friendliest and most sincere expression and walked toward the man.

This passage contains no metaphors. The language is as literal as ordinary language is ever likely to be. Yet the mind interprets it in much the same way as it would a text that is replete with metaphor. The words alone, with their dictionary meanings, are not enough to provide an unambiguous message. Readers must apply their real-world knowledge about stereotypical "friendly and sincere" car salesmen, and generate hypotheses, some weak, some strong, that are modified or discarded as the passage is perused. A reader who interprets the first sentence with a gas station schema is likely to weaken it when he reads the word *elegant* in the second sentence, and abandon it altogether at the word *showroom*. A reader who begins with a hypothesis that the story is about the economy in general discards it when it is clear that a specific episode is being described. This process of interpretation, the active recruiting of hypotheses and schemas, is typical of what we do when we understand language of any kind, whether literal or metaphorical. Simply compounding the definitions of words to derive the meanings of sentences will not suffice.

A figurative passage such as

> When the sun sets the earth does drizzle dew,
> But for the sunset of my brother's son
> It rains downright.

requires much the same sort of juggling with weak or strong hypotheses, a similar use of relevant world knowledge to reconstruct information that is either missing or indirectly hinted at, as the story of the car salesroom. The metaphor of raining is a clue to the intended meaning of the lines, sorrow for the death of a young man, but it is only a clue.

All this suggests that one reason why it is so difficult to build a machine that translates from one language into another is that there is no translation without understanding. But also, and more ominously for the future of artificial intelligence, there is no understanding without interpretation. In order to read and comprehend literal English text, a computer program would need to have a competence rich enough to interpret metaphorical text; it would have to possess an intelligence closer to that of a poet than to that of a logic engine.

The Greek word *hermeios* was used to refer to the priest at the Delphic oracle, whose pronouncements were supposed to explain a state of affairs but which in turn needed to be interpreted. It was also associated with the winged messenger god Hermes, who was able to express ideas out of reach of human understanding in such a way that they became intelligible to mortal minds. Hermes made the strange familiar to the world's inhabitants. Such a process of explanation, of making clear what would otherwise be obscure, was not limited to language. Whereas hermeneutics was originally a tool of theology and later a set of devices to understand literary texts, it has taken on a broader role, as a way of explaining interpretation in general. It proposes that the mind is a great deal less literal-minded than we might suppose, in all its various and sundry dealings with the world. Richard Palmer, in his study of modern hermeneutics, maintains that interpretation is the most basic, rather than the most evolutionarily advanced mode of human thinking, and goes on to say: "From the time you wake in the morning until you sink into sleep, you are 'interpreting.' On waking you glance at the bedside clock and interpret its meaning: you recall what day it is, and in grasping the meaning of the day you are already primordially recalling to yourself the way you are placed in the world and your plans for the future; you rise and must interpret the words and gestures of those you meet on the daily round... existing itself may be said to be a constant process of interpretation."

It is hardly surprising under these circumstances that today Terry Winograd is radically pessimistic about the prospects for a machine that can comprehend ordinary language. Many programs have been created that claim to be able to understand stories, explain decisions, and write plots for novels, but in the vast majority of cases what such programs are advertised to do is greatly in excess of what they can actually do. They give the illusion of understanding language, but only because they work with carefully confected samples of prose and representations created especially to handle them; they cannot deal with new information that is not anticipated, nor with real-world tasks. A completely fresh approach is needed, Winograd thinks. "The alchemists said you can turn lead into gold," he said. "In some sense they were wrong, but of course in another sense they were right. If I take a chunk of lead and carry it over to the Stanford linear accelerator near me and shoot the right kind of ions at it, it will in fact turn into gold, or at least some part of it will. So if someone in the era of the alchemists had said 'It is philosophically impossible, you cannot turn lead into gold,' that person would have been wrong, strictly speaking, because we can do it now. On the other hand, we would have been right to say 'You, the alchemists, are not dealing with the philosophy, the physics, the hard discoveries that lie between where you are now and where you want to be.' I believe that in one hundred or two hundred or five hundred years' time there will be things in the artificial-intelligence field that would be as unfathomable to me as linear accelerators would have been to the alchemists. But today science, like the alchemists, is facing a problem that is much larger and much more complex than the simple models researchers are working with. It is not just a matter of making faster and bigger machines, as many people seem to suppose."

Others, like David Rumelhart, think that promising avenues

are opening up toward the goal of a hermeneutic machine. But such a machine must resemble more closely than traditional ones the actual design of the human brain, because it is by evolutionary design, not by accident, that the brain is "naturally" hermeneutic. In particular, an intelligence that understands ordinary language, which we do with such thoughtless ease, needs to be radically global in its operations. It may be capable of the sort of local processing that is the hallmark of deductive logic, but such local thinking by itself is not sufficient if it is true that all comprehension involves interpretation and there is no such thing as a "literal" sentence. The essence of deductive logic is that the strings of symbols are processed step by step and are uninterpreted while they are being worked on. Meaning is in the form of the argument, not in the content of the message.

To make a machine an understander, therefore, and to use it as a window into the workings of the mind, means delocalizing it, breaking away from the traditional idea of intelligence as a logic engine, and transforming it into a worldly device in which knowledge is stored, organized, and activated in an entirely new fashion. Knowledge would need to be almost Jamesian in its immensity, its generality, and its hermeneutic power.

10: THE WORLDLY MACHINE

If an engineer were to design a mind, ridding himself of all metaphors based on existing machines, shunning philosophy, suspending common sense, beginning at the beginning as if he were the great god Evolution Himself, what sort of blueprint would he write? A promising approach might be to fashion his creation with an eye to what human intelligence does well, spontaneously, and naturally, rather than to what it does poorly and with a noticeable sense of strain. To do so would mean abandoning the notion of an ideal logic device in the head and studying instead the very different ways in which the mind makes sense of the world. The engineer would need to come to terms with the fact that the mind is not a perfect instrument. Its imperfections are not only the best clues we have to the mind's evolutionary history, but in a curious way are indispensable to its extraordinary efficiency and generality. The universal elements of human intelligence includes vices as well as virtues, and they are universal because they are related to the architecture of the brain as it has evolved over millions of years. Being intrinsic to the nature of the human machine, virtues and vices are not separate, detachable elements that are unrelated to one another. A virtue often implies a vice, and a vice frequently entails a virtue. Our engineer-god might decide that the best way to build a mechanical mind that is naturalistic in a deep way is to base it on an overarching design that respects these interlocked strengths and weaknesses.

I have tried to sketch a portrait of a good-bad intelligence of this kind in the foregoing chapters, one that might serve as a model, a metaphor, for the thinking machine of the future. Such an intelligence is a bundle of qualities and defects that, taken together, can be described as "worldly." The mind can be unworldly, to be sure. It was G.K. Chesterton who argued that too much worldliness can unbalance the best intellect. "In the main, and from the beginning of time, mysticism has kept men sane," Chesterton wrote. "The thing that has driven them mad is logic." The man had a point. Yet, as we have seen, worldliness by no means implies logical thought, and may be the very antithesis of it. *Intellectual* unworldliness is an aspect of the modern mind, but that would not be a good place to start for someone who is trying to model the mind from the floor up, following the agenda of human evolution. Among the properties of a natural intelligence we might include the following:

Economy. An intelligence husbands its resources, which means that it trades a general effectiveness for a certain amount of quirkiness and distortion, and an easygoing tolerance of inaccuracy. It makes a little information go a long way, by means of theories, opinions, stereotypes, and other types of schemas, which are forms of economy.

Baker Street reasoning. Making sense of the world by building rococo palaces of plausible artifice on a gimcrack foundation of a few quick observations. Fitting morsels of new information into rich structures of preexisting knowledge and in general "judging the whole piece by the pattern."

Making the strange familiar. Generalizing, putting an unknown object into a category that contains many known objects, is as natural to us as breathing. The mind is an expert thrower away of unnecessary information, and it knows when to stop throwing it away. Since the world is fairly regular, instead of being a chaos, we can use those regularities to tame and manage the world's novelty, banking on the reasonable premise that if two or more things are similar in some respects, they may be similar in other respects. That is why we predict the future with such breezy nonchalance.

Bypassing logic. A schema can sometimes behave like a syllogism. Leaving a ten-dollar gratuity at the end of a meal in a restaurant is not the result of a logical deduction: "All waiters like large tips. Henry is a waiter. Therefore Henry likes a large tip." Instead we apply a stereotype of a waiter to Henry which includes the information that small tips are usually treated with contempt. Logic is only of use in everyday life if we know everything, because deduction can do no more than make implicit information explicit. It cannot fill gaps in the data. That is the task of schemas, which are devices for getting by with incomplete but relevant knowledge.

Thriving on poor-quality information. Since the mind ignores much of what the world tells it anyway, so as to avoid the peril of computational explosion, it is at home with data that is impoverished, ambiguous, incomplete, or contradictory. This virtue carries with it the vice of being content with bad evidence when good evidence is there for the asking.

Giving prejudice a good name. A perfectly open mind is a mind that may not be able to discover anything interesting about the world.

No comprehension without interpretation. An important part of understanding is not local but global, and that means mobilizing enormous amounts of relevant world knowledge, all at once, to provide a spacious context to the words we hear or read.

Without that knowledge, even something as simple as a pronoun has no clear meaning.

Reason not an independent agent. An intelligence does not wake up one fine morning to discover it is "rational" in all circumstances and on all tasks. It does not acquire a single set of rules for solving any puzzle the world may set. A mind can be impeccably rational when a puzzle is encoded in one form, and childishly irrational when it is encoded in a different form.

A new class of artificial-intelligence machines, called connectionist models, or neural networks, revived in a new form in the 1980s after going into eclipse for almost thirty years, does reflect, in very striking ways, some of these properties of natural reason. Because they use the brain rather than the logic machine as a metaphor for the mind, these models have a certain biological plausibility. They mirror in some respects the agenda of evolution, instead of starting with Bertrand Russell's mind and working backward, as many traditional approaches do. Connectionism is in its infancy, and its future is a question mark, but if it grows up it will deserve to be called the science of the worldly machine.

One result of this drastically shifted view of how a natural intelligence works is to downgrade the importance of logic, and upgrade—we might almost say revolutionize—the role of knowledge, and of memory, which is the vehicle of knowledge. With some hyperbole, a leading connectionist, Leon Cooper of Brown University, maintains that in psychological terms memory and logic are one and the same thing. Memory *is* logic. A glance down the list of properties of the worldly brain will show how memory has dethroned reason in the new theory of the mind.

In early artificial-intelligence models, memory was relegated to a fairly minor place, which is one reason why programmers relied on general rules rather than on large amounts of knowledge to solve problems. Computer memories were expensive, and small. They are still puny in comparison with the memory we carry around in our head. Even in the latest, most powerful machines, the memory is only about one four-millionth as capacious as our own. David Waltz has estimated that to bring it up to human size would cost roughly twenty trillion dollars, about ten times the US national debt in 1988. If prices of components fall as they have been doing, such a memory could be built for only twenty million dollars by the year 2017.

Size and power of memory are not the whole story, however. It is the way memory is designed that is of critical importance. In the brain, and in certain kinds of connectionist models, the physical anatomy of memory is strange, almost bizarre. And anatomy is destiny as far as memory is concerned. How it is distributed in the brain determines how it operates as the instrument of reason.

In the standard digital computer, memory is psychologically implausible. Evolution would never have dreamed of producing such an unnatural system. You will not be surprised to learn that it was the work of a committee. In the 1940s, at the start of the computer age, a team of scientists pooled their ideas about what sort of physical design the new information machines should have. Among the members of this team was the brilliant and gifted mathematician John von Neumann. Formerly one of David Hilbert's students, von Neumann had helped to draw up questions about the basic properties of formal systems, questions which had led Alan Turing to imagine the first computer. (Hilbert was the leader of the formalist school in mathematics, which aimed to rid all symbols and operations of the last vestiges of meaning, so that the proof of a theorem could be tested by a series of mechanical steps, specific and precise, as if the system were a mindless logic machine.)

Like Turing, von Neumann realized that computers were more than superfast calculators, and could become general-purpose machines. Yet the first electronic digital computer, the ENIAC, for which von Neumann acted as a consultant, was very much a single-purpose device. As its name, Electronic Integrator and Calculator, implied, it was a number cruncher, which was exactly what its sponsors, the US War Department, wanted. The ENIAC was about five hundred times faster than any existing mechanical calculator, and it broke through the constraints on the human power to compute like a jet plane crossing the sound barrier. One of its successes was to show that the H bomb would not work as designed, a feat that human calculators, no matter how numerous, almost certainly could not have matched. The ENIAC was not a universal machine, however, as Turing's was. The instructions for solving a particular problem were built into its circuits, so that when the problem changed, the machine's switches had to be reset, a laborious task that could take days to complete.

If the new machines were to be more general in their operations, they had to be given a different sort of architecture. Their mental anatomy had to evolve, as the anatomies of primitive living creatures had evolved, into a more versatile form. In particular, a new concept of memory was needed. Turing's imaginary machine was universal, in part, because its "memory," a paper tape, was in principle endless, and did not make a distinction between the data—say a set of numbers to be computed—and the instructions telling the machine what to do with the data, what logical operations it must perform in a step-by-step fashion. The machine was able to compute anything that is computable, because instructions for any and every task it will ever undertake could be encoded on the tape. The actual limits of space and time were ignored in this purely theoretical description of what a universal computer can do.

In a now celebrated working paper released in June 1945, which has been called the most important document ever written on computers and computing, von Neumann and the other members of the team set out their ideas about the design of the new generation of computers. One of their recommendations was to treat memory as "one organ" in the anatomy of the computer, even though it had to perform more than one function.

The Olympians had spoken. Memory was to be a single organ. It turned out to be a momentous decision in the history of the computer. Equally significant, however, was the decision that the logical control device—the general executive that sees to it that the instructions, no matter what they might be, are carried out in the proper sequence—should be another, separate organ. This distinct and independent component in the anatomy of the computer is known as the central processing unit.

A central processing unit is like a director standing on the stage of a vast theater, asking members of the audience for a message. A member of the audience in the first seat of the front row of the orchestra may tell the director to add together the numbers given to him by the two people in the second and third seats of the same row. When the director has added the two numbers, the person in the fourth seat might tell him to write the number and give it to the person in the seat to his right. The theater audience represents the computer's memory, and the man standing on stage takes items of information, whether data or instructions, one at a time from the members of the audience, and then does to the data what the instructions tell him to do. He is solitary, aloof, and active, while the audience is separate and passive.

This arrangement, curious as it may seem, is certainly versatile. The man onstage, who directs the sequence of operations, is general-purpose in the sense that he is independent of the meaning, the content, of the information he collects and acts upon. He needs no extra knowledge to help him perform his task. He simply does what he is told. He takes information from members of the audience sitting in specific seats, reads it, performs certain operations on it, and gives the result to certain audience members. In a computer, the stage director is made of logic circuitry. The central processor makes no leaps, skips no steps, makes no spontaneous judgments. Like a mathematician writing a proof, he makes one move at a time, observing the rules at each move. Messages from the audience are expressed in a code, and the manner in which the man onstage decodes them is determined by his "state of mind," which in turn is determined by previous instructions. If he is told by a member of the audience to add the next two messages, those messages will be treated as numbers. As a result of this arrangement, what comes out of a standard digital computer—and its basic anatomy has not changed significantly since that founding generation of von Neumann machines—is a fairly predictable product of what went in.

The theater audience, the memory of the system, is also general-purpose, because it encodes information of all kinds. Instructions such as "Add the numbers given to you by the two people sitting in the next seats," and data, say, "the numbers 54 and 71," are stored at arbitrary seats in the theater. The seat is the "address" of the item. A number in the computer program gives the specific address of an instruction or an item of data, and the computer reads the number. This is a versatile arrangement because any item can reside at any address. For purposes of memory retrieval, it matters not in the least what the message says. Only the number of its location matters. There is no reason why the content of a message at a given address may not change while a computation is in progress. Any member of the audience can store any kind of message, provided it is not too large for his memory, and his message can be altered by the director while the performance is going on, because the program specifies only his seat number, not what his message says.

In an important class of connectionist models that seem to bear certain resemblances to the anatomy of the brain, memory behaves in a completely different way. There is no central processor, no man onstage taking messages one by one, working on them, and then returning the result to a member of the audience. Instead, each member of the audience is a processor, receiving messages from other members and acting or not acting on them. Cognition in such a system is global with a vengeance, arising out of the somewhat anarchic activity of myriads of individual units working all at the same time on a problem in concert or in competition and settling down into a solution that may not be logically correct but "feels right" to the system as a whole. This curious arrangement means that a memory can be made immensely large without slowing down the system. In a von Neumann computer, pulling items out of a huge memory takes longer than pulling them out of a small one, but in connectionist models of this sort, information is not "retrieved" one small piece at a time, but all at once, collectively, in what is called a "massively parallel" fashion.

Connectionist systems consist of a network of simple processors called units, linked together in such a way that each unit receives signals from other units, perhaps dozens of them, and sends signals to the same or to other units. On its own a unit is not intelligent. It performs quite simple tasks. It does some elementary arithmetic on the signals it receives, and interprets them as a message to transmit or not to transmit a signal of its own. When a signal arrives at a unit from elsewhere in the system, the unit multiplies the signal by a number, called a weight, before passing it on to other units. The weight determines whether the signal the unit transmits is weak or strong. A weak signal links a unit to other units loosely, while strong ones make tighter connections.

A paradox of connectionist models such as these is that each processing unit by itself is a rather ignorant device, and somewhat parochial to boot, yet crowds of them in action together become intelligent. The system is locally dull but globally interesting. Because the links are local, a unit knows only what it is told by the units to which it is connected. There is no omniscient executive who knows what the system as a whole is doing, no overall program to coordinate its various parts. What is more, a unit transmits very little information at any one time. Sending long strings of symbols, standard practice in a von Neumann computer, is out of the question. A unit sends a signal if the total input it is receiving increases its activation to a certain threshold. How a unit behaves, whether it sends a signal, whether that signal is weak or strong, is decided only by its present state of activation and by the sort of signals it receives. Essentially, the information broadcast by each unit to others is the terse message: "I'm turned on as strongly as this or as weakly as this." In some cases, units can send signals that either excite or inhibit other units.

The memory of certain kinds of connectionist networks turns out to have some surprising properties. An item of knowledge, a concept, a fact, any bit of experience lodged in the mind, is not stored in a specific place, as in the familiar type of computer. Instead, it is represented by a whole pattern of activity, the frenzy of numbers of units turning on and off like lights on a Christmas tree as they signal to one another along the weighted links that connect unit with unit. A simple concept like "grandmother" may be spread out across a region of the network. Just how large that region may be in the brain itself is a matter for debate.

Not only is an item of knowledge smeared out across an expanse of the network instead of being at one pinpoint location; it is also superimposed on other items, so that at any given place in the network thousands of different memories may reside, one on top of another. A single unit is involved in encoding many memories, and many units take part in the representation of a single memory. It might be thought that superimposing memories would lead to muddle and confusion. We might mix up a grandmother memory with an aunt memory, or a word with a color, which would lead to chaos. In fact, the system seems to work in such a way that memories that are sufficiently different are kept separate, but memories that are sufficiently similar interact.

From a purely practical point of view, this is a sensible arrangement. It ensures durability and toughness. The brain, which has billions, perhaps trillions of processing units, called neurons, can afford to squander them, letting millions be wiped out in the normal wear and tear of everyday thinking. Even gross insult can leave the brain more or less in working order, as in the famous case of Louis Pasteur. Pasteur was stricken by a cerebral hemorrhage at the age of forty-six and nearly died. His left arm and leg were paralyzed permanently. Yet Pasteur's mind remained luminously clear and he went on to accomplish some of his most brilliant scientific work.

Another useful feature of a distributed, superimposed memory is economy. A single unit is used and reused to process thousands of different items. Economy of this kind is typical of many natural information systems, including the coded biochemical messages in the genes, where a single sequence of symbols may code for two different types of proteins, depending on how it is read. It appears, too, in natural languages, which are able to express an unlimited profusion of ideas with a limited vocabulary because the same word may have different meanings, depending on context. Words do multiple duty. In English, the words *set* and *run* each have about 140 possible alternative meanings. Such economy makes language ambiguous by its very nature, and an unsuitable vehicle for logic.

As a result of the robustness and economy of a distributed connectionist memory, certain surprising properties emerge. One such property is that the "address" of an item of knowledge is not a unique, arbitrary number, independent of content, as it is in a von Neumann computer. Instead, the address of an item is another item, which is related to the first item by its content. For this reason such a memory is called "content addressable." The words *Richard Nixon* set off a pattern of activity in the network, turning on some units. Since similar memories interact, due to the multiple role of single units, the *Richard Nixon* activity sets off a *Watergate* pattern and pretty soon a memory of the entire Watergate scandal is brought to consciousness. This is what Henry James called "judging the whole piece by the pattern." In the same way, hearing the words *Scarlett O'Hara* summons up the whole world of *Gone with the Wind*, possibly including the first time we saw the movie, Clark Gable's last exit, and the circumstances of Margaret Mitchell's tragic death. Often what appears to be computation is simply the completion of a pattern as a result of being given part of the pattern. If I say "Six times seven" you say "Forty-two," not because you are a natural calculator, but because the address in memory of 42 is 6×7. A content-addressable memory can simulate a mathematical operation.

A distributed, superimposed memory behaves a little like a troupe of summer-stock actors. (This is an analogy suggested by Earl Hunt of the University of Seattle.) The actors and actresses perform plays from a large repertory, a different play every night of the week. There is no director to prompt them, or remind them which play they are in. On Monday, the company opens with *The Rivals*. An actor speaks the first lines of the play. As he finishes, the final words of his speech cue the next actor to speak his lines, and he in turn cues a third. Thanks to content-addressable memory, the address of an actor's line is the cue spoken by the previous actor, which is part of a pattern that activates the complete pattern, just as *Richard Nixon* is the cue for *Watergate*. On Tuesday, the play is *Macbeth*, and on Wednesday *Man and Superman*, but the actors are the same as they were on Monday. The memory of *The Rivals* is superimposed on the memory of *Macbeth*, and both are superimposed on *Man and Superman*. The plays are sufficiently unlike one another, however, that they are separated in memory, and a cue always activates the correct patterns.

11: A NEW GHOST FOR A NEW MACHINE

In a connectionist network, knowledge is a processor of information. The dividing line between memory and reasoning, already blurred by Sir Frederic Bartlett's landmark studies of the way people "recollect" the past by constructing a reasonable interpretation of it, seems to break down altogether. Remembering is not essentially different from solving everyday problems, because in each case, fragments of incoming information wake up networks of interacting knowledge, resulting in a pattern of activity that represents a memory, or the answer to a problem, that is most consistent with the evidence.

In logical reasoning (to recapitulate the story so far), argument goes one step at a time. If all elephants are gray and Dumbo is an elephant, then Dumbo is gray. A network, on the other hand, seems to operate by considering a tremendous number of different pieces of evidence, weak as well as strong, all at the same time, which is why it is called a parallel system. Given the following facts

1. Ambrose wanted to win the election.
2. His opponent was ten points ahead in the latest opinion poll.
3. Ambrose hired a private detective.

most people rapidly conclude that Ambrose, his hopes of being elected dimming, plans to uncover a scandal in the personal life of his political rival. It is highly doubtful that they arrive at this answer by logical deduction. More likely, the statements act as cues that provide an "address" for knowledge about how things normally fit together in the world, and such knowledge is encoded in the connections among many processing units in the brain. To think in a logical way, the brain, at each step in the chain of reasoning, would have to consider every possible next step, and this would take far too long, even for a high-speed serial computer. Nor do we appear, in general, to use heuristic rules to reduce the number of possibilities. Instead, what seems to happen is that the knowledge encoded in the network provides a multitude of different constraints, quite apart from the restrictions imposed by the rules of logic, on what might be a sensible step. In general, these constraints are based on experience of how the world usually goes, of what is plausible under this or that circumstance. Many considerations, perhaps hundreds of thousands, may go to determine what is plausible and what is implausible, but since a connectionist computer is parallel, not serial, like the audience in the imaginary theater all voicing their opinions and influencing their neighbors simultaneously, it "makes up its mind" on the spot. The most plausible interpretation of the evidence wins.

The constraints are encoded in the strengths or weaknesses of the connections that link units in the network, in the loudness or softness of the voices of the members of the theater audience.

Units corresponding to the concept of "elections" will have strong excitatory links to units that correspond to the concept of scandals, guilty secrets, and disgrace, because that is the way things are typically connected in the world, and knowledge of the world is stored in the weights of the links that connect units with units. The learned links among elections, opinion polls, private detectives, and scandals all come together in an instant to produce an interpretation of the information that is firmly hemmed in by the constraints of what constitutes a reasonable story, given the evidence. Since each item of knowledge is spread out over many, many processing units, the relevant items interact, and are reinforced, while the irrelevant ones tend to cancel each other out. The resulting story is no more than reasonable, however. It is conceivable that Ambrose engaged a detective to investigate his own wife.

In a connectionist network, memory is a form of reason, and reason is an aspect of memory, because each processing unit is not just a memory device. It is also a decision-maker. It is involved in solving problems. In the brain, the processing units, nerve cells, are soft and wet, intricate, and come in various different types. In a connectionist computer, units are hard, simple, and all exactly the same. They are cartoon versions, rough models, of the real, biological thing.

A neuron in the brain is very slow in operation, about a million times slower than a switch in a digital computer. In a tenth of a second it can pass only about six digits of code to other neurons. Yet the brain can complete an intelligent thought, recognize a face, understand a sentence, in less than a second. A serial computer, engaged in the same task, would still be thrashing through its lines of code, having carried out only about one hundred of the many thousands of instructions needed for a similar kind of task. Speed of this sort is possible in a connectionist system because its hordes of processors go to work on the problem all at once, collectively. Processing, as well as memory, is spread out over the network.

What the network knows, as well as what it can do with that

knowledge, is determined by the connection strengths. They are the long-term memory of the system. In this way knowledge plays a unique role in perceiving, thinking, and remembering. It is inextricably involved in processing information. In a standard artificial-intelligence system, the information stored in memory, the "inference engine" that makes logical deductions from information, and the interpreter, are separate and distinct elements. That is not the case in a connectionist network. The connections, the strengths of the connections, and the units, encode more than just the knowledge of the system. They determine how the parts of that knowledge interact with one another while the computation is going on. Knowledge and inference are both encoded in one and the same network, which is why a system that knows is also, automatically and as a matter of course, a system that infers.

Nothing could be more unlike the digital view of a memory as a piece of information, encoded in symbols, either correct or incorrect, stored in one specific place. In a standard computer, information sits there, waiting to be used, and is the same entity while it is waiting as it is while it is being used. Something far more exotic and ethereal is going on in a connectionist network. The information cannot really be said to exist at all when it is not being used. It is only potential, latent, a wraith implicit in a myriad connection strengths which are simultaneously engaged in representing other kinds of information by patterns of activity. It is a ghost in the machine. As John Tienson puts it: "In a connectionist system, information is actively represented as a pattern of activation. When that information is not in use, the pattern is nowhere present in the system. Information is not stored as data structures. The only symbols ever present in a connectionist system are active representations."

"Information is stored in the weights. And because the weights are as they are, representations are *created* in response to internal or external stimuli. Memories are not stored, they are recreated over and over again in response to whatever reminds you of them. Information that is not presently active—not in use—is only in the system potentially. Thus, there is no distinction internal to the system between recreating old representations and creating new ones in response to the situation."

All this means that in a connectionist network memory becomes interpretation. It is not a filing cabinet, nor a set of index cards, but a hermeneutical system. A cue that triggers a memory is a sort of puzzle that has to be solved, a riddle with multiple possible answers that must be disentangled so that the right answer pops out. The network constructs a pattern of activity that fits the cue most plausibly, just as it constructs a scenario for Ambrose that is most consistent both with the evidence provided by the three statements and with what the network knows about how the world typically behaves.

A very simple way of thinking about a network, in which single units, rather than patterns, represent aspects of the world, is to regard each unit as a hypothesis or opinion about some aspect of an object or event the network is trying to remember, recognize, or reason about (the difference between remembering and other forms of cognition grows increasingly hard to define). A unit can be thought of as representing a feature or property of a given concept, and units whose opinions are relevant are strongly connected. In a pattern of activity corresponding to the concept of *clown*, for example, units standing for features such as *circus, big red nose, funny, children* would be sending strong signals to one another, while irrelevant items connected to children, say *school* or *parents*, are suppressed. If a unit is "confident" about the truth of the hypothesis, it fires. Two units representing hypotheses that support each other are linked by a connection that is strong and excites both units, whereas if two units stand for hypotheses which contradict each other, one unit sends a signal that tends to inhibit the other. A unit listens to the "opinions" of units to which it is connected, and influences other units with its own opinion. By a process of repeated mutual adjustment of opinions, the system settles down into a stable pattern of hypotheses that is consistent. Suppose the network were shown this partly obscured word:

WORK

The information is poor in quality, but the network can make sense of it. There are units for all four letter positions in the word. Units are set to detect a certain part of a letter, an entire letter, or a complete word. The more confident a unit is of its "opinion" that what it is supposed to detect is actually there on the page, the more active that unit becomes. Units for parts of the first three letters, sure of their hypotheses that the parts belong to *W, O,* and *R*, respectively, excite units that detect entire letters. In the last letter position, however, units for both *R* and *K* are activated, since units that detect parts of letters have put forward two hypotheses. Letter units now excite units that detect whole words that contain these four letters, and inhibit units that detect words made up of different letters. Several words are partly consistent with the active letters, and receive encouragement from the letter units, but only the word *WORK* supports the opinions of active letter units in the specific order that they appear. As a result, *WORK* becomes more active than any other word, reflecting the confidence of the word units in their hypothesis, and these send feedback signals down to the letter units for *W, O, R,* and *K,* exciting them still more, increasing confidence in the hypothesis that *K* rather than *R* is the fourth letter so much that finally *R* is suppressed altogether. *K* wins, and *R* loses the debate.

This process of building up confidence in plausible opinions that fit the evidence and breaking down confidence in opinions that do not fit explains why people usually read the word *F O Y E V E R,* when it is flashed briefly onto a screen, as *FOREVER,* because the hypothesis that the third letter is *R,* though untrue, is more consistent with the opinions of the other letter detectors than the hypothesis that it is Y.

A parallel, distributed network interprets the world in a curious way. It adapts to new information coming into the system from outside, and yet the outcome of its deliberations reflects not just the information itself, but also the constraints on what is a plausible interpretation and expansion of it. The knowledge implicit in the strengths of the connections that link units to units and determine directly how the units interact, is influenced by perceived reality, but at the same time that knowledge also influences the perception of reality.

In such a network, memory is intensely active on a global scale. This is quite unlike a von Neumann computer, where only a small part of memory is active at any one instant. "Memory traces in the brain are dynamic objects trying to impose themselves on input," said James McClelland, one of the leading pioneers of connectionist computer models. "When a particular piece of information comes into the system, it tends to wake up the traces that it is similar to. And when they get woken up, they try to tell the input what it should be. Memory traces feed back onto the input."

Scott Fahlman, a cognitive scientist at Carnegie-Mellon University in Pittsburgh, emphasizes the assertiveness of knowledge in brainlike networks. "Look at it this way," Fahlman said. "Say you are standing in a library and there is some piece of knowledge out there you need, and it's in one of the books. One way to find the information is to start with book one, open it at page one, and begin reading until you find what you need. That could take some time. A second way is to spend a lot of effort creating a card catalogue and use that. Standard artificial-intelligence programs are essentially about making card catalogues. A third possibility, which is the approach of massively parallel connectionist networks, would be to stand in the middle of the library yelling out your question, and one of the books, or perhaps a conspiracy of several books, shouts back an answer. Active knowledge in a network computer or a brain is like those books calling out relevant answers, because it's not a dead memory on the shelf that some active agent has to go and find for herself. It's all vibrating and collaborating and trying to see if it fits into a given problem. It's an entirely new ball game, and that is what brought me into this kind of research."

This is an "unscientific" way for a brain to behave. It means that the sort of knowledge Karl Popper assigned to World 2, produced by opinions, conjectures, intuition, imposes itself on the facts, rather than trying to disconfirm conjectures by checking them against the facts. Only when World 2 knowledge has been made explicit and placed cheek-by-jowl with reality, Popper said, can it be regarded as genuine knowledge, the battle-tested, reliable variety that inhabits World 3. Distributed knowledge in a network does not observe this rule; reality is checked against World 2 knowledge, as well as vice-versa. The product of a recollection, a perception, an act of comprehension is a mixture of mind and world, each entangled with the other.

Is this a deplorable way for a mind to behave? In some respects, perhaps. On the other hand, it does ensure that the mind and the world are thoroughly engaged, one with the other. One weakness of a conventional artificial-intelligence machine is that it tends to be aloof from the world. It is fed precooked information by the programmer, who has abstracted some thin assertions about a reality shorn of its natural richness, stripped of context, and on these assertions the machine operates with some formal rules which are also context-free. Stuart and Hubert Dreyfus have criticized this approach as "passing over" the world as such, making a futile attempt to "free aspects of our experience of just that pragmatic organization which makes it possible to use them intelligently in coping with everyday problems."

A novelist's reluctance and even refusal to spell out in explicit detail exactly what he means, his instinctive reluctance to load his descriptions with exhaustive detail, instead deliberately creating gaps that the reader must fill by means of plausible scenarios and re-created knowledge, are strategies aimed at trying to pull the reader into the world of the story, to engage his interest by making him assist in the work of world-making and impose his own interpretation on the "reality" of the narrative —though the author may not be aware of what he is doing, or why he is doing it. That is exactly what happens in everyday life when we use World 2 knowledge to make sense of what is going on around us.

William Bechtel of Georgia State University has made the interesting point that because standard artificial-intelligence programs spell out explicitly all the information the system is to use, they pay the price of being cut off from reality. Since what they do is determined solely by internal representations, such machines are not closely linked to the external objects, events, people, to which the representations are supposed to refer. They lack what philosophers call "intentionality," a jargon word which means that thoughts are *about* something, and this "aboutness" is a hallmark of mental as opposed to physical systems. Intentionality implies meaning and purpose, knowing what objects are for and how they are to be used. A machine may be able to store and manipulate an abundance of facts and symbols, and combine them in clever, accurate ways, but if it does not know what all the facts and symbols are about, what they mean in terms of the real world, if the symbols are defined in terms only of themselves, as in formal logic, the system is not intentional. Human beings do have intentionality; barring an extraordinary mental impairment, it is universal to our species. For that reason, we can "lose" ourselves in a work of fiction and identify with the joys and sufferings of the characters the author has created. Intentionality also explains why the mind matches new things to familiar, worldly things so naturally and easily.

The absence of intentionality in most thinking machines is a spur to robot researchers like Rodney Brooks to build intelligence from the bottom up, starting with such basic forms of knowing as hearing and seeing, moving around without bumping into the furniture or tripping over the dog, taking space and time into account, using the world as a model of itself instead of prepackaging a highly simplified model of the world. Brooks's robots are thoroughly engaged with their physical surroundings.

A connectionist system does not rely on internal representations as its processing units. It constructs representations as *responses* to incoming information, and it is possible to develop networks that adjust their weights in such a way that they categorize on their own, instead of letting a programmer do it for them. The machine tunes itself to its environment. It is not too fanciful to say that the intelligence of a connectionist network is more genuinely *about* things in the world than is the intelligence of a classical thinking machine.

It is no coincidence that connectionist models have been most successful in such basic "world-engaging" skills as perception, seeing and hearing, mobility, recognition of faces, classifying and matching patterns. Connectionism made its false start thirty years ago with network models that were built to learn about visual patterns. In the 1960s, Frank Rosenblatt of Cornell University created a machine called a Perceptron, based on a simple network of computing units connected up together. Rosenblatt cautioned that his invention was a highly simplified model that exaggerated certain properties of the brain and ignored others. In June 1960 the first Perceptron was unveiled amid considerable publicity and fanfare. It had an eye made of photoelectric cells that scrutinized letters inscribed on cards, and passed messages about what it saw to an array of 512 units randomly hooked up together, which in turn sent the messages on to a set of response units. Then the Perceptron made a guess as to what letter was on the card. If the machine made a wrong guess, it was punished by having the weights responsible for the mistake weakened. After several punishments, and as a result of trial and error, the Perceptron made the correct choices.

The Perceptron was an early attempt to do crudely what the new connectionists of the 1990s are accomplishing with more sophistication and ingenuity, namely to build intelligent machines by using the brain, rather than the von Neumann computer, as a metaphor of mind. In a brain that evolved in a real environment, with survival an item high on its agenda, perception would have taken precedence over luxuries like logic. The brain is poor at logic, but since it has been doing perception for all these millions of years, it ought to be pretty good at it by now. Note well, then, that perception, to an important extent, is a matter of matching patterns, not of solving syllogisms. And matching and classifying patterns is exactly where connectionist networks excel. The Perceptron, the primordial *Machina sapiens* of the new age, was essentially a pattern-recognizer, a classifier.

The von Neumann computer amplified aspects of human intelligence that are luxuries from an evolutionary point of view: calculation, logic, brute force search of possibilities. Connectionist systems, by contrast, amplify the more bread-and-butter mental faculty of classifying. That is why they are promising devices for such tasks as shutting down enemy search radars when flying against a heavily defended target. Sorting out hostile from friendly or neutral radar signals means categorizing pulses into separate lists, based on a number of radar pulse-train features. No human being can classify the small-scale structure of individual pulses in this way; it would be like trying to drink from a firehose, being drenched with more data than the unaided brain can handle and unable to make decisions that come up to the level of the complexity of the data. Connectionist systems are good for determining which signals are unique, never heard before, and which ones are familiar; that is why they are also candidates for detecting possible signals from intelligent sources in outer space.

Neural networks are being considered by the US Department of Defense for such "super" vision-processing problems as finding and following stealth aircraft, which fly low against a cluttered background at varying speeds, and for spotting the presence of "quiet" submarines, a perceptual operation which is similar in certain respects to recognizing speech by classifying the frequencies of speech sounds. Terrence Sejnowski has developed a three-layer neural-network model that seems to be better than humans at recognizing undersea mines on a rock-strewn ocean floor in shallow waters using sonar signal patterns.

As we have already seen, logic is not a "natural kind" of the mind. But classifying may be. "Classification appears to be a rather ubiquitous information processing task," says Balakrishnan Chandrasekaran, director of the artificial-intelligence group at Ohio State University and an expert on speech-recognition machines. "This suggests that classification is not an artifact of any one point of view in artificial intelligence, but rather a natural kind, of considerable cognitive significance. Indeed, classification appears to be a powerful human strategy for organizing knowledge for comprehension and action. The human tendency to classify is so strong that we often classify without being consciously aware of it, and feel we have accomplished something by merely naming entities as categories, even if we cannot do much about it."

Certainly one of the reasons why Aristotle is known as the philosopher of common sense, the worldly philosopher, is that his main concern is to classify what the world contains under basic headings or categories. The *Categories,* the earliest of Aristotle's treatises on reasoning, is in one sense a classification of types of predicates, but it may also be read as a method of classifying things, "the ultimate furniture of the world," in terms of what can be said about them. This was part of Aristotle's attempt to create a theory of reality, one strongly opposed to Plato's otherworldly doctrine of the ideal forms.

An interesting question is whether pattern-matching and classifying, which hook us to the world so tightly, and natural reason, are really as different as they seem. In the history of thought, perception is something we share with brute creation, and is therefore a lesser faculty, while reason is something else entirely, unique to our species, a special gift, a guarantee of our semi-divine status in the animal kingdom. Chaucer put it most charmingly in his translation of *The Consolation of Philosophy* of Boethius: "man is a resonable two-foted beest."

It may be one of connectionism's most important insights that thinking and perception are not as foreign to each other as tradition dictates; if so, it would point the way to a new understanding of the unity of intelligence, and of the unwisdom of creating theories of the mind that brush aside the history of the brain.

12: TELLING AN EGG FROM A WALNUT

Frank Rosenberg's Perceptron boom collapsed as suddenly as it began, in part because the contraption, exciting and headline-grabbing as it was, needed perfect information in order to be intelligent. The one-eyed device was not able to deal with the real world of ambiguity and change. If a letter was partly hidden, or printed in an unfamiliar typeface, the Perceptron could not identify it. Asked to recognize an elephant, the machine needed to be shown the entire animal, always the same size and against a white background. That made it very inferior to human intelligence, which can spot an elephant by a glimpse of the end of its trunk, by its trumpeting sound, by a poster advertising the film *Dumbo*, or by the incomplete sentence "An ———— never forgets."

Today's neural networks are brighter than the Perceptron.

The processing units are not crude yes-or-no devices, like the switches in a standard computer. They vary the strength of the signal they transmit in a smooth, gently increasing fashion, which makes it possible to write sophisticated rules for teaching the network to make correct guesses by altering its connection strengths, and therefore its knowledge. When the system makes an error, perhaps by falsely recognizing an elephant as a giraffe, an elegant mathematical procedure, which assigns the mistake a number, enables the machine to change its weights so as to make the pattern of activation correspond more closely to an elephant. At the same time, feedback gives the new connectionist models more versatility, and hidden units, not directly in touch with the outside world, give the machine a "mentalism," an ability to represent the world, that the Perceptron lacked.

Diane Ingraham and her colleagues at Simon Fraser University have designed a network model, simulated on a standard IBM digital computer, that is able to recognize an egg and know that it is different from a walnut. The machine does not need to be given detailed descriptions of eggs and walnuts, as a traditional program would. "A neural network acts like a small child," Dr. Ingraham says. "If you try to teach a child what a ball is, you don't give her the mathematical formula for spherical objects. You just keep showing her different kinds of balls. A network's software 'learns' how to recognize an object, without a formal description of it. You just keep presenting it with examples. You buy a couple of dozen eggs, small and large, brown and white, and keep showing them to the computer. You train the network by giving it examples, and telling it what you want its response to be. The first time you show it an egg, the computer will output garbage. So you do essentially what you would do with a small child. You say, 'No, that's not correct.' You put in the correct response and the computer then looks at its answer, and compares it with the answer you want. The machine attempts to change the weights on its connections in such a way that its output patterns match your input patterns more and more closely."

The model still behaves intelligently when the egg is seen from a new angle or placed in an unfamiliar setting. Put the egg in a different room, in front of a decorated screen, and the machine "knows" it is an egg and not a walnut. Ingraham and her team have created a neural-network model that can recognize a person's face, whether or not that face has been shaved yet this morning, and even when it is wearing sunglasses, and the model can fill in the missing features that the sunglasses hide. That would be extremely difficult to program in a standard artificial-intelligence system; usually such a system, shown pictures of the same face, first smiling and then frowning, thinks the face belongs to two different people. "That gives neural networks all kinds of possible spooky uses," Dr. Ingraham says. "Out here we have police cameras that take pictures of your automobile registration plate if you are driving faster than the speed limit. If you had mud hiding part of one of the numbers of your plate, a neural network could reconstruct the number. It could also identify an incomplete fingerprint. Standard computers have to break down a fingerprint into lines and squirls and cusps and scale it to a typical size, and then search through a data base of millions of fingerprints on file to try and find a match. A neural network can make a judgment about a partial fingerprint without searching a data base. It makes an instant match to a pattern it has learned. That is very much the way the brain works, which is not so surprising, because we are using the brain as a model for our machines."

Networks are at home with imperfect information, just as the brain is. It is a natural property of such systems to be able to respond to defective, ambiguous patterns, or patterns that are not exactly the same as those for which the machine has been trained. The network responds to a new or defective item in the same way that it responded to an item already seen, that matches the new item most nearly. It does not need to be given special instructions about how to deal with this particular new or defective piece of information. Bad cues can lead to the activation of good knowledge. But the system does not promise to be exact, only usefully approximate. "Neural networks excel in those situations where close is a good enough answer," Dr. Ingraham says.

Suppose a network is asked to recognize the letter *A* under the sort of conditions that prevail in real life, when the brain must be prepared to treat as familiar letters crayoned by a child, typed by a secretary, scribbled carelessly by a busy executive, or printed in extravagantly ornate form in a magazine. A single letter can wear all kinds of exotic disguises, like a person wearing a new hat, or sporting sunglasses:

A a a **A** a *A*

The distortions and embellishments can be quite outrageous, and a reader still knows at once what letter is intended. A network can be trained to behave in the same way. It does not need to be told that *A* is a letter of the alphabet, or be given a specific description of each different form. After it has been taught with examples of all the distorted letters, the machine will simply print out a clean capital *A* whenever it is shown any one of the typefaces shown above. The network is taught by example to recognize them all as being the same letter, by typing *A* on the computer keyboard every time an example is shown. The machine knows *A*s in general, not just each *A* in particular.

In a conventional computer program, the letter would have to be broken down into its component parts, and the machine would then compare what it is shown with the parts. Usually, it could recognize an *A* only if it is printed in the same typeface every time. A network, on the other hand, learns like a child to respond in the same way to patterns that are similar in some respects but different in other respects. If such a machine is taught to recognize the first five letters of the alphabet, and it is then shown the sixth letter, *F*, perhaps scribbled roughly by hand, the machine will recognize it as a pattern it has not seen before. At the same time, it will try to classify that unfamiliar letter as one of the patterns it has already seen. It treats it as being similar to E. "It could be an E, but . . . ," the machine says in effect. The pattern of connection weights for an F is fairly close to the pattern of weights for an E.

In the case of some recent, sophisticated models emerging from Boston University, created by the veteran network theorist Stephen Grossberg, seeing an F after learning only the first five letters of the alphabet results in the spontaneous creation of a new category of patterns just for Fs, into which the unfamiliar letter is placed.

What networks often do when they are confronted with information that is corrupt, or strange, or ambiguous, is to interpret it in terms of a prototype. One of the curious features of connectionist systems is that the initial mathematics, multiplying by weights and then summing and passing the result through a nonlinear function, is remarkably simple. Yet when a hundred or so units are hooked up together, in themselves just adding and multiplying devices, and not nearly as complex as neurons in the living brain, unexpected properties emerge, rather as large-scale effects like temperature and pressure emerge from a gas. In itself, a gas is just a collection of molecules, no one of which on its own can be said to have either pressure or temperature. Category formation seems to be one of the emergent properties of a network.

And here is the crux of the matter. Category formation and prototypes, which in psychology are now seen in an entirely new and more naturalistic light thanks to the work of Eleanor Rosch and others, are the bridge between low-level modes of intelligence, such as seeing and hearing, and the more lofty domain of thinking and reasoning. I have already tried the reader's patience by showing that how the mind forms categories of the things the world contains is intimately connected with how it thinks and reasons about those things. Making categories need not involve logic and symbol manipulation using precise rules, but may be a type of pattern recognition. As William Bechtel and others argue, pattern recognition may indeed play a role in high-level intelligence, the kind we usually think of as symbol manipulation. It could be much more important than we realize.

A connectionist network that recognizes patterns does not use a set of rules for putting new items into categories. One way in which it works is to create a prototype, and make sense of new or ambiguous information by virtue of its closeness to or distance from the prototype, by how "typical" it is. To take an imaginary example, a network might read all the English Romantic poets and decide that Lord Byron is the prototype of the category. Then, it would classify new poems according to how Byronic they are. Sometimes the prototype does not exist in reality; it is something the network constructs on its own. James McClelland devised a network model that was given a list of members of two notorious New York street gangs, the Sharks and the Jets. The list included their names, ages, occupations (burglar, bookie, pusher), marital status (married, single, divorced), and education. The network was able to describe a "typical" Jet as being single, in his twenties, with a junior-high-school education. In fact, however, the typical Jet did not exist. There was no member of the gang who matched that description exactly.

Another program, created by McClelland and David Rumelhart, learned the past tense of English verbs by forming prototypes. The model was something of a prodigy, and surprised its inventors by responding correctly to verbs it had never seen before, as well as to verbs that were deliberate fakes. The model did not use explicit rules of grammar, since it had never been shown such rules. Instead, it extracted the samenesses shared by various verbs and threw away the differences, generating a typical past-tense form. At first the network overgeneralized. The prototype reflected the "experience" of the network that most verbs are regular, and so it gave verbs regular endings indiscriminately. It made gaffes such as *bringed* instead of *brought*, and behaved in a childish fashion, saying *camed* and *tooked*. Only when a set of connection weights had been acquired that captured the predominant sameness, and the patterns of activation in the network that represented irregular past-tense endings became sufficiently different from patterns representing regular ones, were both kinds able to coexist in the same network without confusion.

Some connectionists talk about a network's memory as if it were a physical surface, a hilly landscape onto which items of information are dropped. These items then fall down the hills into a valley where the prototype item resides, so that an instant match is made between the new and the typical. For example, a scrawled *A* would roll downhill to where a prototype clear capital *A* is located. A close, but not perfect match is made. The process can also be described as the result of the collective and competitive opinions of large numbers of units, influencing one another and being influenced by the strong or weak signals transmitted along the connections. "Suppose you see an elephant at the zoo," Scott Fahlman says. "It's never going to look exactly like your prototype of an elephant. It has a trunk and a tail and it's gray sure enough, but the wrinkles are in the wrong places. It may be bigger or smaller than your ideal. Yet you look at the animal and it's a whole lot closer to your prototype elephant than it is to a prototype hippo or giraffe. All the units in the brain's network that are little detectors for various aspects of elephants are all going crazy and saying 'This is pretty good.' They are all adding up and voting in the same way. A few other ones may be pointing out the differences between the actual elephant and the prototype in your head, but they get outvoted." In both metaphors, the match is made as a sort of settling-down process that happens naturally.

A surprising feature of network models is that they form prototypes almost as a matter of course, without being told to, but they do so to a significant extent only when they are under a certain amount of strain, and need to stretch their resources. This is another example of cognitive economy dictating the character of natural intelligence. If a network has thousands of processing units, and is being taught to recognize a thousand different patterns, the model will assign one item to a specific set of units and it will not generalize very much. If a severe bottleneck occurs, however, in which the number of different patterns the machine must recognize greatly exceeds the number of its units, the network starts to practice economy by using some of its units to form prototypes.

One such model, built by Geoffrey Hinton, now at Toronto University, was taught the family trees of two families, one English and the other Italian. At first, when it had plenty of units, the system simply memorized all the names and relationships in the two trees. Later, a bottleneck was deliberately created, leaving only six units to handle thirty-two names. When its resources were drastically limited in this way, the network became a generalizer. It used some of the information to construct the rest of the information. Shown the complete English family tree, but only part of the Italian tree, it was able to fill in missing parts of the Italian line, deciding that here was a grandfather or an uncle, there a grandchild or a nephew. The same units were used to represent the same relationships in both trees. The model reused a unit that represented "uncle" in the English family, applying it to the Italians. On the face of it, the system seemed to be doing logic, making inferences from one tree to the other, but in fact it was merely generalizing as a result of not having enough units to encode each person in each tree uniquely. It was practicing economy. With only six units, the system had to resort to some clever encoding to make the most of scarce resources.

One reason why generalizing happens spontaneously in a parallel distributed network is that memories are superimposed, so that a single unit is involved in the processing of multiple memories. When remembering the concept "Fire engines are noisy," the connections between all the units that correspond to *fire engine* and all the units that correspond to *noisy* are strengthened. The network generalizes the concept as a matter of course. It now knows, without being told, that ambulances are noisy, because most of the units that are used to represent fire engines are also used to represent ambulances.

Human beings live in a world where things that come in various disguises must be treated as if they were the same, so that generalization is a key to making sense of life. That applies to something as mundane and basic as the sounds of everyday speech. A New York cabdriver speaks the same language as an Oxford professor or a Maine fisherman, yet the actual sounds they make are as different as various typefaces of the letter *A*. In spite of this, we communicate efficiently for the most part. Henry Higgins could understand Eliza Doolittle, and she could understand him, from start to finish of her education. It is said that in the heyday of the Brooklyn Dodgers, when a player named Hoyt was hit in the head by a rogue ball, an alarmed spectator in the stands, a resident of Brooklyn, jumped up and cried: "Hurt is hoyt!" Everyone at the game knew immediately what the anguished spectator meant, even though the vowel sounds in the two words were exactly reversed.

Some network models are so lifelike in their ability to make sense of data that is incomplete or new that they become "bored" when given too much information, and cease to absorb it. Adding more of the same sort of information does not improve the efficiency of the machine. Showing a network a million examples of *A* may produce no better results than showing it a thousand examples.

It is hardly likely, however, that this is the way all human thinking works. Prototypes and categories, excellent devices for making sense of a world that is too ambiguous to know in detail, are the stuff of perception and of reason too, unifying the two types of intelligence. But that does not mean the mind has given up all its secrets. Science does not advance at such a breakneck speed. Network models, which amplify the pattern-classifying aspect of intelligence, just as von Neumann computers amplify the symbol-manipulating aspect, are least satisfying when they attempt to mimic certain uniquely human powers of the mind, such as language.

"The state of the art in neural networks is nowhere near the thinking machine you read about in science fiction," said Dr. Ingraham. "You're not going to see R2D2 any time soon. One of the problems with networks is that we still don't really understand human thought mechanisms, so that the underlying theories are not complete. The models we simulate on a computer are at best broad generalizations, and each deals with only one aspect of thought processes in the brain."

There are certain inherent limits to what connectionist models can do, and the limits arise from one of the peculiar strengths of these systems, the fact that knowledge and interpretation are both embodied in one and the same network. In traditional artificial-intelligence machines, the data structure that represents aspects of the world, and the program which interprets, and in a sense "understands" the data, are separate and distinct. Knowledge is split between these two vehicles, the data and the procedure for looking at the data. That is not the case in a connectionist system, where there is one physical device, and it contains the data as well as the interpreter. As a result, everything the system must know about a person, an object, or an event in the world must be represented explicitly in the network.

Such an arrangement means it is possible to have symbols in a connectionist network, but the symbols cannot exist in isolation, divorced from meaning, separated from the associations to which they are linked; they cannot be free variables, simply x or y. A symbol that is cut off from its associations is not even a symbol any longer. It represents nothing at all. A constraint of this kind on the cognitive powers of networks has interesting things to say about how the mind represents the world. Computer scientist Lokendra Shastri thinks it gives us insights into the universal principles at work in the way the brain, as a parallel processing system, actually organizes knowledge.

One of the most telling criticisms of connectionism is that it fails to do justice to one of the most important properties of the mind, its unlimited expressive power. The number of brand-new sentences we can speak, sentences never spoken before in the whole history of the world, is potentially infinite. That unboundedness is a hallmark of natural languages, which are able to convey an inexhaustibly rich font of ideas and meanings with a limited apparatus of words and rules. Unboundedness cannot be explained in perceptual terms, as the completion of partial patterns, or as associations based on content. Language is a system that is "recursive." In other words, a rule can be used over and over again on the same finite number of elements to combine them and build larger units out of them, generating an unlimited number of novel sentences. Jerry Fodor, a philosopher and linguist at the City University of New York, said, "There's not a snowball's chance in hell that connectionist models will provide anything like a general architecture of cognition. The argument against associative theories of learning has always been that they can't account for the expressive power of the mind, and it still is. These things are just lists, really. They have no way of handling recursion. And that is why B. F. Skinner's theories of learning were rejected in the 1950s. It's a bit embarrassing that it should be necessary to make these kindergarten points again after thirty years, but the kindergarten points still hold. I don't know why it's true, but Anglo-American psychologists have been carrying on a love affair with associationism for about three hundred years now, and it's awfully hard to get them off it."

Any sort of template device will enable a system to complete partial information, in Fodor's view. Merely matching the pattern of a trunk and ears to a stored pattern of an elephant is not productive, however, in the sense that a language, and perhaps the inner language of thought as well, are productive, because of their unlimited expressive power. English is productive because it is able to embed groups of words inside other groups of words to make new sentences, and this is possible because sentences have grammatical relations between parts and wholes. The sentence "The girl is walking in the park" can be expanded into the sentence "The girl who ate the ice cream is walking in the park" by a recursive rule, because grammar can preserve the original connection between *girl* and *walking*. The error into which connectionists have tumbled, Fodor maintains, is the same one that Kant accused David Hume of making, namely to assume that thoughts are made up of sets of elements, with no structural relation. If a "mind," natural or artificial, merely deals with finite lists of thoughts, and does not have the ability to use rules recursively on elements which are grouped together syntactically to generate new concepts, then it cannot be productive. Connectionist networks seem to be that sort of device.

"The question is, how do you put the elements, whatever they are, together to make new combinations of thinkable thoughts?" Fodor said. "It's the problem of how to put the word *pen* together with *my aunt* to make *the pen of my aunt*. You can't do that if sentences are just lists of words, without syntactic structure. It's a very old-fashioned point, and it's been made over and over again by rationalists against associationists, and they don't seem to be able to get it." Others believe connectionists will be able to meet the criterion of recursiveness, which they were not aware of needing to do as recently as the early 1980s.

If language is boundlessly expressive, and is based on a device that generates thoughts that are newly minted rather than copies or associations of existing thoughts, it gives human beings a certain autonomy, a degree of freedom, because they are not so dependent on experience as are creatures that do not have language. Some artificial-intelligence researchers believe that, even using the new ideas thrown up by connectionism, it will be a long time before a robot can be built that is truly, independently intelligent, for the very reason that today's connectionist models are so heavily reliant on their designers and trainers. The message of modern linguistics is that experience by itself is not enough to produce language in a child. There must be devices in the brain that enable the child to acquire a productive language system without intense training. At first glance, James McClelland's network, which learns the past tense of English verbs by being exposed to examples, without an inbuilt "supertheory" of the structure of languages, seems to suggest that experience *is* enough, that a child learns to speak by classifying and matching the patterns it is given. That has led to the breathtaking statement by some connectionists that a network need not be intelligent in order to learn.

On closer inspection, however, the McClelland model is not the linguistic prodigy it appears to be. It needs to be set in such a way that it recognizes what are speech sounds and what are not, what is a word and what is not a word. All the network does is to take messy, fuzzy data and clean it up. What is more, it seems to be merely reflecting back to its trainers the structure of the information they fed into the system, and that is not the way the human mind behaves. The network violates the basic tenet of modern linguistic theory: that language, even at its most prosaic and mundane, is a creative activity, and for that reason it is difficult to link language to lower-level cognitive processes such as perception.

In general, a dilemma for connectionism in its present state is that the amount of training needed to make a network model thought in an interesting way may be exorbitant. The big dream of the connectionists, which is that if you can train a small network with a few hundred units to perform simple cognitive tasks, then there is no reason why a huge network with billions of units cannot be trained to perform complicated tasks, is haunted by a specter. It is the old hobgoblin of combinatorial explosion in a new guise. This time the risk of explosion occurs not in a search of possibilities, but in the number of training runs required, which may be unmanageably large. There are mathematical results which suggest that the training problem is intractable.

Another question mark over the connectionist enterprise is that the codes of the brain may be more elaborate than was once believed. The visual system, for instance, seems to transmit information by "multiplexing"—adding together more than one signal, combining them into a single complex wave, and then disentangling each signal when the wave reaches its destination. This is roughly how an FM radio is able to broadcast music in stereo. If the brain as a whole turns out to use such intricate codes, it would pose a challenge to the connectionist doctrine that processing units send only very simple signals to one another.

"To assume that experience does everything in the brain is totally false," said Jack Cowan of the University of Chicago. "Connectionists think in that way because they don't have anything else to work with. The necessary algorithms haven't been devised yet. When connectionists build models they start with a blank sheet, essentially, a randomly connected network, and train the machine in such a way that its output corresponds to what they want. But clearly there have to be innate, hard-wired structures in the nervous system, embodying prior knowledge, before intelligence is manifested. We are decades away from understanding how that is implemented in the actual circuitry of the nervous system. Connectionists are good at engineering, but they are naïve about biology. They underestimate by orders of magnitude the complexity of the brain, and the sort of tasks the brain does easily.

"I don't see any simple way in which a machine can do these tasks just by being trained. There has got to be an enormous amount of stored programming, and that has been done in the human brain by evolution, during more than a billion years. If we can understand some of the principles we might be able to telescope that long evolutionary process, compress it into a few decades, but what we produce will still be only a faint reflection of the actual complexity of the living brain."

13: THE SOFT ABYSS

In a connectionist network, "intelligence" seems to emerge from the activity of crowds of units that in themselves are simple and uninteresting. Intelligence cannot be located in a particular place, any more than a memory is confined to one spot, but is the result of many, perhaps thousands or millions of units influencing one another and being influenced by one another as they settle into a cooperative decision that is most consistent with external evidence as well as with internal knowledge. An enormous number of constraints, representing strong or weak opinions about what plausibly goes together with what in the world, have to be satisfied almost simultaneously.

A network of this kind has been compared with a market economy, where there is no single, omniscient mind that has access to all the information needed to arrive at decisions for the society as a whole. No digital computer could possibly act as the central planner in a market economy, because the complexity of calculation, let alone the task of gathering the right sort of information, would result in combinatorial explosion. The system would suffer the electronic equivalent of a nervous breakdown. A market economy works because decisions are made, not at the top, but by millions of individuals, each of whom is in touch with a few other individuals and is well informed in his or her own small, parochial way. People receive information locally and transmit it locally. Friederich von Hayek, the champion of free-market mechanisms, recognized that such an arrangement rules out the idea that an economy can be run in a *logical* fashion. A godlike central planner who knows about everything that is going on and possesses unlimited computational resources could reason and decide in a perfectly logical way, step by step from impeccable premises to faultless conclusions. The perfect planner would never make a mistake. In the real world of space and time, however, a system of that sort is unworkable. Strict logic must be thrown to the winds, because all the premises can never be available to a single mind.

The knowledge on which economic decisions are based, von Hayek said, "never exists in concentrated or integrated form, but solely as the dispersed bits of incomplete and frequently contradictory knowledge which all the separate individuals possess." In a market economy, changes in prices are a way of communicating simple, highly abbreviated information, which is passed on only to those involved with buying and selling. Producers of goods and services can act intelligently and appropriately merely by watching a few numbers increase or decrease, without needing to know what it is that causes the numbers to rise or fall. "The most significant fact about this system is the economy of knowledge with which it operates, or how little the individual participants need to know in order to be able to take the right action," von Hayek thought.

In a roughly analogous way, a connectionist network reaches collective decisions which appear to be the result of the complex synthesis of a mass of data, whereby large numbers of individuals mutually adjust their behavior in response to very simple signals that are broadcast locally. The whole is intelligent, but each of its parts is a little stupid. Like a market economy, the network is not perfect, but it works.

If the behavior of a market economy as a whole looks more logical, more centrally determined, than it actually is, so too does the thinking brain when it is studied globally. What connectionists are trying to do is to delve beneath the surface skin of cognition and understand how the individuals interact on the small scale of single units and their connections, hoping that what they discover about the microcosm will shed new light on the large-scale knowledge structures such as schemas, scripts and stereotypes, and the sort of thinking that seems to be based on rules. The motto of many connectionists is: "There are more things between the upper level of logical reason and the lower levels of simple units than are dreamt of in your philosophy." Properties of mind may emerge at the higher levels out of what is going on at lower levels (not all connectionists accept this as a literal description), and these properties are to some extent unexpected; they cannot be understood or predicted by a study of the parts of the lower levels on their own. A newspaper photograph "emerges" out of thousands of tiny ink dots on the page that are meaningless if examined one by one under a microscope. Many of the most stimulating problems of science are nonlinear in this way.

Paul Smolensky, a computer scientist at the University of Colorado, describes the space between the highest levels of thought, where explicit logical reasoning is performed, and the lowest levels, where the senses process information arriving from the world outside, as "a conceptual abyss." We know a great deal about deductive logic, and sense perception is no longer a baffling puzzle, but in between, where most of the interesting mental activity goes on, there are question marks, mysteries. Conventional artificial-intelligence researchers tend to assume that what happens in this gap between the top and bottom of knowing is the manipulation of symbols, which is a digital computer's stock-in-trade. Smolensky imagines these classical theo-

rists as daring Alpinists, mountaineers who explore the uncharted terrain of the mind by starting at the top and climbing
down into the abyss, "clutching a rope of symbolic logic anchored at the top, hoping it will stretch all the way to the bottom."

Connectionists, by contrast, climb up the abyss on a ladder
anchored at the bottom, hoping it will extend all the way up to
the peak. They do not begin with symbols or with logic, nor do
they expect to encounter such a refined apparatus of thought as
they ascend the abyss. Logic is at the very top of the mountain,
and describes only a few mental processes in which thought
proceeds by means of explicit rules of argument; the air is thin
and rarefied at this altitude, and it almost seems as if the top of
thought, like the summit of Mount Everest, is an inhospitable,
alien place where the going is difficult, full of strain and effort.
Oxygen masks should be worn. Lower down, cognition is easier,
more "natural," and better suited to the everyday task of making
sense of the world.

On the mountaintop, Smolensky thinks, knowledge is "hard,"
in the sense that it is governed by complex systems of specific,
yes-or-no rules, that tightly constrain what is valid reasoning
and what is not. In the subsymbolic realm, where most of
human thought occurs, knowledge is "soft." The connections
that link units in a network are constraints on opinions about
what is connected with what in the world. These soft constraints
are quite different from the hard rules that govern thinking in
the upper galleries of the brain, where logic prevails. Logic is as
brittle as barley sugar. One wrong move can cause the entire
system to grind to a halt; a single contradiction may be fatal,
because any conclusion, no matter how absurd, can follow from
it. A rule can be used again and again to manipulate a string of
symbols, quite independently of all the other rules in the system, to arrive at a valid statement which is true forever, no
matter what may happen later.

Knowledge in the abyss, in the domain below the mountaintop, is not brittle, but adaptable. No one constraint by itself
leads to irrevocable conclusions, because other constraints in the

network, if they represent strong opinions about a plausible interpretation of what is in a word, a face, a scene, can override it. Whose face is that? What word do these letters spell? A decision of this sort is the result of all the constraints, working in concert, globally. A conclusion is not set in concrete. It can always be reversed by introducing additional soft constraints. The process is not in the least like deductive logic, but resembles more a branch of mathematics called the statistics of inference, which makes statements that are inexact on the basis of information that is incomplete. An opinion poll rating a candidate in a presidential election campaign is an example of soft inference of this kind. The poll samples the opinions of a tiny fraction of the total population of the United States, and it does not pretend to be one-hundred-percent accurate. Only the margin of error it contains can be specified precisely.

It is sometimes unclear at first sight whether an intelligent system is operating at the hard, upper level of symbol processing, or at the soft, lower one. Terrence Sejnowski and Charles Rosenberg built a machine called NETtalk, consisting of hundreds of units and thousands of connections, which was taught to read aloud from a simple English text. The machine was a sensation; it was invited to appear on the NBC *Today* show. Anyone listening to its childish but astonishingly accurate pronunciation of English sentences might have supposed that NETtalk had been programmed with explicit rules of language and used the rules to manipulate symbols one after the other, in a perfectly logical way. That is not the case, however. NETtalk was not given any hard rules at all, but learned by example, stopping after speaking each word to check its pronunciation with the correct speech sound supplied by its human trainers, adjusting its connection strengths so as to reduce the error. The machine began by babbling incoherently, then recognized consonants and vowels, and finally caught on to the fact that there were spaces between words. After a night of learning, it was able to speak intelligible sentences. NETtalk was not programmed, but simply came to recognize, after repeated exposure to samples of text, the regular patterns that are implicit in spoken English.

Terrence Sejnowski regards NETtalk as a triumph of soft constraints over hard rules in what might seem to be a task that involves the pure manipulation of symbols: finding correspondences between letters and sounds. That is the secret, he believes, of the spectacular and curiously "natural" ability of a simple network of processing units to deal with a certain kind of communication system, namely speech, that is notorious for its tangled complexity. The explicit rules that govern the pronunciation of English words are immensely intricate, and they are riddled with exceptions. For example, the rule that "a final *e* is silent" is true of most words but untrue of extremely common words such as *he* and *she*. A whole family of words that come from the French, like *café* and *negligée*, violate the rule. Among exceptional rules there are exceptions, and exceptions to the exceptions.

"This formal apparatus of rules for recognizing the sounds of speech is like the Ptolemaic system of astronomy, which described the movements of the heavenly bodies in terms of circles within circles within circles," Sejnowski said. "The whole convoluted system became incredibly simple as soon as the celestial movements were described in terms of ellipses. It was a more appropriate formalism. In a similar way, a simple network like NETtalk was able to capture ninety-nine percent of the complexity of the huge armamentarium of thousands and thousands of rules and exceptions in speech. What can be more symbolic than words? Yet when we used a formalism based on patterns rather than on symbols to match words to speech sounds, the complexity turned out to be much less than we thought. There are various levels of processing in the brain, and at each level I believe we are going to have to reconsider all our previous assumptions."

The subsymbolic domain is below the level where whole symbols are manipulated with hard rules, but above the basic hardware level of neurons and their electrical and chemical properties down on the floor of the abyss. In the subsymbolic realm, the brain is a connectionist network, where crowds of individual units reach decisions en masse, making statistical inferences that satisfy the largest number of soft constraints. A plausible speculation is that such decisions constitute the "atoms," or elementary building blocks, of the symbols that emerge full-blown at a higher level. What sort of mental activity goes on at the subsymbolic level? Much of it is not the kind of cognition that is unique to human beings, for example mathematics and logic, but is evolutionarily more primitive than these. It includes seeing and hearing, recognizing faces, finding one's way home, handling objects, playing Frisbee, all very difficult to imitate with a standard computer but easy and natural for many species of animals of which Homo sapiens is just one. Thinking at this level is intuitive rather than explicitly logical.

Terence Horgan and John Tienson have suggested that the kind of "thinking" a skilled basketball player does while in action on the court, which is well captured by a connectionist metaphor, underlies much human cogitation that has a more intellectual flavor: solving puzzles, reasoning about moral choices, understanding in general. This may sound strange, because basketball seems so physical, whereas the intellect, we like to think, is airy, insubstantial, gossamer. Yet a basketball player making a pass as he runs down the court must consider a large number of soft constraints almost instantaneously, including which player to throw to, whether to lob or bounce the ball, whereabouts his teammates and the opposing players are in relation to the basket, and where they are likely to be when the ball actually reaches its target; what is the shooting range and ability of each member of the team, the state of the score, the minutes and seconds left on the clock. Anything, literally anything, that has to do with basketball may influence a decision, and as the situation changes, so do the constraints. Horgan and Tienson think it is "crazy" to imagine that hard rules govern a basketball player's mental processes at this level, and yet intelligence that works in sequence, like a digital computer, and seems to be driven by rules, emerges out of it. Some of the information a player must consider is encoded in sentences that have a subject and a predicate, the stuff of logic: This teammate is a good shooter. That one has a hot hand. A third is impeded by a bad knee.

Are basketball players "dumb jocks"? Evidently not. They have specialized cognitive systems which make quicksilver decisions that satisfy a myriad of constraints on what is possible, many of which can be overridden, and anticipate what is likely to happen in the next seconds or fractions of seconds. A player's behavior is far from predictable, because he often invents a new play on the spot, and a small change in the state of the game can result in a big change in what he decides to do. There is no way in which the factors that influence a decision on the court can be specified in advance. Most basketball players may not be very good at the sort of thing philosophers do, but their brains are marvelous cognitive engines that are probably more difficult to imitate with a machine than the cognitive engines of philosophers, Horgan and Tienson think.

A skilled basketball player's mental apparatus for playing the game is what Smolensky calls a "soft machine." It is a network that simultaneously considers many different factors, some of which constrain more tightly than others, and it adapts with admirable flexibility to a world that is always changing and a body that is constantly on the move. The basic form of cognition in such a system is not logical reasoning, but perception, "recognizing" the right pass to make instead of deducing it in a series of steps. A soft system of this kind is so complex that if we stand back and observe it from a higher level, it sometimes looks like a hard machine, one that manipulates symbols with exact, obligatory rules that are systematic enough to be written out in the form of a program. Complexity at one level gives rise to hardness at another level, but softness is fundamental, and there is no way in which we can use the hard rules in the symbolic domain to describe completely the soft machine in the subsymbolic realm. Symbols and symbol manipulation in the brain, Smolensky playfully proposes, are built out of "connectoplasm," the squishy-soft networks that produce the sort of intelligence that is closer to perception than to logic.

The idea that one type of machine can be transformed into a different sort of machine is basic to computer theory. Alan Turing proved a theorem showing that a certain class of his imaginary Turing machines are universal; that is, they can be made to imitate any other symbol-manipulating machine, no matter how sophisticated, by writing a more complex list of instructions. A universal machine programmed to add numbers can be given new instructions that will turn it into a machine that does word processing, or plays video games. Such instructions are said to describe a "virtual machine," which the physical device mimics simply by doing what it is told. The universal machine is not some Platonic ideal, but is the familiar digital computer we all know and love, though in practice it is restricted in the range of machines it can imitate by limits on the size of its memory. Today a universal machine may imitate a virtual machine which in turn is instructed to imitate another virtual machine at a higher level. Impersonation is piled on top of impersonation, layer upon layer, so that there is no way of telling which is the "real" machine.

In fact, most of the connectionist models that recognize faces, read handwriting, or pronounce words are simulated on conventional von Neumann machines instead of being run on a neural network computer, since network technology is in its early childhood, and cheap, special-purpose connectionist hardware is not available yet. An intriguing speculation is that nature may have engineered the brain in exactly the opposite way, by first developing a connectionist machine as the basic hardware, and this later simulated a virtual machine that manipulates symbols serially like a digital computer. Hard symbolic thinking may have evolved out of soft perceptual intelligence. As in the case of man-made computers, there may be no way of telling which of the brain's virtual machines is the real one. This is rank speculation, of course.

Certain kinds of mental operations, notably logic and mathematics, can be understood best in terms of von Neumann machines, while other more intuitive and fluid ways of thinking are better explained as connectionist networks. The relation between these two types of biological computers may not be the same for all kinds of knowledge; a theory of how we do mental arithmetic could be entirely different from a theory of how we recognize faces.

In the subsymbolic realm the bedrock, the foundation on which knowing is built, is perception. And classifying, generalizing, sorting information into categories and matching it to prototypes, exactly what connectionist networks do best, is a basic chore of perceptual systems. Expert systems, which encode knowledge in the form of if-then rules, do not need to be able to see and hear, since they merely process predigested information, and dwell, blind, deaf, and dumb, in the symbolic realm. They have no idea what the world is like outside their little corner of expertise, or how to interact with it. Increasingly, however, cognitive scientists are coming to believe that perception, and the incessant traffic with the world that seeing and hearing naturally entail, are the underpinning of common sense. Start with perception, the argument goes, and you have a firm platform on which to construct the higher flights of intellect.

The brain, with its highly evolved perceptual apparatus, interacts with the world in such a way that world and brain are two aspects of a single thing, flip sides of a coin. As Terrence Sejnowski puts it, "The world is your friend. If you want to build intelligence, you have to come to grips with the world, and if you come to grips with the world then the problem of representing knowledge becomes very different, because you're not working in a vacuum. You are building on top of a structure that is interacting with the world already. You have layers of processing. You have a system that is engaged with the world at all times. And you can't really discuss the top layer until you specify the bottom layers first. This approach is very fresh. I think it is heading in the right direction. A layer of cognition represents objects in the world only by virtue of its interactions with other layers that are also representing the world and interacting with it."

A connectionist system works from the bottom up, processing millions of competing hypotheses, opinions, and conjectures, settling into a decision that represents a global synthesis of all the local contributions. The knowledge structures described in earlier chapters, however, the schemas that we impose on reality in order to reduce its complexity and predict its behavior, are large-scale, top-down devices that are clumsy and slow compared with the frenzy of activity down in the abyss. The lower system is a medium where massive uncertainty and ambiguity are easily accommodated. A global "thought" synthesized by a network in response to an ambiguous piece of information, or a novel experience, may be inconsistent with certain aspects of that information or experience. Top-down schemas prefer greater exactness and simplicity, and fewer and tighter constraints. Hans Berliner of Carnegie-Mellon University, who builds computer chess programs that compete with master players, sees connectionist networks as "percolating" plausible patterns of activity upward, while large-scale knowledge structures such as schemas examine downward, noticing the global patterns while ignoring the small-scale local contributions in their teeming millions, trying to explain what is happening in terms of symbols and rules and to eradicate the uncertainty that is the stuff of which a network is made. A computer that aspires to be a world chess champion, Berliner believes, must be able to examine its own workings so as to alter course when appropriate, and this means it will probably need to have a connectionist base and an upper level of large-scale knowledge structures or "explainers," to look down and redirect the process when needed. "Although the answers are far from clear, it does appear that competence at the highest levels of intellect is dependent on knowing the bounds of uncertainty on almost everything one knows, and being able to proceed to eliminate uncertainty in the case at hand," Berliner says. "Paradigms that are rigid in their approach can all be shown to have 'seams' or 'ridges' where a process without much understanding of itself will fall through, or become a ridge-follower forever."

In the philosophy of Kant, a schema has one foot in the world of the intellect, another in the world of perception. It mediates between the raw data of the senses and the abstract operations of the understanding, thereby making knowledge of the world possible. A Kantian schema is activated by the experience of seeing and hearing, and at the same time supplies an interpretation of that experience. It is partly a set of rules, partly a provider of images. A new view of the schema is emerging in cognitive science today that reflects this dual Kantian aspect. Up to now, schemas have been depicted as hard structures in the symbolic domain, suitable for running on a von Neumann machine. Increasingly, however, the notion of a schema is being "connectionized," so that schemas are seen not as Tinkertoy assemblies, but as emergent properties of the soft, subsymbolic realm. A schema is not a "thing," in this view, but a manifestation, a sort of oversimplified summary of the activities of a network which settles into a stable interpretation of the world by satisfying as many as possible of a vast number of different constraints, some implicit in the long-term memory of the system, others contained in the new information the network is trying to interpret. Only in the most superficial sense can a schema of this kind be described as a mental object, a ready-made interpretation that is stacked in memory like a book on a shelf, always the same no matter how often it is taken down from the shelf and read. In fact, it is more like the pattern of waves on the surface of an ocean, reflecting the countless influences and forces at work beneath the surface of the water, and in the shifting, restless depths.

This means that a schema is different each time it is constructed by the mind, because the network out of which it emerges is not subject to exactly the same constraints from one moment to the next. In traditional, symbolic artificial intelligence, a schema is treated as if it were purely a surface structure, with no hidden depths of complex processing underneath, and hence is a fairly simple, large-scale, and static device by means of which, it is supposed, the mind interprets the world.

A fresher, more modern approach is to think of a network as starting without any schemas, which emerge later as a result of the networks "experiences." Once a schema has emerged, the network must be able to recognize it and represent it explicitly, in a form that resembles the traditional symbolic schema. Only if schemas are made explicit in this way is it computationally feasible to manipulate them and compose simpler schemas into more elaborate ones; but they will be very brittle and limited if they are regarded as disembodied objects, cut adrift from the immense complexity of the network that gave rise to them, a complexity that reaches down into the depths of the abyss where perception, learning, and other subsymbolic processes go on. Making schemas explicit without disembodying them is a ticklish challenge for artificial-intelligence researchers, and one that many have not faced fully yet.

Detached, disembodied schemas, the building blocks of thought in traditional cognitive psychology, are cartoon versions, travesties, of the far richer and more flexible knowledge structures that emerge from the abyss where perception is the basis of cognition. Perception is as swift and agile as a bird in flight, and it is so partly because we ourselves are always in motion, always actively exploring the world and interacting with it, seeing it now from this angle, now from that, resolving ambiguity by a change in perspective. So, too, intuitive thought is mercurial, fluid, adaptable, "recognizing" answers to problems in a flash. By contrast, the schemas, scripts, and stereotypes of the traditionalists are like toy gliders, stiff and rigid, liable to crash as soon as they meet an unexpected obstacle.

The attempt to make machines think like people by means of classical, top-down knowledge structures has been in large part a disappointment, some would say a failure, and nowhere more so than in artificial vision and the understanding of natural language. This has been a spur to the development of more brainlike computer architectures rather than new software to run on the old hardware. It was disillusion with the conventional theory of schemas that led David Rumelhart to explore connectionist models, whose most conspicuous successes have been in simulating perception. These new machines are likely to be as bad at doing logic as they are good at recognizing faces and objects;

whether they will be able to mimic intuitive thought as well as they can mimic vision is an open question. What they have done, at this early stage, is to suggest an entirely fresh approach to intelligence as being not one thing, but a many-layered edifice whose topmost pinnacles are anchored and undergirded by rich, mobile cognitive systems perfected by millions of years of evolution. Such systems may be the basis of the deep, implicit worldliness that Tolstoy saw as the ultimate framework of understanding—not describable by the rules of logic—within which human beings live, as a fish swims in the sea.

14: THE REPORTER IN THE CORRIDOR

If a connectionist network is like a huge parliament or congress in the throes of debate, then the alert, conscious mind is like a newspaper reporter hanging around outside the locked chamber, notebook in hand, waiting to be told what happened. The reporter is not allowed inside the room while the debate is in progress. She is informed only about the result of the vote, and is quite ignorant as to the opinions expressed by particular members of the congress. All the ferment and frenzy of individuals exciting and inhibiting one another, forming coalitions, sending messages back and forth, takes place behind closed doors. When we recognize our grandmother wearing a new hat, we are aware of the fact that it is she and not our aunt or sister, but have no idea how that decision was reached. It is as if a newspaper printed the bare fact of the defeat of an amendment to a tax bill, without its parliamentary correspondent being able to reach her contacts inside the chamber for news of floor speeches, intrigue, bargains struck, or even the final tally of votes. An actual reporter would hardly win a Pulitzer prize for such uninformed reporting.

One reason why the conscious mind is reduced to the role of outsider, waiting in the corridors while the real business of cognition proceeds in camera, is that so much is going on in the network, and that so much is all happening at once. A vast number of constraints must be satisfied in order to arrive at a single decision, involving the activity of perhaps billions of processing units, and in a distributed network a single unit is supposed to be a pretty ignorant individual. It knows only a tiny fraction of what the network as a whole knows. A modern digital computer goes one step at a time, at high speed, which is why it is good at sequential tasks, and a born logician. Yet such a machine is so poor at simple perception it might take days to tell the difference between a dog and a cat. The brain, by contrast, is able to recognize a cat as a cat in about half a second, because it can juggle immense quantities of evidence, some weak, some strong, nearly simultaneously. All the chattering and conjecturing that goes into a decision is over in a flash, too fast for the conscious mind to detect. Only the finished product, the thought "cat" is dumped into consciousness. What other possibilities were voted down? Which opinions were overriden? We do not know. Connectionist networks test so many hypotheses in such a brief span of time that usually we are not aware, and cannot be aware, of what hypotheses are being tested.

When thinking is difficult and slow, it tends to be done in the bright glare of full awareness, but when it is easy and fast, the doors slam shut and the conscious mind must wait outside in the corridor for the result. That is why early artificial-intelligence programs did the kind of thinking humans find difficult, like mathematics and logic. Even simple arithmetic—say, adding 4,317 and 5,826 without using pencil and paper—is laborious and tough; sorting out a Lewis Carroll puzzle in one's head can be a headache, literally. In each case we are painfully aware of what we are doing, and of how complex a procedure it is. Because mathematics and logic are activities of the conscious mind, these forms of knowledge are very well understood, and for that reason it is quite a straightforward matter to program them into a machine. On the other hand, we are able to read and make sense of a newspaper headline held upside-down, glimpsed through the smeary window of a subway train as it is pulling out of the station, and do it with so little conscious effort that it seems simple, whereas in fact it is so complex that for a long time visual perception was a deep mystery, and scientists had no idea of how to imitate it with a machine. We imagine such tasks are easy because we have almost no conscious insight into how they work.

Normally a single, final decision is sent up to consciousness, but if a task that is usually easy becomes difficult because the information to be interpreted is highly ambiguous, or due to some other quirk or oddity, the conscious mind may be aware of more than one interpretation, because the network cannot settle on a definite decision. It votes first this way, then that way. In the sentence

The astronomer married the star.

the word *astronomer* seems to constrain the meaning of *star* to that of a celestial body. It is a reasonably strong and plausible hypothesis given just those two words. When all the pieces of evidence from the entire sentence are considered, however, a more plausible hypothesis is that *star* has the sense of a movie actress. A reader may be dimly aware that first one, then the other interpretation was dumped into consciousness, because the difficulty presented by the ambiguity is sufficient to slow down the process. A connectionist computer network model actually behaved in this fashion, choosing first the wrong interpretation of the sentence, then settling on the correct one by simultaneously bringing to bear knowledge about astronomers, marriage, and stars, observing the constraint that astronomers do not marry heavenly bodies. This slowing-down effect can also be seen in the famous optical illusion of the Necker cube, which seems to flip back and forth, now outside-in, now inside-out, because there is not enough information in the figure for the brain's networks to vote once and for all and have done with it. So they debate endlessly, back and forth, throwing one decision into consciousness, then the other, which knocks out the first.

"What we are discovering," said Terrence Sejnowski, "is that beneath the surface of awareness, an enormous amount of unconscious processing is going on. One reason why it is unconscious is that a lot happens very fast. But there is also active suppression of knowledge. Possible interpretations compete, and less plausible interpretations are inhibited by more plausible ones, by a process of adjustment. If one idea is more powerful than the rest, it dominates the rest. The brain must have some way to suppress information that is not relevant for a particular moment, and link together only those pieces of knowledge that are directly relevant. Those relevant items are all that enter consciousness from instant to instant." They are small bubbles of froth on the surface of a great ocean of unconscious mental activity. But that is not the whole story. Since content-addressable memories, which are natural, "emergent" properties of a parallel distributed network, fill in the missing parts of information that is incomplete, the version of the world that is tossed up to consciousness may be largely fictitious. And since only the product, not the processes, of a decision by a network's behind-closed-doors parliament is open to inspection, the conscious mind may have no way of knowing which part is fact and which part is fiction.

Freud portrayed the unconscious mind as disorganized and unreasonable to the point of ignoring even such rock-bottom rules of logic as the law of noncontradiction. He saw it as an irresponsible, unsociable brat, incapable of learning or improving itself, remaining childish all its life, powerful and indestructible. The true Freudian unconscious, as opposed to merely preconscious thoughts that do not need to be repressed, is a repository of information that the conscious mind does not want to know, and puts as far out of its reach as possible.

Memory is the agent that disposes of inconvenient knowledge in this fashion. In Freud's theory, memory is quite unlike the memory in a von Neumann computer, which is a mere container, indifferent to the nature and meaning of its own contents, not acting, but being acted upon by the central processor. The Freudian memory is a different creature altogether. It is highly sensitive to content, and it is active, not inert. It accepts or rejects ideas, thoughts, and feelings according to the meaning they have for the psyche, nice or nasty, bearable or unbearable. Unwanted material is rejected by being forgotten, but such forgetting is not simply a matter of letting thoughts disappear. Freudian forgetting is not nearly as passive as that. Memory pushes unacceptable thoughts into the unconscious, wanting to be rid of them altogether, but having to settle instead for a compromise in which the objectionable matter is still present in the mind, but is hidden from awareness. Some of the repressed information escapes from the limbo of the unconscious in the form of neuroses. To cure a neurosis, the conscious mind must release the banished memories of a lifetime and vanquish their power with the sword of reason, a difficult task to accomplish.

Freud compared the conflict between the id, home of unconscious drives, and the higher centers of the mind, with the tensions that wrack a modern state, in which "a mob, eager for enjoyment and destruction, has to be held down forcibly by a prudent superior class." Later in his career, Freud divided the mind into three domains: the unruly, chaotic id; the superego, seat of conscience which tries to keep the mob under control; and the ego, an agent of reason whose unenviable chore is to mediate between the mob and the strict, ever-critical, and constraining edicts of conscience. The ego is a go-between, a roving ambassador with a passport to the chaotic underworld of the unconscious, and yet is also persona grata at the court of the superego, which, in Freud's theory, is as irrational in its own way as the id.

Quaint as this picture of the mind may seem today, it does contain the germ of a modern view of the unconscious that has nothing to do with guilt, repression, and a psychological police state. This view, which is gaining ground on the brink of the 1990s, suggests instead that much if not most of our reasonable and constructive, even highly intelligent thinking goes on below the level of awareness. It is foreshadowed by Freud's evolving theory of the ego—the worldly, rational agent of the mind, a realist which is capable of learning from experience, unlike the id. The ego is in touch with what is happening outside the organism, in the environment. Yet this ambassador of realism is not exclusively conscious. In some of Freud's later writings much of the ego is unconscious.

For many years, unconscious thought was mainly of clinical interest, and it was studied on the psychoanalyst's couch. Serious people trying to build a science of the mind considered the unconscious was too fanciful. William James spoke for many of his colleagues when he called the unconscious "a tumbling ground for whimsies." Some of the early insights into hidden memories, information that is noticed and stored in the mind without awareness, came from accounts of crystal-gazing and automatic handwriting, a field where cranks and charlatans abounded, about as distant from scientific psychology as fortune-telling is from physics. Crystal-gazers "saw" scenes in their glass globes and automatic writers penned messages that were interpreted as visitations from the spirit world, or as intimations of the future. In the light of what we know today, these pictures and words were almost certainly fragments of past experiences lodged in the mind that had never entered conscious memory. At the time, however, since these relics of the past were not part of the gazer's or writer's known autobiography, it was tempting to assume that they appeared from nowhere, which was an invitation to conclude that they were otherworldly. Hypnotism was another early source of speculation about the existence of hidden domains of memory and learning.

Lately, hidden memories, unconscious thinking, learning that goes on behind the back of awareness, have become respectable in cognitive science. Even computational theories of the mind make room for mental processes of this kind. A new interest is being taken in what Freud called the preconscious, a sort of halfway house into which material from the unconscious could move and eventually become conscious as a result of deliberate mental effort. The mind, considered simply as a very fancy computer, hides many of its operations behind an opaque screen. Far from being otherworldly, many of these backstairs operations are "this-worldly," in the sense that they are part of everyday intelligence, enabling us to deal with the complexities of ordinary existence in a partly automatic way, as if life were a bicycle and we have learned to ride it. Worldliness is not restricted to the tiny fraction of thoughts that are explicit, sitting high up on the tip of the iceberg of the mind. Unconscious thinking seems to be different in kind from conscious thinking, but that does not mean it is irrational, in Freud's sense of the word.

One of the mind's most basic ways of making sense of the world, the creation of categories and prototypes, appears to be, in part at least, an unconscious process. Some striking studies have been done at Cambridge, England, where words were flashed onto a screen so briefly that no one could read them. The words appear for such a small fraction of a second they seem invisible, and are at once replaced with a meaningless abstract pattern. Yet people can form mental categories of words even when they are unaware of having seen them. If *queen* is flashed onto the screen, and viewers are then asked to guess what the word was, they will often say "King," or hazard the answer "Blue," if *yellow* was the word. All they have seen is the abstract pattern. Yet viewers classify the words on the basis of meaning.

Certain kinds of memories that are accurate records of actual objects and events may enter the mind quite unawares. These implicit recollections, which could account for the ghostly apparitions of knowledge that occur in crystal-gazing and automatic handwriting, manifest themselves indirectly, in the form of likes and dislikes that seem to have no clear explanation, and in improved performance on some mental task. Henry Bennett, of the University of California at Davis, thinks that patients who are lying anesthetized on the operating table, to all appearances completely out of it, can understand and commit to implicit memory the chitchat of doctors during surgery. By the sound of it, surgeons are not the soul of tact. In one case, a doctor walked into surgery while a woman patient was unconscious, exclaiming, "My God, they've dragged another beached whale up onto my operating table." After the operation, the patient was irritable and tense, with poor appetite and a fever. Seven days later she suddenly remembered the remark and complained to a nurse about it. Having got it out of her system, she went on to make a good recovery and was soon able to go home.

Knowledge that is consciously acquired may become unconscious once it is thoroughly assimilated, and it seems to change its form. Once made implicit, the knowledge often resists heroic efforts to make it explicit, as writers of expert-systems programs know to their cost. Southern California Edison, for example, spent two years and three hundred thousand dollars in an attempt to create a computer program to diagnose faults in Vermilion, a large hydroelectric dam in the Sierra Nevada, by tapping the brain of a civil engineer, Thomas Kelly. Highly experienced at spotting symptoms of trouble in the dam, Kelly could tell serious omens, like water seepage due to a blocked drain, from nonserious ones, as when escaping water was merely a result of the huge structure "breathing."

Quizzing Mr. Kelly so as to transfer the wisdom in his brain to a system of if-then rules in a computer's memory was a marathon affair, simply because this intelligent and highly skilled man did not have conscious access to his own thought processes and found it difficult to put them into words. Two knowledge engineers from Texas Instruments started by grilling Mr. Kelly for seven hours in a windowless room, putting every word he spoke on tape and then transcribing it. Mr. Kelly was wonderfully cooperative, but his explanations were too brief to be really helpful. His inquisitors spent more and more time with him, even eating meals together and drawing him out on a pet topic, skindiving. The program writers realized that Mr. Kelly used bits and pieces of evidence to detect faults in the big dam. What baffled them was how he put them all together to make a diagnosis. Logic was of little use. Months elapsed, and only twenty rules were written, which gave no more than trivial advice. A year went by, and a third knowledge engineer was added to the interviewing team. At the end of two years the Kelly system was still not in regular operation and needed more work to be really useful. The power company, once hopeful that a program could be written that would apply to dozens of different hydroelectric dams, scaled down its expectations and settled for a more limited system with a smaller number of rules that could be used only on the Vermilion plant.

Clearly, the unconscious, once thought to be the seat of unreason and unworldliness, is a player in the game of reason. The unconscious remembers, categorizes, solves ticklish problems. It is intelligent. Yet when a conscious mind asks the hidden reasoner to reveal *how* it reasons, good answers are extremely hard to come by. The whole process seems unnatural and strained. The computer in the brain that thinks in terms of explicit rules and step-by-step procedures, and the intuitive computer that processes unconscious knowledge, seem to be foreigners to each other, speaking different languages. Once the deliberate thinking of the novice has been transformed into the implicit wisdom of the expert—once logic is converted into art—the process is extraordinarily difficult to reverse.

Psychologists suspect that implicit intelligence works by rules that are not the same as the rules that underlie explicit thinking. There is strong evidence that the unconscious mind is able to consider a wider range of possibilities, to juggle a larger number of weak hypotheses, than the conscious mind can manage. As early as the 1960s, researchers noticed that a word flashed onto a screen too briefly to register in consciousness set off a series of associations in the minds of viewers. It became clear that the network of meanings suggested by a word is richer and denser when the mind is unaware of having seen the word, than it is under normal circumstances. Awareness seems to shrink the horizon of meanings, while unawareness extends the horizon, so that a word becomes surrounded by a halo of ideas that are related to it in sundry different ways. A well-known device to improve conscious memory for a list of unrelated words is to create, deliberately, a context of associations for the words. As we might expect, this does not work for implicit memory, because implicit memory adds context automatically, as part of its basic mode of operation.

The "mystery" of intuition may be nothing more magical than the conscious mind's dim awareness that a certain vote in the secret parliament of the unconscious is more likely to go one way than another. The reporter waiting out in the corridor puts an ear to the keyhole and listens to the members voicing their opinions, forcefully or feebly. What she hears is not much, but it is enough to persuade her that the session will eventually deliver a plausible decision and slip the result under the door.

Kenneth Bowers, a psychologist at the University of Waterloo, calls this almost irrational sense that certain problems have good answers, even if the answer is too difficult for the conscious mind to arrive at, the "presentiment of coherence." Like all presentiments, it seems to come from nowhere, out of the blue. Yet it may actually arise because the hypotheses being considered by the network of connections below the level of awareness influence the conscious mind without fully surfacing into plain view, just as hidden memories reveal their existence indirectly, in the form of inexplicable likes or dislikes.

Often, Bowers finds, people have an intuition that certain ideas hang together, are connected in some way, even if they are not able to give explicit reasons for their hunch. When someone is shown the string of words

Democrat   birthday   girl

and is then asked to add a fourth word which is related in some way to each of the others, she may not be able to solve the puzzle, which requires her to discover the idea that connects the original three. Given a choice between that string and

Saucer   stamp   Scissors

however, most people have a presentiment that the first three words are more likely to be related than the second three, even though they cannot say why. They are right. The word to which *Democrat, birthday*, and *girl* are all related is *party*. No such word exists for *saucer, stamp*, and *scissors*.

Presentiments of coherence are part of the mysterious process of scientific discovery, which engages the global, submerged orchestras of thought, as well as the higher, thinner solo violin of logical reasoning. Jeremy Bernstein says of Einstein that he did not arrive at his results by sweating through long calculations, but by a "phenomenal intuitive instinct as to what the results *should* be." Einstein used to say "I have a nose," meaning that he possessed a sense of the direction to pursue and could recognize a correct answer when he saw one. There is a famous autographed cartoon of Einstein by Ippei Okamoto entitled *Albert Einstein or The Nose as a Thought Reservoir*. The nose did not operate by the strict canons of logic. Young scientists who became Einstein's assistants at Princeton started with high hopes of learning how the great man's mind worked, but their hopes were usually dashed, because Einstein did not reason explicitly in a way that could be described by rules. An intuitive nose would be exceedingly difficult to program into a modern expert system.

Psychologist John Kihlstrom thinks the presentiment of coherence can be explained rather nicely in terms of a connectionist network in the brain that is considering plausible opinions as to how a list of words which have no explicit association can be made to fit together by means of an idea they share in common. The network is filling in gaps. "What is happening is that connections are being activated in the network for the words that really do cohere, and they are generating hypotheses, but the network has not settled on a final answer yet," Kihlstrom said. "Coalitions of neurons are lighting up, even though the network as a whole is undecided. That activity impinges on awareness and gives us an intuition that the words really do hang together in some way, exactly how we do not know. It is as if we can feel the neurons discharging. When words have nothing in common, as is the case in the second string, there is no activation in the network for consciousness to detect."

This suggests that the intuitive computer, which presumably is distributed and parallel, can connect ideas and find chains of associations more freely than the conscious computer, which has a narrower focus. Some of these connections may be audacious and original, leading to new insights, and this often happens when the conscious mind is distracted or tired, or asleep. Important discoveries have been made by scientists who were in a state of reverie, almost daydreaming, arriving with a shocking suddenness that seems like magic, as if brought by a visitor from another world. Intuition, Kenneth Bowers thinks, is a matter of linking ideas that are in the mind already, but have never been put together before; the new synthesis may or may not be dumped into consciousness. Implicit intelligence does not communicate directly with the alert mind, but slips messages under the door at unpredictable moments, when the reporter in the corridor least expects them. She had better not be out to lunch.

There is an inscrutable quality to a connectionist network that sets it apart from the more transparent models of standard artificial intelligence. One of the selling points of a conventional expert system is that it is unmysterious in its thinking processes and does not lock a door of privacy on the human being who is using it. By design, an expert system provides "audit trails," step-by-step explanations of how it arrived at any given piece of advice. That is possible because each step was determined by specific rules, written into the program. A connectionist network does not and cannot explain itself in this way. It works, not by rules and programs, but by the interaction of large numbers of units. An item of knowledge is not in one place, but distributed over many units, and superimposed on other items. This intermingling and spreading out gives the network some of its most interesting properties, such as robustness and content-addressable memory, but it also confers opaqueness. You cannot point to a particular place in the network where a specific piece of information resides.

Since knowledge is all over the place, and interacting with other knowledge, a neat description of exactly how a decision was reached is out of the question. "You really don't know why the network ended up where it ended up," says James Anderson, a psychologist at Brown University who is one of the pioneers of the new connectionism. "The reason is that so many different things are going on at the same time. And just as accurate knowledge is spread out over the system, so too is erroneous knowledge. Error is as robust as truth in these networks, which makes it very difficult to remove. Since error is distributed, unpredictability is built in, and that is both an asset and a liability. It is a real source of concern to people who work with these systems."

In Smolensky's view, the contents of the conscious mind reflect only the large-scale patterns of activity in networks, patterns that extend over sizable spaces and persist for relatively long periods of time. Fleeting coherences, thoughts that flair into life and die out quickly, knowledge that occupies only a small space, are not dumped into awareness. If true, this suggests that what reaches consciousness is a highly simplified and static version of the richness and fluidity of the debate that goes on behind closed doors.

Connectionism is an infant science, and at present it does not offer a satisfactory theory of what it takes to make unconscious information conscious. It is more comfortable, for the time being, with modeling mental operations that are almost entirely hidden from consciousness, such as the mechanisms of seeing and hearing and motor activity. Yet until we discover how fast, implicit thinking is able to coexist with slower, deliberate reasoning, intelligence will remain a mystery, and there will be no overarching theory of how the mind works.

Why is it that so much of the mind's work is unconscious, and so little of it is conscious? That is not a question for connectionists alone. Many cognitive scientists who believe the mind is more like a digital computer, using rules to manipulate symbols, than a system of soft constraints, nevertheless maintain that most of the interesting mental processes go on out of reach of awareness. The philosopher Jerry Fodor says the sheer quantity of the hidden machinery is something of an embarrassment to science, and it suggests that perhaps we should treat the unconscious as normal, and consciousness as a sort of aberration, a pathological mental condition. Thought, Fodor concludes, "isn't primarily intended, I suppose, for introspection. What it's for is the organization of behavior and getting around in the world. Fundamentally that's the biological basis of the thing. So it's not clear what massive introspectability would buy one. It would just make psychology a lot easier."

Perhaps one reason why it is such a surprise to discover that consciousness is an outsider loitering in the corridors, picking up what shreds of information it can, while the real business of cognition proceeds in windowless, soundproofed rooms, is that we expect the mind to be a general-purpose device. We assume that all the members of the parliament are milling around, chatting with reporters, in a single huge arena, and that everybody knows what is going on everywhere in the arena all the time. That idea is quite mistaken, however. There are many separate rooms, each one occupied by specialists in some domain of cognition. The specialists in one room, speaking their own impenetrable jargon, do not share knowledge easily with jargoneers in other rooms, and communicate only indirectly with the press. Even if a reporter managed to insinuate herself into one of the sessions, she might be little the wiser, as she would not be able to understand most of what the members were talking about.

A network in the brain, specialized for some aspect of intelligence, is doubly inscrutable to awareness. First, there are so many interactions going on all at the same time that to track them all would amount to an intractable problem, like exploring all possible moves in a chess game while the game is in progress. Second, the network and the brain systems that are trying to gain access to the network may compute in entirely different ways, so that free and full communication is impossible. To complicate matters even more, it is not unlikely that there are scores, hundreds, or even thousands of different computers in the brain, each with its own quirks and peculiarities, and ways of learning. Contemplating this medley of devices, the surprise is not that there is so little consciousness in the brain, but rather that there is so much.

Seymour Papert has written adversely, but affectionately, of the "quest for universality of mechanism" that has pervaded the culture of artificial intelligence since the beginning, and is a source of its theoretical energy, in spite of the fact that universal machines have by and large been failures, and that narrowly specialized ones have by and large been successful. The dream of a machine that is completely general-purpose arose, Papert says, partly from the "mythic nature of the enterprise—mind building mind!"—and partly from the fact that the people who created artificial intelligence as a science were mathematicians; it is second nature for mathematicians to think in terms of universals. Yet it is now abundantly clear that the brain is not a universal machine, whether connectionist or serial, and that tells us something interesting about consciousness.

Papert and his colleague Marvin Minsky see the brain as a network of networks, each one an agency designed in specific ways to perform special tasks, operating by different principles, and talking to each other, not in a universal language, but in the "classical" way, serially, by means of symbols, through a narrow communication channel. The communication is not fast, as networks are fast, but slow. Limited control over the networks is imposed by serial, symbolic systems added later in evolution. The networks do most of the work. Each network must learn to exploit the abilities of other networks without having direct access to what happens inside the others. Communication is thin and superficial, because different networks speak different languages. A network always "knows" more than it can divulge. The best that a given brain system can do is to try to build its own model of other agencies based on presuppositions and generalizations it already possesses. "Because of this," Papert and Minsky write, "what appear to us to be direct insights into ourselves must be rarely genuine and usually conjectural. Accordingly, we expect distributed representations to tend to produce systems with only limited abilities to reflect accurately on how they do what they do."

Intuition is really a special case of Baker Street reasoning, where what a person comes to know greatly exceeds the meager evidence of which he is aware. Where does the extra information come from? Presumably it is the result of unconscious networks, which usually know, or hypothesize, more than they can divulge, communicating some of that knowledge due to a momentary widening of the communications bottleneck that exists between them and the conscious, symbolic control systems at a higher level. For a brief time, the language barrier that divides system from system is overcome. If true, this is an ironic reversal of Freud's picture of the unconscious as a sink of repressed and brutish desires, with the power to throw a person's sense of reality out of kilter. Kenneth Bowers, who calls the traditional notion of the unconscious "as threatening and fascinating as Count Dracula," believes that in fact the unconscious systems of the mind may be richer in knowledge of the world than the conscious systems, so that people are often in closer touch with reality than they are able to represent explicitly, to themselves or to others. Thanks to what we do not know that we know, we are more worldly than we suppose.

15: THE EXPLAINING SPECIES

I f there are networks in the brain that know more than they can tell, there are other, conscious systems that are in an opposite predicament: they tell more than they can know. The conscious agencies concoct their own version of what goes on inside the cryptic capsules of unconscious thought. They "guess the unseen from the seen." The reporter in the corridor, frozen out by her sources, barred from entry into the rooms where all the work is going on, presented with only the bare result of a vote, cannot simply call her editor and say, "No story." An outsider, she must produce copy that reads as if it were written by an insider, by relying on presuppositions, theories, large amounts of experience and explicit knowledge, and plausible explanations. She is not really a reporter, but an explainer, and explaining is one of the conscious mind's most highly developed skills.

Explanations of our inner mental processes are interpretations of interpretations. When computer scientist Hans Berliner talks about the need to build an "examiner" into a computer chess player—a large-scale, top-down device that monitors and explains what is happening in a small-scale, bottom-up connectionist network, so as to redirect it if it goes astray—he is quick to add that such a device would have no genuine insight, but would merely be rationalizing, producing plausible stories about the network's doings. The reasons why unconscious intelligence settles on a particular decision are often profoundly obscure. Not daunted, however, conscious intelligence will go ahead and generate reasons it can express in ordinary language, effortlessly and spontaneously, and may cling possessively to such reasons, even if they are completely wrong. One kind of knowledge, conscious, logical, serial, behaves as if it has insight into a different kind of knowledge, unconscious, parallel, distributed, but in reality it is simply engaging in a form of explaining. The result may look like intuition, since there is not nearly enough available evidence to justify the conclusions, but often consciousness is making up stories.

Conscious systems try to understand what is happening in unconscious systems, and delude themselves with false answers. The fact is that in many activities of the mind, there is no need for such understanding, which may even be an impediment and a nuisance. It is easy to tie a shoelace, think of a rhyme, get the point of a joke, but being aware of the cogs and wheels of the mental machinery behind these spontaneous skills can lead to paralysis. Many learned skills involve orders of things that are quite arbitrary. The letters of the alphabet, for example, are arranged in a sequence for which there is no meaningful explanation, but, as Donald Norman has noted, once the sequence is fully learned and automatic, it does not matter in the slightest that the order is meaningless. That is not the case, however, with the higher-level, conscious systems which supervise the performance of automatic skills, and intervene if anything goes wrong. An intervening consciousness *does* look for order and meaning and understandable relations between things, and that is part of its uniqueness.

Humans are the explaining species. Nobel prize–winning physicist Leon Cooper thinks the desire and need for explanation is older than science, and that the psychological necessity for explanation, one of the "built-in primitives of our mental apparatus," is a prerequisite for the emergence of science. Homo sapiens possesses a remarkable facility for taking things that have no apparent logical connection and linking them up together in a causal chain that seems to make sense. When an explanation is formed, it becomes an active processor of information, in the sense that we tend to select new evidence according to whether it fits into the explanation. People make inferences on the basis of their explanations, and the more coherent the explanation, the more confident they are likely to be about their inferences. Studies of criminal trials show that members of a jury reconstruct the scrambled, piecemeal, incomplete evidence presented by witnesses into a narrative story wherein events have clear causes, and people have intentions. A juror may construct more than one explanatory story, but he is likely to base his verdict on the one that is most coherent and plausible.

Explanations are a means of bringing an uncertain world under control. They can make random events seem to reveal a hidden, rational order, and tame the wild beasts of mere chance. Every day, experts on the stock market come up with at least one plausible explanation of why the index went up or down on the previous day, with definite causes neatly producing logical effects. Yet if there is an underlying order to the gyrations of the stock market, economists have been unable to discover it. One promising approach is to apply to the market the new theories of turbulence in physical systems, where seemingly chaotic processes like breaking ocean waves or cloudbursts are regular enough to be described by a complex set of equations. The fly in this mathematical ointment, however, is that a minuscule change in one variable can shift a system from a stable state to a chaotic one; in principle, the smoke curling up from the cigarette of a sailor standing on the deck of a ship on the Pacific Ocean can set into motion a chain of events that results in a hurricane in the Caribbean. Thus a single event, so obscure and seemingly trivial nobody paid any attention to it, could have precipitated the stock-market crash of October 1987. Some economists speculate that the market is "neither rational nor irrational, but inscrutable," because, like a connectionist network, it is a system where a vast number of small elements contribute to the behavior of the whole. If that is true, it is fruitless to chase after neat explanations for its ups and downs. No satisfactory account has yet been given for the great crash of 1929.

A fascinating study by Gideon Keren and William Wagenaar of blackjack players in an Amsterdam casino shows how important explanations can be in affairs where chance plays a leading role. This is especially true of blackjack, because a blackjack player is not a passive bystander, as in roulette, but is constantly making various decisions that influence his chances of winning, such as how much to bet, whether to take a hit or stand, to double or not to double. Blackjack players seem to be poor at coping with the uncertainty inherent in the operations of luck. They misunderstand the nature of chance, assuming that some mysterious set of interconnected causes still lurks in a pack of cards that has been shuffled into a meaningless sequence; if a high card is dealt, they expect the next card to have a low value, and vice-versa. So they increase a bet after winning and reduce it after losing. An illusion of control is created.

Some of the players in the Amsterdam casino made an interesting distinction between chance and luck. Chance, they decided, is impersonal; it manifests itself in events and outcomes, whereas luck is something a person does or does not possess. Luck confers her favors unequally. Some individuals are luckier than others, but chance is more democratic. Chance is the same for everyone. Luck cannot be predicted, but it can be detected, and you can manipulate luck when it appears, which is not the case with chance. Expert blackjack players deliberately break a run of bad luck by drawing an extra card where otherwise they would stand. Detecting the presence of luck is regarded as a skill, a mark of cleverness, a rational strategy for bringing uncertainty under control, even though luck itself is an illusion. Luck is made to serve as an explanation that eliminates the uncertainty which actually rules the game, inventing spurious large-scale causal connections for a world in which events are actually determined by many small-scale factors.

The mistake these gamblers make is to confuse explanation with prediction, because they misunderstand the nature of luck. An explanation is radically different from a prediction. It can be used to make a chance sequence of events seem predictable after those events have taken place, but it cannot be used as a guide to events before they happen. Yet in blackjack, as in life, explanations are made to play both roles.

One reason for the human passion for explanations may be that the idea of cause and effect, which logic is poorly equipped to handle, seems to be inborn. A modern digital computer does not "know" about cause and effect, but an infant aged only about twenty-seven weeks does know. This is a recent, surprising discovery, and it was made in part by scientists who were interested in finding out what children's minds can do that computers cannot do. What seems to happen is that a child acquires the idea of cause all of a sudden, instead of developing it gradually, as she grows up and experiences the world. The child "sees" cause without much in the way of learning or experience. Ann Leslie and Stephanie Keeble believe that a distinct mechanism in the brain, which takes information from low-level systems of motion perception, operates independently of general knowledge and reasoning, so that whatever an infant does not know about the world, at least she knows that effects have causes. She does not even need to know what a cause "really" is. When babies of six months are shown films of causal sequences of events, interspersed with a rare noncausal sequence, such as a billiard ball seeming to make another billiard ball move without making contact with it, they show unmistakable signs of surprise. Heart rate speeds up and blood pressure rises.

If that speculation is true, the implications are intriguing. It would mean that in humans the concept of cause is primary, a mental engine pushing the mind of the infant into learning and reasoning, rather than emerging as a result of learning and reasoning. The power of causal knowledge in the development of mind would be somewhat akin to that of language, which is also an inborn faculty that drives children toward intelligence rather than intelligence driving them toward language. The psychologist Jerome Bruner argues that not only cause, but the idea of intention as well, is a primitive, basic building block of human thinking, hard-wired into the brain. In fact, intention may be even more primitive than cause. Shown a film of a small moving triangle or circle, a large moving square, and a boxlike empty rectangle, people cannot help seeing the action in terms of a big bully pursuing two lovers, barging into a house where the lovers have taken refuge, and breaking up the house when he cannot find them.

Putting a disconnected world together by explaining it in terms of effects and causes may be as natural to us as breathing. If the world does not provide coherent information, the mind is apt to impose its own coherence on the world, with an abundance of explanations, and it does so almost of necessity, because of the way the brain is engineered, just as the nature of memory, and the mind's ability to amplify impoverished data, are determined by fundamental features of the brain's design.

Dreams may be one extreme case of this gift for tying together bits and pieces of evidence into a narrative story. J. Allan Hobson, a Harvard psychologist, has developed a new theory of dreaming that is based in part on the idea that the mind imposes order on experience by means of explanations. Freud saw dreaming as a mechanism degrading and distorting unconscious thoughts, repressed during the waking day, that break out at night and threaten to enter the sleeper's conscious mind, disrupting his sleep. Dreams, Freud believed, protect sleep by scrambling the messages these rogue wishes represent, rendering them harmless by making them bizarre, disguising their true meaning. Hobson takes quite a different view. He proposes that the brain generates the raw material for dreaming internally, in the form of information that is poor in quality to begin with. Instead of destroying the coherence of good information, as Freud thought, the brain tries to make sense of what is essentially junk, in the form of signals emanating from an evolutionarily ancient part of the brain stem called the pons. Nerve cells in the pons are switched on periodically during sleep, as part of the chemistry of sleep itself, and send strong signals to the higher brain centers in the cortex concerning the sleeper's eye movements. What seems to happen is that the brain processes the internally generated messages from the pons, which are partly random and refer only to the wild twitching of eyes whose lids are tightly shut, as if they were sensible messages from the outside world. The sleeping brain acts under the illusion that it is awake. It interprets the chaotic signals by matching them to knowledge stored in memory. Since the memories may be remote, time in dreams is topsy-turvy, and the past is represented as if it were the present.

It may be, Hobson thinks, that the profundity of dreams, the way in which they make contact with the deepest and most universal aspects of experience, is a result of the mental strain of finding connected explanations to make sense of highly disconnected data. The mind is doing what comes naturally—putting a world together out of bits and pieces of new information and information it already knows—but it is operating at full stretch because the new information is so severely degraded. All the brain's windows onto the outside world are tightly closed and shuttered, so that no messages from reality can enter. The brain is thrown back entirely upon its own internal resources. "The brain-mind may need to call upon its deepest myths to find a narrative frame that can contain the date," Hobson suggests.

Interpreting dreams, in this theory, is doubly difficult, because in sleep the brain makes incoherent data coherent by means of patterns of preexisting knowledge, and later, on awakening, the mind attempts to make sense of the dream narratives by conscious analysis and reasoning. A dream itself may be, at least on one level, an attempt to explain the unexplainable. But like the mind's creations that make up the knowledge in Karl Popper's World 3, dreams, once they are out in the open, dissected and discussed in an objective way, may reveal properties that are wholly unexpected and surprising.

In fact, the ability of the sleeping brain to connect up partly random, internal messages into a plausible narrative, may be related to the power of the waking brain to explain what it sees in the world of external reality. Martin Seligman, a psychologist at the University of Pennsylvania, and his colleague Amy Yellen, asked a number of students to describe their dreams of the night before, and gave them a high rating if the dreams were tightly integrated into a coherent story, a low rating if the dreams were loosely integrated. Then the students were asked to look at a random series of pictures and tell a story about them as they were flashed onto a screen, one by one. Each student was told to be sure to *explain* the sequence as a whole.

The results showed that the dreaming brain and the waking brain are alike in the way they explain information that is so disconnected it seems to have no rhyme or reason. Awake, people whose vivid images in dreams are highly constrained by the plot of the dream tied the randomly presented pictures into a closely woven thread of narrative while awake. By contrast, the students whose dreams lacked coherence and consisted of one unexpected image after another, with no story linking them, constructed nothing much in the way of a plot when they looked at the pictures. "Waking has many of the properties that dreaming has," the two psychologists conclude.

One of the curious properties of causal explanations is that they are easy to create, but once created, they seem to take on a life of their own, and not just a life but a kind of immortality. They become so robust as to be almost indestructible in the face of devastating logical argument. All the evidence on which an explanation is based can be shown to be utterly worthless, yet the explanation itself survives unscathed. Trying to kill an explanation can be as futile as going after Dracula with a water pistol. This remarkable breed of knowledge structure seems to be amazingly resilient and longlasting.

A causal explanation is an impostor. It may be built out of flimsy or contradictory data, but since the data fall away and disappear once the explanation has been constructed, leaving it freestanding, it becomes independent of the facts on which it was originally based, and so can easily resist the most powerful onslaught against those facts. In fact, some research suggests that weak but vivid evidence, exactly the kind that tends to be discredited later, is also the most likely to start the mind spinning out a plausible explanation. Such an explanation may be dead wrong, but is armor-plated against disproof, and laughs at logic.

It might seem that we cling to our stories about the why of things because they are important to us in some way, and involve our emotions. But that is not the whole story, by any means. Like other kinds of knowledge structures, an explanation can be uncoupled from emotions and motives and stand simply as a creature of the thinking mind. Craig Anderson and his colleagues at Stanford University have tested this theory by asking people to explain a topic so supremely irrelevant to their daily lives and concerns that they could not possibly have strong feelings about it one way or the other: the astonishingly uninteresting question of what qualities go to make a good firefighter. Bogus case studies were concocted, some suggesting that a man who likes to take risks goes on to become a successful firefighter, and others suggesting exactly the opposite, that a taste for risks leads to career failure.

All of the people who took the test expressed their beliefs as to the connection between a risky temperament and success or failure in a firefighting career, depending on how the material had been manipulated. They were not told they were reading fiction. Then half the people were asked to give an explicit, written explanation of the connection they had discovered. These often took the form of scenarios in which a successful firefighter braves immense personal risks to rescue a victim trapped in a blazing house, while his timid counterpart stands helplessly by as lives are lost. When the deception was finally revealed, and the case studies and profiles were shown to be pure inventions, worthless as evidence, members of this "explanation" group nonetheless were more likely to persist in their beliefs, now shown to be completely without foundation, than the others who had not been asked to explain. It hardly seemed to matter that the evidence, weak to begin with, turned out to be entirely fictitious.

Explanations, like stereotypes, are so powerful that they can seem more real than reality itself. They are lenses through which the mind looks at the world, reasons about it, and predicts what it will do next; but the cost of seeing clearly through a lens is to magnify some aspects of reality at the expense of making others virtually invisible. What is striking about explanations is that they rule out much more information than they rule in. That is why some experts on crime are actually hostile to new explanations of the causes of crime: because all such explanations, no matter how plausible, are incomplete. In fact, explanations in terms of external causes like television and permissive parents have often been a barrier to finding out why crime "really" happens, because they rule out possibilities that may be more relevant than the possibilities they rule in.

Martin Seligman believes our explanations for events may have a more powerful and long-lasting effect on our lives than the events themselves, because the way we explain the present guides our expectations of the future. Since the reasons for the bad things that happen to us are often ambiguous, more than one plausible explanation can be constructed, and that explanation becomes a psychological force in its own right. It may be the key to staying in control. If a love affair breaks up, a person who sees the cause as being an ingrained personal shortcoming —"I always screw up my relationships"—may expect to fail in future love affairs, and the prophecy is often self-fulfilling. On the other hand, a causal explanation such as "We had different tastes, and besides he was too short for me," does not preclude success in the next relationship. If the causes selected are external rather than internal, temporary rather than permanent, specific rather than general, the bad thing that happens is to a certain extent tamed, just as the blackjack players in the Amsterdam casino tamed the wild beasts of chance by assigning simple, definite causes to a process which is actually so complex it defies brief explanation. Such explanations do not need to be strictly rational; in fact, it is often good for a person to have an unreasonably favorable notion of his or her own social skills, because success begets success.

In a fascinating study of the explanatory styles of politicians, Seligman and Harold Zullow found that explaining bad events as external and temporary, and good events as internal and permanent, can be a winning strategy. Explanatory style strongly predicted the winners of the ten US presidential elections from 1948 to 1984. It seems to have been the secret of Harry Truman's upset defeat of Thomas Dewey in 1948, when he started as an underdog, and John F. Kennedy's hair's-breadth win in 1960 against Richard Nixon. Adlai Stevenson, who lost twice in a row to Eisenhower, had an almost perversely pessimistic explanatory style. Stevenson spoke of the "ordeal of the twentieth century—the bloodiest, most turbulent era of the Christian age," as being far from over, and likely to continue far into the future, a classic example of explaining a bad event as permanent rather than temporary. In sharp contrast, Ronald Reagan explained that the causes of America's problems were temporary, specific, and external, and could be corrected by voting Republican. He blamed Democratic leaders and the bloated government bureaucracy for the state of the nation. The energy shortage, for example, could be ended as soon as the Democrats removed the controls and regulations that crippled enterprise. In 1980, Reagan won a landslide victory over Jimmy Carter, whose explanatory style left a good deal to be desired. Carter's political fortunes began to plummet after the Camp David domestic summit in 1979, when he spoke of a "malaise" in the land and said: "The erosion of confidence in the future is threatening to destroy the social and political fabric of America."

Explanatory style is part of psychological reality, and as such it can determine actual behavior, shaping events. How a child explains her performance on a school task can influence strongly whether she gives up after a failure, or presses on. Students who see the causes of a setback as external and specific usually go on to get better grades in exams than those with the opposite style. Insurance salesmen with good styles stay longer with their firms and sell more insurance. Racing swimmers rebound more quickly after a defeat. Seligman speculates that good explainers tend to be healthier and live longer than poor explainers, and that thinking about new kinds of causes can help people in the grip of depression. The causes we select, the way we chain them together to interpret an ambiguous and unpredictable world, may determine whether we take chances in life and rise above our potential, and even whether our lives will be long or short.

Explanations are devices that make sense of the world from the top down, imposing themselves on the data rather than, as connectionist networks do, working from the bottom up, considering vast amounts of information all at once in a massively parallel fashion and sending the finished product "up" to consciousness. They are more rigid, simpler, and entertain less uncertainty than a network system, and they reduce the openness of the mind by turning possible outcomes into probable ones. Explaining some hypothetical future event, which may look highly improbable at first glance, often makes the event seem more likely to happen. An explanation may give a false picture of reality because it connects up in the mind things that are not connected that way in the world.

One curious feature of an explanation is that it appears to be supremely conscious and rational, supported by the facts, accurately describing the processes of thought, whereas in reality it is something else entirely. In the first place an explanation considers too few possibilities and is much too cavalier in its use of evidence to be entirely rational. Also, the machinery of putting an explanation together, as opposed to the actual words in which the explanation is couched, may not be conscious at all.

In the head, there are various kinds of unconscious cognitive processes. Some, like the perception of objects and the detection of speech sounds, are so important to survival and so intricate that they are largely hard-wired into the brain, little independent computers manipulating the information that comes in from the senses, their inner workings a total mystery to the conscious mind, which has no say in their operations at all. Certain optical illusions still deceive the eye, even when the conscious reasoning mind knows they are illusions and tries to correct the distortion. We cannot help but see the world in the form that the encapsulated computer of visual perception dumps into our consciousness.

Such self-contained modules are innate and unconscious from birth to death. Yet there are other mental systems that begin by being conscious and then are pushed down into the unconscious, not for reasons of Freudian repression, but because of cognitive economy. The mind cannot afford to waste precious resources of attention and effort performing a mental task deliberately, thinking about every step, when the task can be done automatically, outside awareness. A child learns to read with painful concentration, speaking the words out loud, creeping through a text like a tortoise. One reason why reading is so difficult may be that it requires a child to try to open up and "look inside" an encapsulated cognitive process, to make explicit the operations of the little computer in the head that identifies speech sounds, so that the child can connect the sounds with the shapes of the letters on the page. Silent reading is a comparatively recent achievement: Julius Caesar was thought unusual by his contemporaries for his ability to read without moving his lips.

Yet if a child is to make progress, reading cannot remain a fully conscious process. Some of its operations must become to some extent automatic—as a basketball player dribbles, passes, and catches a ball automatically, or an experienced driver weaves his way home through rush-hour traffic listening to the radio with one part of his mind and wondering what is for dinner with another part. The mind must remove learned routines from awareness, so that awareness, with its limited capacity, is left free to deal with what is unlearned, new, and surprising. Yale psychologist Robert Sternberg thinks that certain people are learning-impaired because they are slow to make consciously learned skills automatic, or make them only partly automatic. In such children scarce resources of attention are squandered on tasks that normal children have already mastered and pushed down beneath the level of awareness. In fact, Sternberg suggests that intelligence should be measured by the sort of tasks that are "nonentrenched," in the sense that they call upon ideas and operations that are outside a person's ordinary experience.

Familiar knowledge that is submerged in this way—whether it is "intellectual," like reading, or a motor skill such as driving a car—setting the conscious mind free to attend to an entirely different task, turns out to have a curious property. It takes on a life of its own. The explicit facts and rules that were involved in learning such knowledge, when learning was painful and deliberate and conscious—the context of places and times and people—all drop away, leaving the skill itself freestanding, and independent of its origins.

An explanation, like a skill, takes on a life of its own. It, too, becomes independent of the evidence on which it was based, and to an extent, automatic. A person who has explained an ambiguous happening can often resist the most potent logical arguments discrediting the explanation, in somewhat the same way that the conscious mind cannot undeceive the eye when it looks at an optical illusion, even when it brings to bear its whole armory of thought and reason. That is what makes explanations so efficient, so powerful, so surprising and paradoxical, and so skilled at creating their own special kind of reality.

16: BEWARE OF GOOD STORIES

One of the ways in which the mind excels is in its effortless ability to treat the world as if nothing it contains is entirely strange. We interpret what is new in terms of what we already know. That strength is built into the very architecture of thought, because in the brain, memory, which encodes the past, and the processing of information here and now, in the present, are not independent elements located in different places, separate, as in a digital computer, but instead are inseparable elements of a single system. Making sense of the present, in an act of perception or problem-solving, is essentially the same as making sense of the past, in an act of recollection.

Making the strange familiar is not a talent reserved for the higher flights of the intellect, but is basic to such bread-and-butter modes of intelligence as being able to recognize a simple scene that contains some ambiguity. Often, the visual system must supply information that is missing in a scene in order to make sense of it; speaking in metaphor, it "interprets" what it sees using presuppositions, opinions, schemas. In the figure below, the mind actually clamors to interpret what it sees as a white triangle lying on top of a black-bordered one, which is going well beyond the bare data. It assimilates what is vague and potentially odd to structures of knowledge that are based on plausible assumptions about how the world normally behaves. In cases of scotoma, where a hole appears in the visual cortex, knocking out of action neurons that normally process information from a certain part of a visual image, patients are still able to perceive the image as a seamless whole. The brain interpolates what is missing, with the right colors, the right shape and edge, papering over the blemishes.

Some connectionists stress the survival value of a brain that deals in close but not exact matches between a new experience and the memory of a similar one. It might pay a creature living in a dangerous world to react to a new event in the same way as to a previous but slightly different event. The creature might live longer than if he treated every experience as brand-new. If he was out walking one day and a yellow-striped animal ate his friend while he himself escaped by skinning up a tree, it would be prudent behavior when on a later occasion he came face to face with a khaki-striped animal, to skin up a tree just in case the beast with stripes of a slightly different color had similar eating habits.

It is not surprising that the brain should want to reduce the newness of the world in this way. Making life more predictable means making it more manageable, and is often an efficient way of dealing with a reality that provides too much data, or too little, or the wrong kind, so that interpreting that reality is like reading a book with words and pages missing, sentences scrambled, ink stains blotting out words. What is remarkable is our ability to tolerate quite extreme kinds of novelty, severe distortions of what is usual and normal. We have a built-in propensity to accommodate to almost anything the world may throw at us, no matter how bizarre and disjointed it may be. The mind leans over backward to transform a mad world into a sensible one, and the process is so natural and easy we hardly notice that it is taking place. The novelist Anthony Burgess has suggested that writing pure nonsense may be an impossible task, although many authors have made a brave try at it, for the very reason that there are always knowledge structures in the head that will interpret nonsense as sense. For instance, the famous question asked in Lewis Carroll's *Through the Looking Glass*, "Why is a raven like a writing desk?" may appear quite meaningless, but ravens are black, black ink flows on a desk, and you can dip a raven's feather into ink.

Burgess tried to suppress all his logical inclinations and compose a random string of words completely devoid of sense: "Perspex vulture cognac keyboard gamboge inimitable werewolf inhabit." Nonsense, yes, but Burgess found there was something at the bottom of his unconscious mind that would not let meaning disappear so easily. He was tempted to order the elements into something like "The keyboard emits a sound which both suggests the color gamboge and imitates the roar of a werewolf (thought to be inimitable); a vulture inhabits the perspex inside of the instrument, which is thought to be full of cognac." That is an improbable sentence, Burgess acknowledges, "but it is just about a possible one. I do not think it is all that easy to produce genuine nonsense."

We can turn nonsense into sense because that is the way the brain has been designed for a world where a fast, plausible interpretation is often better than a slow, certain one. The mind thrives on imperfect data. Yet this strength of our everyday intelligence carries with it an unexpected liability. By making the world more coherent than it actually is, by taming its wildnesses and disorderliness, by construing the outlandish as normal, we weaken our capacity to learn from experience. Paradoxically, our very experience, our worldliness, closes the mind to certain kinds of input where it should be open, so that we ignore rather than absorb the lessons the world teaches.

Daniel Kahneman and Amos Tversky, in a celebrated series of studies, showed that people are not just irrational in many of their decisions, but are systematically, predictably so, even when they are trying hard to be rational. We might almost say that there are "rules" of irrational thinking that can be written out and itemized, like the rules of logic. One of the reasons why intelligent adults persist in their follies, the two psychologists believe, is that when confronted with a puzzle to solve, they are immoderately inclined to make sense of "worthless" information. They seem unable to discard rubbishy data, which means that they fail to learn that other, higher-quality data are the key to an intelligent solution of the puzzle. The fact that certain information is worthless does not bother them nearly as much as it ought to. This is one of the chief obstacles in the way of rational thinking.

A surprising insight of Kahneman and Tversky's is that, when answering questions about another person they do not know, people are more likely to think logically if they are given no information whatever about that person, than if they are given information which is of dubious value. In the now-classic test, described in an earlier chapter, people are given a brief profile of a woman named Linda that mentions that she campaigned against social injustice at college. Subjects are then asked to say which is more likely, that Linda is a bank teller, or that Linda is a bank teller and an active feminist. Overwhelmingly, they chose the second statement, even though their answer flouts the logic of probability. They ought to discard the information that Linda took up certain causes as a student, but the mind finds it impossible to discard such data, because it matches a plausible scenario in memory.

If the question about Linda were converted into the notation of logic, "Which is more probable, x alone or x and y?" most people are quick to agree that x by itself is more probable. But even trained statisticians fall into the trap when the puzzle is written out complete with Linda's profile, because they process the information, not by using the rules of logic, but by applying their connected knowledge of the world. Training seems to work no improvement in their ability to think logically if useless information triggers a preexisting knowledge structure.

Another striking example of the way experience seems to run off the mind like water off a freshly polished car is the tendency for people to say "I knew it all along." An abundance of research, much of it penetrating and original, has been devoted to this quirk of human reason, which seems to be one of the universal laws of irrationality. It explains why so many Americans believe that any simpleton could have foreseen fiascoes like the Vietnam War, the Watergate scandal, the Iran-contra affair, as well as the stock-market crash of 1987. Wasn't it perfectly obvious to the merest imbecile that these events could have been avoided with a modicum of foresight?

As in the case of Tverksy and Kahneman's studies, work on the "I knew it all along" effect shows that IQ has little to do with whether or not people commit this particular kind of error. That is part of its universal character. Highly intelligent people as well as not-so-bright ones do what a computer would never do, which is to overestimate vastly their own ability to have solved a puzzle—once the puzzle is already solved by someone else. If they are told the correct answer in advance, they decide that they could have found that answer easily all on their own.

Baruch Fischoff, a psychologist who studies the way people make decisions, discovered that in hindsight, the mind fancies itself as something of an intellectual prodigy, clever and deeply perceptive. Fischoff devised a number of tricky general-knowledge questions, such as "Was Aladdin Chinese or Persian?" and asked players of this game to assign a probability to each alternative answer. In fact, Aladdin was Chinese, but most players gave "Persian" a very high probability of being correct and

"Chinese" a very low probability. After some time had elapsed, the players were told the right answer and asked to remember what their previous answers had been. True to the rules of irrationality, they almost reversed themselves, falsely recalling that they had said Aladdin was very probably Chinese.

Once a surprising answer to a puzzle is part of history, the mind is deluded into thinking it was not really so surprising. The shock of an unexpected outcome has to be felt in the present, or it is hardly felt at all. Looking back at the past has the curious effect of quelling novelty. That is because memory is biased, and psychologists are finding out just how biased it is. Memory is not a clear, transparent window onto the past, made by a perfect glazier, without bumps or flaws. It is much more like a storyteller, a partly deaf interpreter, or a rewrite editor in a newspaper office. It tends to remake the past in terms of what is plausible, given what is known about the world in general, trying to fit clues into a network of schemas, themes, stereotypes, and explanations. Memory is a Baker Street reasoner. In a standard digital computer, memory has none of these deplorable weaknesses. What comes out of memory is a faithful copy of what went in, and only a small part of the total memory system is active at any one time. In the mind, what comes out is a reconstruction, and much of the entire memory system is active in the manufacture of the product.

As a result, people find it easy to succumb to the illusion that the most improbable happenings or facts were actually quite easy to predict. Fischoff demonstrated this fallacy by showing some students an account of an actual historical event, the struggle between the British colonials and the Gurkhas of Nepal in 1814. In part, the story read as follows:

> The campaign began in November, 1814. It was not glorious. The Gurkhas were only some 12,000 strong; but they were brave fighters, fighting in territory well-suited to their raiding tactics. The older British commanders were used to war in the plains where the enemy ran away from a resolute attack. In the mountains of Nepal it was not easy even to find the enemy. The troops

and transport animals suffered from the extremes of heat and cold, and the officers learned caution only after sharp reverses. Major-General Sir D. Octerlony was the one commander to escape from these minor defeats.

Readers of the passage were split up into five parties. The first party of readers was told that the British had won the struggle, the second that the Gurkhas had emerged victorious, the third that a stalemate was followed by a peace treaty, the fourth that the result was a stalemate without a treaty. Each reading party was told that the version given was true history, whereas in fact, the British won this particular campaign. All readers were asked to rate their particular result for likelihood and give reasons for their answers. A fifth party was left dangling, without being given any outcome, true or false.

In general, readers who were told how the story turned out were about twice as likely to say they knew it already, even if the answer was wrong, than readers in the fifth group who were completely in the dark. What is more interesting, they also interpreted the text in ways that fitted the ending they were given. Readers who were told the British had lost, for example, placed special emphasis on the extremes of hot and cold weather in the mountains, to which the British were unaccustomed. In this way the connections between the supposed ending of the story and the reasons that support it are strengthened, making the outcome seem more plausible.

Fischoff thinks that the brain is so adept at integrating new information into its web of knowledge structures that it assimilates the outcome of an event, or the answer to a tricky question, into whatever else the mind knows about that particular topic. This is all quite natural and spontaneous in a content-addressable memory. In the twinkling of an eye, question and answer, event and outcome, all become woven into a single, seamless mental fabric. That is why we think we "knew it all along." As part of the process of creating coherence in material that contains gaps and unstated assumptions, the mind reinterprets evidence in such a way as to make it more consistent with the outcome.

In remembering, people not only distort and interpret information from the past so as to make it fit what they know or believe in the present; they seem to add new information. The more distant the event, the more material the mind adds from its store of world knowledge. Beliefs are notoriously hard to shift by means of argument and logic. People who have read a magazine article on a controversial topic and are then shown certain facts supposedly excerpted from the article, which are actually fakes, pure inventions, "remember" them as having been mentioned in the original text, as long as the spurious facts support their particular belief. They mistake falsehood for truth, if the falsehood buttresses their views. Also, the mind has a way of remembering the strong points of evidence that confirms its beliefs, and the weak points of evidence that disconfirms them.

In everyday thinking, the mind is very good at brushing aside information that a logician would regard as being of the utmost importance to correct thinking. What is more, people do not seem to learn, easily or at all, the rules of probability and statistical reasoning just by having repeated experiences of them. Even after long exposure to chance processes, most people are not much wiser in the ways of probability at the end than they were at the beginning. Why should this be? One answer seems to be that the rules of statistics and probability fly in the face of common sense. And "common sense" in many cases turns out to mean the way in which human memory is organized and how it processes information.

Consider this conundrum. In English text, does the letter *k* appear more often as the first letter of a word, or as the third letter? The answer is that *k* appears about twice as often in third place, but common sense suggests, wrongly, that it is more frequently found in the first place, because it is easier to remember words by their initial letter than by letters somewhere in the middle. For much the same reason, the more easily an event is brought to mind, the more probable it seems. That is why many people think murder is more common than suicide in New

York, in spite of the fact that suicide is far more common, because murders are vividly reported in the newspapers and so are readily available in memory.

Sometimes, the very act of explaining that an event is unlikely actually makes it seem more likely, due to the role of memory in everyday reasoning. Decision researcher Paul Slovic has noticed that the public is seldom won over by elaborate explanations of why nuclear power stations are safe, because the explainer describes all the many small ways in which things could go wrong, hoping to show that the probability of so many small glitches happening all at once to produce a big disaster is extraordinarily low. The mere description of such an unlikely concatenation of events, however, makes a big disaster more memorable, and by the curious laws of common sense, more likely. Ironically, coherence appeals vastly to the mind, because the mind is so good at imposing coherence on reality, yet the more a set of events is coherent, the less that chain of events is likely. The greater the number of links there are in a narrative, the more realistic the narrative seems, but the less probable it is. The statement "The stock market crashed today and it made a lot of investors unhappy" is more plausible but less likely than the sparer statement "The stock market crashed today." That perhaps is the basis of the old newspaper adage, "Never spoil a good story by checking the facts."

This failure to learn about the ways of probability from experience is connected with the remarkable difficulty human beings have in understanding randomness. A computer programmed to generate numbers by sheer chance and a person asked to do the same thing will produce strikingly different results. People tend to think a random sequence must be as irregular as possible. Difference is what they insist upon. Yet one of the curious features of a random series is that irregularity, carried to extremes, becomes regular. In actual random strings of numbers there are streaks of sameness amid the differences. Suppose we toss a coin six times. There are twenty possible sequences of heads and tails, and in a sense every one of them is random. Yet few of these sequences *look* random. During World War II, it was thought that the German bombing of London was not random, because certain parts of the city suffered more than other parts. In fact, scientists who studied the distribution of bombing hits on London found it passed mathematical tests of randomness surprisingly well.

University of Wisconsin psychologist Lola Lopes finds that someone who has no formal training in probability theory is usually quite unable to produce random strings of numbers or letters. Such a person even finds it difficult to pick just one number truly at random; when asked to say the first number that pops into his mind, he often says "Seven." This is quite a predictable answer. At the same time, randomness is not clearly defined or well understood even by the experts. Dr. Lopes seriously doubts whether inhabitants of other worlds, monitoring signals from television broadcasting antennas on the planet Earth, would be able to distinguish an orderly message from meaningless, random noise. "A fundamental problem facing extraplanetary eavesdropping—human or otherwise—is to know, having intercepted some stray energy, that it has been generated by intelligent beings rather than by a natural process," she says.

What seems to happen is that in ordinary reasoning, people have a stereotype of randomness which they use to detect or produce random events, just as they have stereotypes for the "typical" feminist, banker, secondhand car dealer, politician. Like those other knowledge structures, a randomness stereotype may fall far short of being faithful to reality. A stereotype of randomness is one in which each event in a series is different from the event that precedes and the event that follows. Yet in actual randomness the same event may occur over and over again. In the irrational number pi, for example, which looks as disorderly as any sequence produced by a random number generator, a string of seven threes, one after the other, occurs when pi is expanded to nearly a quarter of a million places of decimals. A cynic would say that this is the mathematical equivalent of finding an honest politician. Seven threes in a row seem so untypical, so implausible, that no layman would dream of writing down a "random" sequence that violates the stereotype in that way.

Recently, three psychologists decided to investigate the stereotype of randomness by studying the "hot hand" effect in basketball. Basketball enthusiasts are apt to believe that a player has times when every shot he makes goes through the hoop, and other times when every shot misses. The belief is so strong that players will try to pass the ball to a teammate who seems to be on a winning streak. The psychologists pored over the records of the Philadelphia 76ers and interviewed the team's coach, Billy Cunningham, to find out whether the hot hand hypothesis had any basis in statistics. The players clearly had a causal theory of the phenomenon. They thought that a hit increased the probability of another hit on the next shot, and estimated that they were about twenty-five percent more likely to score after a hit than after a miss. The psychologists wanted to know whether this estimate by the players had any basis in statistics. What they found was that the players' view was nearly the reverse of the true state of affairs. A player is actually six percent more likely to score after a miss than after a hit. The streaks of hot and cold in forty-eight games of the 76ers 1980–81 season were simply due to chance, like a run of heads when a coin is tossed many times, or the string of threes in the expansion of pi. When a coin is tossed only twenty times, there is a twenty-five-percent likelihood of a sequence of five heads and a ten-percent chance of a streak of six heads in a row. Since a basketball player makes about twenty shots during a game, the laws of probability can explain the hot hand myth.

What is interesting about this study is that it shows how difficult, how almost unnatural, it is for people to learn about the logic of probability just from experiencing its effects, no matter how ample that experience may be. Experience does not discredit the mistaken causal theory of the hot hand; in fact, experience seems to reinforce it. The more basketball people watch, the more likely they are to believe in the myth. Players often take more risks when they think the hot hand is exerting its magic spell on the game.

When dealing with uncertainty, people ordinarily rely not on the sciences of uncertainty, but on how knowledge is organized in memory. They assume that the world is causally connected, put together in a certain way, and they conclude that an event is probable if it is plausible and typical. The mind is designed so that it forms prototypes and constructs scenarios based on what usually goes with what more easily than it searches a space of possibilities and manipulates abstract quantities. Even when the statistics of an uncertain problem are known, even vaguely, the mind still prefers to think in terms of a stereotype. When intelligent adults are asked a question like "Is it more representative for a Hollywood actress to be divorced more than four times than to vote Democratic?" they usually reply yes, because multiple divorce is part of the stereotype of Hollywood. Yet the same people certainly do not think that there are really more actresses in Hollywood with quadruple divorces than there are actresses who vote Democratic.

Interpreting the world in terms of causes rather than chance, of typical cases rather than exceptions, of good stories rather than hard data, works well much of the time, but it tends to dampen curiosity as to what the world is really all about. Berndt Brehmer, a psychologist at the University of Uppsala, Sweden, noting the stubbornness with which people insist on using causal schemas rather than statistical ones, thinks the idea of cause and effect is so basic in the human mind that schemas for chance and probability appear only when causal thinking is already firmly established, and as a contrast to it. "For a person with a firm belief in the deterministic character of the world, there is nothing in his experience that would force him to discover that the task is probabilistic," Brehmer says. The probabilistic nature of a problem is often concealed behind a facade of determinism. It can be detected only by someone who already has a schema for probability in his or her head. It cannot be learned by experience alone. In short, probabilism must be invented before it can be detected, in Brehmer's view. It is very hard to come by from experience: "Our faith in experience is far from well grounded, because we have an untenable concept of the nature of experience, one that assumes truth is manifest, and does not have to be inferred."

If information, no matter how unreliable, scanty, or out of date, fits a mental model of the world we carry in our head, we are apt to become quite unreasonably confident that we can predict what the world is going to do next. So robust is our confidence that awkward facts, instead of derailing the prediction, are simply absorbed into the model. We behave like the eighteenth-century astronomers, who had such faith in Newton's theory of the heavens that new observations that did not fit the theory were rejected, and consequently nothing significant about the universe could be learned. This means that the mind seldom grows out of its illogical ways of thinking as a person becomes mature. The systematic biases that Tversky and Kahneman catalogue are for the most part *lifetime* biases, which repeated failures of judgment do not correct. To some extent, this has genuine usefulness as a goad to human achievement. If the mind worked like a pocket calculator, computing probabilities, human beings might never embark on any enterprise that involves risk. The facts show that for every business in the United States that makes money, four others will only break even, lose money, or go bankrupt. Yet in the past five years about three million new businesses have been started, creating ten million new jobs. Couples go to the altar in record numbers, in spite of the fact that the venture is literally a toss-up. According to the US Census Bureau, the projected rate of divorce to the end of the century is about one out of every two marriages. A computer might refuse to accept such odds. But optimism of this kind is possible for humans because the mind constructs models of successful businesses and happy marriages, stories rich in detail, episode linked to episode in a way that makes the story seem highly plausible, yet, according to the laws of probability, less and less likely to come true. In this way the mind suppresses uncertainty and makes action possible.

The result is that the mind operates rather as the English

establishment is said to operate, rendering rebels, dissenters, and assorted intellectual firebrands harmless by welcoming them into its own ranks on equal terms, going to see their plays, looking at their paintings, marching side by side to protest this, that or the other injustice, thereby ensuring that no radical changes take place in the society that would seriously and permanently disturb the establishment's comfort. In a similar fashion the mind takes the sting out of rebel facts and figures by fitting them into a context where they will cause least trouble. Tversky and Kahneman gave some of their students a description of a fictional character, Tom W., which ran as follows:

> Tom W. is of high intelligence, although lacking in true creativity. He has a need for order and clarity, and for neat and tidy systems in which every detail finds its appropriate place. His writing is rather dull and mechanical, occasionally enlivened by somewhat corny puns and by flashes of imagination of the sci-fi type. He has a strong drive for competence. He seems to have little feel and little sympathy for other people and does not enjoy interacting with others. Self-centered, he nonetheless has a deep moral sense.

The students were asked to predict what Tom W. would do when he graduated from the university, listing nine possible careers in order of likelihood. Most said that Tom was highly likely to go into computer science or engineering, and unlikely to choose social work, the humanities, or education. Then they were told a surprising fact: Tom W. had actually begun to train as a teacher of handicapped children. How could they explain that event in the light of what they had just read?

Most of the students did not use the surprising, anomalous fact of Tom's choice of career to revise the schema of his personality they had formed by reading the profile. If they had done so, they might have learned something about Tom and about the doubtful validity of such potted biographies as a basis for predicting the future. Instead, they absorbed the unlikely fact of Tom the teacher of handicapped children into the schema of Tom the cold fish. They did so by selecting a few relevant parts of the profile, such as the mention of Tom's deep moral sense. Some actually reinterpreted his decision to teach as an example of his need to dominate. Even though they had been rather skeptical of the profile at first, the students did not use an incongruous fact to alter their existing model of Tom. They failed to learn from experience, and simply stripped the new information of its novelty and importance.

This shows, Tversky and Kahneman think, "both the reluctance to revise a rich and coherent model, however uncertain, and the ease with which such a model can be used to explain new facts, however unexpected." The description of Tom was a good story, and good stories, like stereotypes and explanations, ride roughshod over the principles of logic and the laws of probability, immunizing the mind against surprise, and consequently blocking the path to wisdom.

17: THE SELF AS BIG BROTHER

Do we possess a self? Or is the mind so good at explaining what goes on in its deeper recesses that it simply builds a coherent story out of bits and pieces of information and calls that story the self? Does our knowledge, and our amazing knack of using knowledge to make sense of dubious data, lead us to create an "I" which is just a plausible fiction?

The theory of the mind as a sort of secret parliament, deliberating behind closed doors and sending its decisions up to consciousness, casts doubt on traditional notions of the self as the chief executive. In a non–von Neumann brain, there can be no central processor. Knowledge *is* process, and we are our knowledge.

The philosopher Daniel Dennett sees "lots of disturbing evidence" that the idea of a self, an executive who is in charge and knows everything that is going on, must be abandoned. If there were an agent of the kind that we intuitively identify as the self, Dennett thinks, "it wouldn't be the boss; it would be the director of public relations, the agent in the press office who has only a very limited and often even fallacious idea about what is really going on in the system. He's the one whose job is to present a good face to the world, to issue press releases and generally try to tell everybody on the outside what is going on.

"He can be wrong, he can be massively misinformed, he can be massively ignorant. And many results of experiments in cognitive and social psychology now strongly suggest that our own access to what is going on in our minds is very impoverished. We often confabulate, we tell unwitting lies and we are often simply in the dark; we have no idea at all."

The metaphor of the self as a press release may be new to modern cognitive psychology, but it is no stranger to art. Comedy thrives on the exposure of inflated and erroneous ideas about the self. The ludicrous characters in Shakespeare's plays are often the ones who have an explanation of their own personalities that is hopelessly out of kilter with other people's explanations of them. Those who believe their own publicity in this way are frequently led to folly and sometimes to ruin. The pompous misread themselves so badly that others are easily able to dupe them and bring about their downfall. Malvolio in *Twelfth Night* is a figure of ridicule because he does not know himself.

In Shakespeare's plays, the many cases of mistaken identity are more than just conventional plot devices. They are also metaphors for the way comic characters, who have a lofty opinion of their own intelligence, mistake their own identities, and thus make fools of themselves. Paradoxically, the licensed fools often have the sharpest insight into the nature of human folly. A person who think she knows who she is, when all she has is a plausible hypothesis, a good story, is material for laughter, and has been from the classical Greek theater down to the present day. Comedy is born in the gap that opens up between our theories of ourselves and other people's theories of us.

In his celebrated essay *Laughter,* Henri Bergson argues that a person becomes comical when there is some aspect of his personality that he overlooks. And this happens all too easily, because we generalize about ourselves and accept the result as self-knowledge. In fact, such generalizations conceal the truth rather than reveal it. They make the self even more opaque to consciousness than it is already. "Even in our own individual, individuality escapes our ken," said Bergson. "We move amid generalities." We merely imitate ourselves, because there is no way of tearing aside the curtain of description and seeing into the heart of things. That is why comedy deals in general types and stock characters, stereotypes like the miser and the hypochondriac, the cuckold and the ladykiller.

The mind behaves in a curious way when it encounters other people. In his landmark studies in the 1940s of how we form impressions, the psychologist Solomon Asch found that when two people meet, a glance, a few spoken words, are sufficient to "tell us a story" about a mystery as deep and complex as what another person is like. Such impressions are created so quickly, so easily, that the mind is unable to resist them, any more than it can resist recognizing a tree as a tree, or hearing a melody. And just as when we listen to a piece of music we experience it as a connected whole rather than as a series of distinct sounds, so too we connect the various traits of another person into a seamless unity from the very first encounter. Instead of thinking about a stranger in local terms, noticing this or that personality trait in isolation, we see him globally, as one coherent person who makes sense as a whole. What is more, this impression is quite difficult to forget once it is formed. The mind does all this effortlessly, whereas it would make extremely heavy weather of the much simpler task of connecting a series of disconnected numbers or words. This storymaking process that is set off when we come face to face with a fellow human being is not always perfect, Asch found, but it is sometimes extraordinarily sensitive.

Making coherent sense of another person in this way involves the use of schemas, large-scale knowledge structures that may be simplified summaries of the deliberations of small-scale networks. Recent psychological studies suggest that schemas are always constructed in a social encounter, even when psychologists explicitly instruct their subjects to concentrate on details of behavior, and to refrain from schematizing. The mind is not content with noting particulars, but must always form an impression based on schemas of one kind or another. And as we might expect from a mind whose physical basis is the worldly brain, it can do so even when the quality of the information about another person is severely degraded. You can show people a film, say of a man and a woman alone in an apartment, cooking and eating a meal, and run it at different speeds for different audiences, giving them poorer and poorer information the faster the movie runs. When the film is played at twice or seven times normal speed, viewers are worse at remembering what happened, but they are just as good at remembering their schematic impressions of the actors' personalities. Impressions formed by schemas seem to be more robust, more resistant to noise and distortion, more firmly entrenched, than other kinds of knowledge. At high speed, details were lost, but viewers supplied extra information about the actors based on generalizations. They were explaining the man and woman using severely impoverished data.

There is increasing evidence that the way we explain ourselves to ourselves is not so very different from the way we generalize about other people. The schemas we use to understand the self, like those we use to interpret the personalities of others, are also imperfect but are sometimes acutely sensitive. They are a strength and a weakness, a means of discovery as well as a source of delusion, a striking example of the fact that insight and error are back to back in our everyday thinking, two sides of the same coin of the mind's economy. Self-schemas reflect the connectionist premise that nature prefers a good guess that is sometimes wrong to an infallibly correct deduction with perfect data that might take all day, or a whole lifetime, to complete.

Psychologists have puzzled for years over the remarkably weak connection between what people say they believe and how they are likely to act. In 1957, Leon Festinger developed the theory of cognitive dissonance, which proposed that if the mind experiences discomfort when it believes one thing while doing another, it can ease the strain either by behaving in a different way, or by adopting a different belief. A smoker who is told that cigarettes are harmful to health, yet goes on smoking them, has a choice between giving up the habit or denying the medical evidence that says cigarettes may kill him. Either way the inconsistency disappears and comfort returns.

Perhaps the effects of brainwashing are an example of this adjustment between belief and action. During the Korean war, some American prisoners of war made false confessions. They said that the United States was engaging in germ warfare. Many prisoners came to believe what they had confessed, even though it was quite untrue. Cognitive-dissonance theory would explain this as a way of bringing beliefs into line with behavior. A prisoner could either admit his cowardice in signing an untrue statement that brought discredit on his country, or abandon his beliefs by telling himself that there was some truth in what he confessed. Many prisoners chose the second course.

Paradoxically, a person seems to be able to change his beliefs more easily when there is little incentive to do so than when rewards or penalties are used. The American POWs readily persuaded themselves that their confessions were true when there was no threat of punishment, because they could explain their behavior by saying, in effect, "If I was under no duress, why would I have written something that was false?" Then they were able to conclude that the statements were true. Festinger tested this effect by paying college students to perform an excruciatingly boring task and then to confide to the next student waiting to do the same task that the experience had been fun and exciting. Later, when the students were asked what they really thought of the task, those who had been paid twenty dollars to say it was thrilling admitted it was boring, but those paid only one dollar maintained that the chore was "fairly enjoyable."

These adjustments were made without the participants having the faintest idea of what was going on in their own minds. Another psychologist, Daryl Bem, has suggested that adjustments between belief and action are not due to a desire to ease discomfort, but are the natural consequence of the fact that when people think they are observing attitudes and beliefs, whether their own or other people's, all they are really doing is making inferences from clues that are often ambiguous, dim or enigmatic. The prisoners who wrote confessions free of penalty and the students who said a tedious task was fun were in fact, according to Bem, inferring from their own behavior and the circumstances of the test that they *must* have told the truth. They were applying causal theories to what meager data was available to them. Far from having privileged insight into their own selves, these people were simply indulging in explanations. A bystander casually watching them and noting what they did and said could have reached exactly the same conclusions, without access of any kind to their inner mental processes.

At one time, it was thought that these "inferences without insight," were logical, almost scientific devices based on careful observation and comparison, drawing rational conclusions from information that is of fairly high quality. But that could hardly explain why the errors people make when they try to explain their own behavior are systematic and predictable, suggesting that universal laws of thought underlie the mind's blunders and biases: the explanations that go awry, the failure to distinguish between inner reasons and outer circumstances.

A more modern approach is to recognize that we identify the self by means of a constellation of knowledge structures or schemas, so that we can no more find the "real I" than the mind, in Kant's theory of knowledge, can know the "real" world. These schemas are generalizations about the self based on past experience, and they are neither logical nor scientific. They guide the interpretation of thoughts, feelings, and behavior, and predict how we will think, feel, and act in the future. A self-schema influences the way in which knowledge is organized in memory, and so determines how information about the self can be retrieved from memory quickly and easily. Like explanations, self-schemas tend to resist evidence that is not consistent with their interpretations. They can also drive behavior. If someone has a self-schema for efficiency, for example, she is likely to be efficient, not by reason of some embedded trait of personality, but because that is a kind of theory she had about herself. Since schemas process information about the past as well as about the present and future, such a person is likely to remember past instances of efficiency better than instances of inefficiency.

Hazel Markus, a psychologist at the University of Michigan, believes that we become "experts" in certain domains of our own behavior by constructing sets of schemas that recognize and explain information bearing on a particular aspect of the self, organizing it in memory. A person may decide she is an introvert, shy in public, a shrinking wallflower at parties, spending much time alone. She becomes an expert in introversion, amassing a wealth of knowledge about it, expecting and even seeking out circumstances that will highlight this aspect of her personality most clearly.

Such people are experts in a domain of the self in the sense that a master chess player is an expert in the game of chess. The popular notion of a superior chess player is someone who has a logical mind and makes deductions on the basis of each move, planning many moves ahead. It is well established now, however, that this is not how a chess player's mind works at all. An expert player's memory is not general-purpose, nor is he usually an all-round genius outside the game itself. He thinks only a few moves ahead, like a novice does. What makes the expert so formidable is the immense number of schemas specific to chess that are stored in his memory, organized there in such a way that the right one can be retrieved instantly. Some fifty thousand different arrangements of pieces on the chess board are memorized in this way, the fruit of years of study, play, and practice. An expert beats a novice because he can recognize, at lightning speed, a pattern of as many as twenty-five pieces on the board, matching it to the same or a similar pattern stored in memory, to which is attached a memory of a suitable move. When an admirer of Capablanca, the former world chess champion, asked him how many moves he usually considered when in a tight spot, the master replied, "One, but it is the right one." By contrast, the novice chess player is like a child learning to read, who looks at a page of text and sees strings of unrelated letters.

If the arrangement of pieces on the board is random, however, not part of an actual game, the chess expert's powers of recognition and memory sink at once to the level of the novice.

In Markus's view, information about the self is organized in memory in somewhat the same way as information about chess is organized in the mind of a chess expert. Self-schemas are acquired as a result of a lifetime's experience of ourselves, just as chess knowledge is built up by years of immersion and scholarship. They enable us to recognize new information that is relevant to a certain domain of our personality, and to make judgments about ourselves in that domain much more quickly and consistently than if we lacked schemas of this kind. We win the game. But having elaborate schemas for a particular aspect of the self does not ensure that we have them for other aspects too. We can be an expert on efficiency, say, and a novice on ambitiousness.

There is considerable evidence to suggest that self-schemas play a role in interpreting not only the self, but other people as well.

If we decide or are told to concentrate on details of what another person does or says, self-schemas will not play a crucial role. As soon as we decide to make inferences or predictions about that person, however, or try to interpret ambiguous behavior—and most behavior is ambiguous—such schemas do exert a powerful influence. It becomes easier and more natural to think in this way. Schemas are increasingly potent as information about the other person becomes less and less clear-cut and connected. Given free rein, they enable the mind to construct a whole biography, a complete profile, on the basis of very little in the way of hard evidence. As the evidence improves in quality, it tends to take control, and self-schemas play a diminished role.

The mind as instant biographer can be seen in action in the reaction of viewers to a film made by Markus and her colleagues of a young student named Jack, alone in a room. Jack's behavior was curious. At times, it was almost a cartoon version of masculinity. He would lift weights, browse through a copy of *Playboy* magazine, crush a beer can between his fingers, and watch a baseball game on television. At other times, Jack was not noticeably masculine. He would eat an apple or put on a record. Viewers of the film, all males, were carefully chosen so that some of them had a strong sense of their own masculinity and others had a weak sense of it. After they had seen the film, they were asked to reconstruct it and write down anything they could remember about the young man. The experts on masculinity filled in and amplified the sparse information about Jack provided by the movie to a much greater extent than the nonexperts. They generalized from slight clues, conjectured about unseen aspects of the actor's personality, predicted the academic fate that was in store for him, and created plausible scenarios to explain his motives. They felt they knew what kind of person he was, even though they had seen him perform only a few simple actions, some of them extremely stereotyped. Out of flimsy data came the confident assertions that Jack was competitive, that his grades were poor, that he was a loser. The nonexperts on masculinity found the young man's actions less coherent and more difficult to interpret.

Schemas do not search possibilities, as a logical device would do, but select information that is consistent with their own version of the world, and add to it from their resources of knowledge and belief. When schemas drive processing, they may provide information that is quite misleading, and do so with great confidence. We are especially prone to make mistakes when dealing with a domain in which we are expert. Knowing a lot about the self and a little about the other person is a recipe for a radical misreading of personality, and this misreading is robust; it resists disproof, because self-schemas influence the way we perceive people, the way we remember them, the way we generalize about them. The mind peers at other people through the sometimes distorting lens of unconscious self-knowledge.

This means that an expert is not open-minded about himself or about other people, and is less open-minded as the information available declines in quality. Opportunities for self-delusion abound, because memory for our own behavior, thoughts, feelings, likes, and dislikes, is not general-purpose, not "pure," but instead is organized in categories and patterns so that relevant information is readily available. But as we have seen, the more efficiently memory is organized, the more we tame the world and make it seem familiar when it is actually quite surprising, the less we are likely to learn from experience.

The self, psychologist Anthony Greenwald thinks, is rather like a totalitarian state that fabricates and rewrites history, controlling information, distorting the way we think about reality. In certain respects it resembles Big Brother in George Orwell's novel *1984*. As a organizer of knowledge, the self is a personal historian, but its scholarship is sometimes decidedly shoddy. The self tends to preserve existing knowledge structures in memory by resisting evidence that might render them suspect, because any disruption in the way knowledge is organized in the mind could make it less useful. Big Brother, the revisionist historian, preserves the illusion of his own infallibility by turning a blind eye to awkward facts.

The biases, obsolete opinions, and inaccuracies with which the self is riddled are normal and healthy. They preserve cognitive organization and make us steadfast in the pursuit of chosen goals. That is why we can change our behavior without going through the upheaval of shifting and rearranging our inner attitudes and beliefs. If we are experts on politeness, a single case where we are rude will not dislodge the self-schema, any more than the loss of one game will transform a chess master into a novice. Between what we do and what we say we are, stands the schema, which is more consistent than the behavior it mediates.

Another bulwark against the need to alter beliefs is the fact that self-schemas are not just summary stores of knowledge, history texts, but are also procedural devices, which include information about what to do with the knowledge. A good chess player stores in memory specific patterns of pieces on the board, but connected to each memory is a plan of action, a good move to make. So it is with self-schemas. They provide expectations and guide future decisions and judgments. They suggest what "move" to make in the game of life.

Some knowledge structures in the mind, Hazel Markus proposes, define a future, "possible" self, and contain plans and strategies for becoming or for not becoming that self. Some possible selves are desirable: the creative self, the rich, successful, thin self. Others are those we are afraid of becoming: the alone self, the incompetent self, the baglady self. Someone who wants to lose twenty pounds, Markus believes, "does not harbor this hope in vague abstraction, but rather holds a vivid possible self —the self as thinner, more attractive, happier, with an altogether more pleasant life."

This is a far cry from traditional philosophy, which talks about knowledge in terms of true propositions, and of beliefs that can be justified by logical reasoning. Possible selves are plausible scenarios that are less constrained by social reality than other types of self-schemas, and though they may provide a measure of self-knowledge, they can also be highly unrealistic. Unlike the classical kind of knowledge, a possible self is indifferent to logic and cannot be expressed in terms of propositions that are either true or false. Awkward facts and contrary evidence are like tiny atomic particles passing straight through a sheet of solid matter; they make no dent in the armor of a possible self. A possible self is intensely private and deeply hidden, so that other people cannot point out the disparity between what we are and what we plan to be. Moreover, because a possible self deals with the future, it is relatively immune to events in the present that contradict that particular kind of self-knowledge. Present reality can be rendered harmless, at least for the time being, by private, future possibilities.

That is why possible selves are apt to produce behavior that, to a detached observer, might seem irrational and even weird. A politician who loses an election but talks as if he had won it might be regarded as odd, and unlike his "true" self, but his behavior is really consistent with the schema of a future self that wins elections and is highly popular and successful. So a gap opens up between our theories of ourselves and the theories other people have of us. We tend to think of ourselves, but not of others, in terms of future possibilities, and in turn others sum us up by considering only our present behavior.

The "real me," therefore, may be a chimera. Our judgments of what we are like, what stable traits of personality we possess, seem to be constructions that are based at least as much on theory as on observation. In fact, the ease with which we are able to explain ourselves to ourselves by means of language suggests that genuine self-knowledge is even more elusive for humans than it is for nonhuman animals. Daniel Dennett thinks that one of the critical differences between us and other animals is that we have opinions and they do not, and we have opinions because we have language. Animals may have beliefs and desires, and almost certainly do, but they do not "bet on the truth of certain sentences." Beliefs are best considered divorced from language, whereas we have opinions for the very reason that we are the only creatures who have language. Dennett says: "Once you have a language, there are all these sentences lying around, and you have to do something with them. You have to put them in boxes labeled 'true' and 'false.'" We collect opinions as we collect paintings or overcoats, "inherit them, fall into possession of them without noticing, fail to discard them after deciding to discard them, take them on temporary loan and forget that this is what one has done." That makes human actions even trickier to interpret than they might otherwise have been, because an opinion does not predict behavior as directly as a belief does. We may cling to an opinion even when our confidence in its truth is severely weakened or almost nonexistent, but that does not mean we will act on it. Only when our opinions are in rational correspondence with our beliefs are they reliable forecasters of the way we will behave.

That helps to explain, Dennett thinks, why dumb brutes, unlike humans, never suffer from self-deception because they lack opinions. Part of what happens when we deceive ourselves is that we behave one way while judging another way, and this is possible because humans are quite capable of being presented with an argument of such irresistible logic on a certain matter that they agree with its conclusions, and thus acquire a new opinion, but do not believe it. "This is what happens, I think, when you follow an argument whose conclusion is that, all things considered, cigarette smoking is harmful, acquiesce in the conclusion ('Yes, that conclusion falls in the set of true sentences'), and then light up another cigarette," Dennett says.

Language may even be a barrier to self-knowledge. Psychologists have found that players of Peter Wason's four-card game, and other puzzles that seem simple but frustrate the efforts of highly intelligent minds to solve them, exhibit a strange obtuseness about themselves. They select certain cards to turn over, and then explain why they chose those particular cards. But the explanations are patent fictions. Players show no insight whatever into the actual reasoning that went into the selection, but simply construct plausible theories that are compatible with the choices. Jonathan Evans, who has made many studies of this curious effect, concludes that two types of thinking are at work in the four-card game. Type one controls the actual decision to turn over this card or that, and is completely nonverbal. Type-two thinking, which expresses itself explicitly in words, is a faker. It purports to make manifest the implicit, type-one thinking that controls card selection, but in many cases it is simply telling stories. It announces what are little more than after-the-fact opinions. Type two is rational, even logical, consistent, and very, very glib. The trouble is that type two is largely fraudulent. It does not control the reasoning that underlies the actual selection of cards. When players are forced to admit in words, in type-two thinking, that their choices of cards were incorrect, many refuse to change their selections, but at the same time appear to be under stress, "as if caught between two conflicting processes."

What we take to be the self is really a network of knowledge, probably the richest there is, that is saturated in language and organized in such a way as to be useful rather than true. Whereas the world is known by means of mental structures, the self *is* a system of structures. It is not a thing to be known, but a process of knowing, which is why it escapes description, and baffles scrutiny, as if we were to look through a telescope in the hope of seeing the telescope itself instead of the sky.

18: NICE
IS NOT
ENOUGH

If we can be experts in the self, as a master chess player is an expert, actually thinking about the game in a different way from a novice because of the organization of knowledge in memory, can we also become experts in goodness? Do we have knowledge structures for moral judgments and decisions?

During the heyday of behaviorism, such questions were highly unfashionable, because the radical behaviorists asserted that what the mind already knows, and the architecture of such knowledge in memory, has little to do with learning. In the work of the main champion of radical behaviorism, B. F. Skinner, independence is not a personality trait in which we become expert, but a behavior that is controlled from outside. If a mother praises her child for being independent, and scolds her for being dependent, she increases the likelihood that the child will repeat her independent actions. To make people more moral, you maintain good behavior by rewarding it and eliminate bad acts by ceasing to reward them. In Skinner's theory of morality, what goes on inside the head, the way we use our world knowledge to interpret and make sense of new experiences, is unimportant. It is pointless trying to appeal to what people already know about goodness in order to make them good; but if you take a hardened burglar and offer him the right kind of rewards, he is capable of becoming an angel of charity and kindness. Free will is an illusion, Skinner maintains, because learning is independent of our preexisting structures of knowledge, our beliefs and expectations, our presuppositions and theories and schemas.

Skinner's idea of a moral utopia maintained by rewards and punishments, "conditioned avoidance reactions," and the rest of the behaviorist paraphernalia, is at one extreme. At the opposite extreme is the traditional view, as developed in neoclassical economics, that people are psychological miracles, ideally rational beings who know their own minds and what is best for them, freestanding individuals who form their own judgments and make sensible decisions. What is more, economic theory regards the choices an individual makes as being, for practical purposes, *morally* correct. This theory attaches such high importance to free will and liberty that it shrinks from the idea that the human mind is not a perfect instrument for making economic and moral choices. Once we admit that people do not always make rational decisions on their own, we leave open the possibility that decisions can be made for them, that they can be manipulated by governments and advertising sharks, that their lives can be shaped by social forces: in a word, that they are unfree.

The new cognitive theory of the mind steers a path between these two extremes. On the one hand, it unites knowledge and learning, which Skinnerism put asunder. In order to learn, what we know already must exceed what we are trying to know, and the structure of that preexisting knowledge has powerful effects on what sort of new knowledge we acquire, and how readily we acquire it. On the other hand, the gist of much psychological research in the last several years is that human beings are nonrational in systematic ways, that they pay too much heed to information of dubious worth in making their decisions, and that this is a universal consequence of how the mind is made; it reflects the weaknesses of natural intelligence, which are inextricably bound up with its strengths. We are not psychological miracles.

Out of this middle way between two diametrically opposed views—human beings as creatures shaped by external forces and as individuals who always make rational decisions on their own—have come new ideas about the nature of human morality. The debate is pitting philosophers against psychologists, and has prompted educationalists to test theories of moral development in the real world of schools, universities, and prisons.

No thinker has been more influential in this debate than the Harvard psychologist Lawrence Kohlberg, who died in tragic circumstances in 1987. Kohlberg strongly rejected the whole behaviorist theory of moral thinking, and took the daring step of asserting that human beings, even small children, are in a certain sense moral philosophers; it is only by starting from this premise that we can understand how people actually behave. Kohlberg decided it was necessary to enter "the den of philosophical wolves" in order to pry out new truths about the moral development of the person.

Since philosophers think in terms of universal principles, the underlying laws and regularities that are to be found beneath surface differences and accidents of culture, marauding into philosophical territory meant Kohlberg was looking for an account of moral actions that would apply to everyone, everywhere, at all times. It would be based on how the mind works and how the mind is made, as well as on how societies impose their various constraints.

Kohlberg began thinking seriously about moral matters when he served with the US Merchant Marine in Europe during World War II. He was deeply impressed by the sufferings of the survivors of the Nazi holocaust, and after the war he became a volunteer helping to smuggle Jewish refugees into Palestine, then a British colony closed to Jewish immigration. Here was a basic moral paradox: Kohlberg was breaking the law in order to accomplish a goal that seemed to him more ethical than the law. "I had no moral conflicts about breaking British law, which was unjust to the Jewish survivors of the holocaust...who had no home country to go to," he said. Yet the experience made him wonder about the nature of moral decisions, the laws that govern them, and the role that knowledge plays in choosing between right and wrong.

At the University of Chicago, where he trained as a clinical psychologist, Kohlberg grappled with this problem for ten years. In 1958 he published a theory he hoped would explain why certain types of moral thinking are universal, but are not necessarily present in all individuals. The answer, he decided, is that human beings develop morally in a series of three distinct levels of thinking. Within each level there are two related stages, six stages in all. Each stage represents a separate moral philosophy. The stages do not vary from one person to another, and in that sense they are part of human biology, but not everyone moves from stage to stage at the same speed, and some never reach the highest levels.

Up to the age of ten, a child in Kohlberg's scheme is something of a behaviorist, a little Skinnerian of sorts, strongly influenced by external forces, interpreting good and bad in terms of rewards and punishments, making his moral decisions out of blind obedience or the fear of authority coming down hard on his head. Much of the time children at this stage conduct themselves with reasonable outward decorum when authority is looking their way, but they can be cruel when the usual apparatus of enforcement breaks down. That is what happens in William Golding's novel *Lord of the Flies*, where a group of boys aged six to fourteen, evacuees from an atomic catastrophe in World War III Britain, are marooned on an idyllic Pacific island. The children are in a sort of wild paradise, with plenty to eat. Without adult supervision, however, the veneer of civilized behavior soon breaks down and the boys become monsters, savages without the redeeming innocence of the savage, blood-crazed, indulging in irrational taboos. The intelligent among them, the intuitive or efficient, the logical, they destroy, and brush aside appeals to what adults might think or do. Simon, the only boy with true insight into what afflicts them, is sacrificed in a subhuman orgy.

Moral crises arise, Kohlberg said, not out of a Freudian conflict between the id and the superego, but when circumstances are socially ambiguous, and typical moral judgments no longer apply. Golding's story makes it clear that morality can be maintained at such times only if it is based on principles that make sense regardless of what the rest of society thinks. That is not the case at the first three stages of Kohlberg's scheme, up to the age of fourteen, exactly the period of growing up depicted in *Lord of the Flies*. A young child at the first stage, for example, might cheat when there is no risk of punishment. At stage three, the same child, who tends to regard morals as a way of fitting comfortably into society, and seeks approval by being "nice"—like Charlie Brown in the *Peanuts* comic strip—might cheat if other nice people are cheating but not if they are not. A stage-three child has a good stereotype of "what most people do." On Golding's Pacific island, there is no punishment, and "most people" are the other boys, who are running around being obnoxious.

It is only during the teenage years, Kohlberg found, that behaviorism recedes and a more rational element enters, as the maturing person begins to construct moral principles that are logical in their own right, independent of authority and aside from any allegiance to individuals, gangs, or cults. Logic makes moral thinking autonomous, in Kohlberg's view (and incidentally makes the streets safer), so that even if there are gaps in the power structure, people at this level of development will act morally.

People will act morally on a desert island, it seems, only if they are at stage four, five, or six. At stage four, thinking is still conventional, a time of fixed rules and a desire to maintain the social order for its own sake. After this, at the final, highest two stages, the individual jumps to a new, "postconventional" level. Stage five is legalistic, seeing morality in terms of a social con-

tract, in which certain ways of acting have been examined criti-
cally and agreed upon by the whole society. Outside the system
of established rules, right or wrong may be a matter of personal
opinion. Laws are not eternal, but may be changed if they do
not reflect the rational needs of society. Kohlberg saw this as the
official morality of the US government, based on the thinking of
the writers of the Constitution. At the sixth, topmost stage, ethical rules are not concrete and specific, like the Ten Command-
ments, but universal principles of justice, of human rights, of
respect for the individual, and these may transcend the laws of a
particular society. Stage six is the most logical and consistent of
all.

Kohlberg used as a test of moral development an imaginary
story of a woman who is dying of a fatal disease, a special kind
of cancer. There is one and only one drug, a form of radium,
that might save her life, and a certain druggist sells it. But the
druggist is greedy and insists on charging ten times what the
medicine cost to make. The sick woman's husband, Heinz, approaches everyone he knows to borrow the money, but collects
only half the cost of one small dose. At last, in desperation, he
breaks into the shop and steals the drug. Should Heinz have
done that?

A stage-one child might reply, "Heinz should not steal. If he
steals, he might get put in jail." Stage two is more pragmatic;
even if Heinz is caught, he could return the drug, and the judge
would be lenient. At the "being nice" or Charlie Brown stage,
Heinz is either right to steal, because his family will think him a
good fellow, or wrong, because nice people don't rob stores:
"He won't be able to face anyone again." Stage-four people
think in terms of rules: Heinz made a vow to love and cherish
his wife when he married her, and he'd better keep it. At stages
five and six, where broader, more abstract principles of human
rights come into play, the life of the woman is seen as being of
supreme importance.

Kohlberg himself faced a dilemma of right action at the end
of his life. For fifteen years, he had been plagued with an intes-
tinal parasite, picked up while on a visit to Belize, which gave

him excruciating pain. Sometimes the discomfort was so great he would conduct tutorials lying on the floor. Early in the autumn of 1986, he began to lose a great deal of weight and seemed discouraged by his illness. One bright winter Saturday Kohlberg drove to Winthrop, a suburb of Boston, parked his Volkswagen where the sea washes up almost at the end of the street, and took his own life by walking into the Atlantic Ocean.

Before his death, however, Kohlberg's theory of moral stages had begun to come under sharp criticism. His project was called a provocative and stimulating failure. Some psychologists now consider that it should be abandoned wholesale, since ten years of experiment have failed to confirm it. Others see some evidence for the first three or four stages, but very little for later ones. It is generally agreed that Kohlberg erred, as Piaget erred, in assuming that the mind develops in a natural, irreversible sequence into a logical instrument, a general-purpose solver of problems—in this case moral problems. He overestimated the rational element in human thinking, and was not hospitable to the idea, salient in modern cognitive psychology and emphasized repeatedly throughout this book, that the way the mind reasons, whether it proceeds in logical or nonlogical fashion, is heavily influenced by the content of the matter it is deciding, and on the knowledge that is available to it. We have seen that the mind can slip back from a late Piagetian stage to an earlier, more childish, less logical one, depending on the content of the problem, the words in which it is expressed.

Kohlberg, like Piaget, studied the general forms of moral thought as they change during the various stages of development, quite apart from the content of particular moral decisions or actions. Whether the action was stealing or cheating or being disloyal, in this circumstance or that, hardly mattered. A problem could be about almost anything, and a mind at a certain stage would work on it in the style appropriate to that stage, as if it were doing algebra. Kohlberg studied the moral development of seventy-five boys at intervals of three years from early adolescence into the late twenties, testing them with imaginary moral dilemmas, some of them taken from works of medieval casuistry. Two boys at the same stage might give totally different answers to a particular dilemma. If the problem was Heinz's sick wife, one boy would say yes, he should steal the drug; another no, he should not. But such variance did not worry Kohlberg at all, because he found that the form of thinking, the mental algebra, that led to the contradictory answers was the same in each case. The first boy would explain his reply by saying that if Heinz lets his wife die, he will get into trouble for not saving her, and the second would assert that if Heinz does steal the drug he will be sent to jail. Both boys, who are at stage one, think of morality in terms of avoiding punishment.

These underlying forms of moral thinking, Kohlberg held, are universal, even if content changes. He claimed to discover the same forms among Malaysian aboriginal teenagers and inhabitants of a Taiwanese village. At this deep structural level, he saw no important differences in the development of moral thinking among Catholics, Protestants, Jews, Buddhists, Moslems, and atheists. Children's moral values in the religious domain ascended through the same stages as their general moral values. "Be good to God and he'll be good to you!" a stage-one child would announce, thinking in terms of rewards and benefits. In effect, Kohlberg was saying that we have a general-purpose intelligence for ethics that applies to any and all circumstances, cultures, and faiths. Someone who thinks Heinz should steal the drug will also think that Americans who helped slaves to escape before the civil war were quite correct to do so.

Ethical thinking, in Kohlberg's theory, is the end result of a program that unfolds as human beings interact with their world, stage by stage, in a sequence that never varies. Some children go faster than others, especially if they are given a chance to exercise their powers of reasoning, but they do not skip a stage. Also, the natural direction is one way: upward, not downward. Children and adolescents understand all stages up to their own, but not more than one stage beyond their own, and they prefer that next, higher stage. Reason and moral judgment do not go forward in lockstep, however. Kohlberg discovered that bright children with high IQs can be slow developers in ethical thinking.

A weakness of the theory is that the moral judgments typical of a given stage, especially at the higher levels, tend to be regarded as "true in all possible worlds," like a logical argument. Kohlberg expressly stated that the answer a person gives to a moral puzzle is not determined by knowledge of that specific case, or of cases similar to it, but rather reflects a distinct, underlying "thought-organization." Knowledge is almost incidental to moral reasoning, just as it is in logic. We are led to suppose that this is all profoundly natural, part of the program of development.

In 1970, Carol Gilligan of Harvard began to look into the ways in which people think about real-life experiences of moral conflict and choice. She and her colleagues found that up to the age of about nineteen, the college students they talked to tended to reason about morality in strictly logical terms. A follow-up study of the same men and women at ages twenty-two and twenty-seven, however, showed they were not satisfied with logic as a basis for understanding their own personal ethical choices. Some very powerful, very difficult dilemmas had arisen in their lives, quite different from the fictional puzzles taken from medieval casuistry, or the story of Heinz. A lawyer found he had unknowingly prosecuted an innocent man. Another person had to deal with the infidelity of a spouse, a third struggled to live up to a principle of absolute truth. These experiences brought them face to face with the limits of their earlier ways of thinking. As one student put it, "My whole world fell apart."

One of these students, a college senior when first interviewed, had reached the topmost of Kohlberg's levels. When solving hypothetical moral problems, he applied universal principles of the sanctity of the individual, as Kohlberg predicted. He decided that Heinz was morally correct in stealing the drug to save a life. The form of thinking was general, true in all possible worlds. But when the "possible" world became the actual world that the student inhabited, Kohlberg's system broke down. The student had a moral conflict in his own life. He was involved with a woman whose husband had not been told of the affair. At first, he recognized that he had violated the universal moral principle of obligation to correct an injustice. The husband clearly should be informed, since "truth is an ultimate thing."

Soon, however, real life began to overwhelm abstractions. The wife, overwhelmed by work and illness in her family, could not face the extra strain of telling her husband of the affair, in spite of her lover's repeated requests. Later, the husband found out on his own. The shock unsettled the student's whole system of moral thinking. He began to examine the "universal" principles he had once taken for granted. Moral truth, he decided, is much less absolute than it might seem, especially in the case of psychological realities as opposed to artificially created dilemmas. Certainty vanished. He began to slip back down the Kohlbergian ladder, from stage five to a mixture of stages four and five. He could not find, and doubted whether anyone could ever find, a satisfactory answer to the dilemma. "Was her right to sanity less important than his right to know?" he asked his interviewers. "That is a good moral dilemma. Now you figure it out." His earlier moral judgments he saw as "high-handed."

Interestingly, the same student, interviewed five years later, at the age of twenty-seven, was uncertain not just about real-life dilemmas, but also about hypothetical cases. His own experiences had led him away from universal logic and made him consider the unique features of each particular case, and the results of a moral decision on the people involved. His earlier, exclusively logical thinking he regarded as a mark, not of maturity, but of callowness, because his dilemma had been at the same time moral and not moral. He had dropped to an even lower stage in Kohlberg's sequence.

Gilligan and her colleagues noticed this "regressive" shift of thinking in many of the people aged twenty-two to twenty-seven that they studied. Answers that were correct in theory had a way of losing their rightness in real-life circumstances. They called this "the dilemma of the fact." It began to seem as if an almost exclusive emphasis on logical consistency in moral judgments

was a sign of a lack of moral development, rather than an eleva-
tion to the highest stage. Formal logic and eternal principles of
justice are useful and effective in freeing adolescents from the
cramping constraints of a conventional mode of moral thinking,
but in adulthood, the choices that arise are too complex, too
much entangled in the uniquenesses of each specific event, of
each character in the drama, in our knowledge of the world, to
be amenable to such an abstract treatment. Form can no longer
afford to be indifferent to content.

There is some evidence that, well before adulthood, children
make sense of moral problems by applying specific schemas to
them, rather than the general-purpose mental operations pre-
scribed by the theory of stages. That means the answer to a
problem, like the solution to the four-card puzzle, may vary
depending on what schema is used. And this is a genuine difference, not a surface one. For example, Carol Gilligan asked two
eleven-year-old children, Jake and Amy, both bright and good
with words, to decide the Heinz problem. In the interviews,
Jake uses logic to arrive at his answer, calling it "a sort of math
problem with humans." He argues that a human life is worth
more than money, and if the druggist only makes one thousand
dollars he can still get by. Life is worth more than money because the druggist can always obtain one thousand dollars from
rich patients with cancer, but Heinz cannot get back his wife if
she dies. Jake takes as his premise that society agrees on moral
values, and proceeds from there by logical argument. This
shows that Jake has a measure of independence in his thinking;
his ability to reason frees him from the need to rely on authority
for answers.

Amy, by contrast, reasons by means of a narrative schema, a
sort of script, which she applies to the Heinz dilemma. She fails
to see it as a self-contained logical puzzle. Rather, she outlines a
series of plausible stories. In one story, Heinz steals the drug
and goes to jail. That does not help, because the wife grows
more sickly and Heinz is unable to procure more of the medica-
tion. Try another story schema: If the druggist could be made to
realize the perilous condition of Heinz's wife, he might relent.

Or other people could be persuaded to help. "If Heinz and the druggist talked it out long enough, they could reach something besides stealing." Whereas Jake sees a world that obeys rules, Amy sees one that hangs together by human talking to human, and relies on the power of narrative to envisage the unraveling of a moral crisis. For Jake, there is a conflict between life and property that can be settled by deduction; for Amy, "a fracture of human relationship that must be mended with its own thread."

Here Amy's moral judgment seems to be a full stage lower than that of Jake. She shows an inability to think systematically about the concepts of morality and law. She is reluctant to challenge authority and examine the logic of accepted moral truths. On the face of it, Amy lacks the independence that logic and rational thought are supposed to confer. Yet her approach may be more "worldly" than Jake's, and perhaps more likely to succeed, because it is based on content rather than form, knowledge rather than logic.

Kohlberg liked to quote a statement by Socrates as expressing the essence of his theory of moral judgment:

First, virtue is ultimately one, not many, and it is always the same ideal form regardless of climate or culture.

Second, the name of this ideal form is justice.

Third, not only is the good one, but virtue is knowledge of the good. He who knows the good chooses the good.

Fourth, the kind of knowledge of the good which is virtue is philosophical knowledge or intuition of the ideal form of the good, not correct opinion or acceptance of conventional beliefs.

The trouble with this manifesto is that while it proclaims the possibility of universal liberation from dictated standards of conduct through the growth of the light of inner reason, antibehaviorist in its every syllable, it fails to accommodate the overwhelming evidence that human beings are inclined to make sense of the world, not by applying a single ideal to all circumstances, but by fitting the facts of a specific circumstance to an appropriate structure of worldly knowledge. Kohlberg seems to think, like the neoclassical economists, that unless human beings are consistently rational they cannot be free. But is Amy any less free than Jake? As the anthropologist Richard Schweder has pointed out, the more rational we try to make our moral concepts, the more we must empty them of content, until, in the limit, they are perfectly rational and perfectly empty. They become disconnected from reality. Because logic is contentless, it can produce "moral" assertions that are technically valid but absurd by the standards of ordinary common sense, which is why people are rightly suspicious of too much logic and too little worldliness in their public figures. One of the criticisms leveled at Robert Bork, President Reagan's unsuccessful nominee for a seat on the Supreme Court, was that he let doctrinaire principles obstruct ordinary human feelings and common sense, and insisted on carrying ideas to their logical conclusions, even when this led to questionable and even perverse moral judgments. For example, Bork opposed the Civil Rights Act on the grounds that it would reduce the freedom of those who wished to discriminate.

It seems unlikely that our moral judgments approach perfect rationality in a program that is part of the natural development of the human species. A more plausible account is that the lower stages represent an implicit world view, a set of "skills" that operate with little interference from consciousness, as a sort of cognitive economy, enabling us to get by in our social environment, but not much else. The highest stages, by contrast, are explicit. Here the conscious mind turns around and reflects on its moral attitudes, in a detached and almost philosophical fashion. It makes explicit and verbal earlier modes of moral judgment that are largely hidden from awareness, because they were geared to action rather than to reflection. Later stages are to earlier ones what Bertrand Russell's mathematical philosophy is to a child's intuitive grasp of number. The highest stages are in a sense "unnatural," which is why few people attain them, and some who do are regarded as dangerous. Kohlberg thought

Martin Luther King was assassinated because he was a stage-six moral thinker.

That may be why the highest level of moral thinking may sometimes seem a little thin and artificial, and too narrow to do justice to the rich possibilities in human nature. It is an example of the restricting effect of awareness that psychologists have noted in connection with the cognitive unconscious. Harvard's John Gibbs suggests that liberalism, as an explicit doctrine, a result of conscious reflection on implicit views of the world at an earlier stage of development, is not powerful enough to satisfy and conquer the full range of our feelings and ideas because, while it may override the "natural" stages of moral judgment, it cannot eliminate them. It can act as a guide for practical social judgment, for the skills that are hidden from awareness, but is not a replacement, because it is radically incomplete. At the explicit level, different moral philosophies may coexist, because they are partial interpretations of the many implicit moral intuitions that are hidden from awareness.

Moral philosophy itself began in the fifth century BC when Greek politics and society were in upheaval. The old agrarian order was in retreat and a brash new commercial class was in the ascendant, trampling on ancient traditions and rising to positions of political power on the wings of money. Because these nouveau riche traders were not brought up through the "natural" tradition of moral thinking in which the landed gentry was steeped since birth, they needed a code of conduct that was explicit and applied quite generally to all kinds of cases. The ethical principles of the old aristocracy were implicit, intuitive, unexamined, acquired spontaneously from home and family, and therefore had to be scrutinized in a clear-minded, reflective way if they were to guide the behavior of the coming class. In Popperian terms, they were World 2 types of knowledge which needed to be brought into the open arena of World 3. Socrates began this task in the hope that he could put together a complete kit of moral tools for Everyman, a set of general-purpose rules based firmly on logic and reason, good for all times and all places. This enterprise, which ended in failure, was the first of many ill-fated attempts to capture the full spectrum of human resources of moral feelings and ideas in a neat, all-purpose doctrine. "Socrates realized the difficulty, bordering on impossibility, of finding adequate answers," Raziel Abelson has written. "He did not find the universal and self-evident code he searched for, but it was his memorable achievement to have revealed to mankind that without such a code its actions will lack justification, and that moral perfection is therefore an ideal to which we can only approximate. Perfect clarity about what constitutes moral perfection is no more of this world than is moral perfection itself."

19: AN AURORA BOREALIS IN THE HEAD

If brevity were to be carried to reckless extremes, and the essence of human intelligence compressed into a single word, that word would probably be: *worldliness*. To say that intelligence is worldly, and to follow the consequences of that assertion, is to have the glimmerings of a theory of how the mind works, where it is strong and where it is weak, why its biases are systematic and deeply embedded, and why the organization of knowledge, rather than the rules of logic, is a key to understanding what natural intelligence is all about.

The long shadow of René Descartes, one of the founders of modern thought, looms over today's debate as to what the mind is and how it stands in relation to the brain. Descartes lived at a time when the whole edifice of medieval thought was collapsing under the impact of new discoveries in science, as well as the voyages of exploration, which radically upset previous ideas about the nature of the world in which human beings lived. A crisis of skepticism ensued, in which all established science and philosophy was eyed with mistrust. Descartes hoped to conquer skepticism by means of a new method that pushed skepticism to the farthest possible extreme, the last frontier of unbelief, by doubting everything except the existence of the intellect. He gave pure mind a unique status as the one thing whose reality no skeptic, however radical, could deny.

The mind, Descartes decided, is self-sufficient. It stands apart from anything material and is an independent domain. The body can be studied without reference to the mind, and the mind can be studied on its own, quite separately from the body. The mind does not need to be embodied, to exist in space, to be realized by a physical device. It does not require a world. In fact, one of the chief properties of the Cartesian mind is its worldlessness. In the act of thinking, Descartes declared, he could easily "feign that I had no body, that there was no world, and no place for me to be in."

The worldless mind of Descartes is rational, special to human beings, and, unlike the body, can never be imitated by any conceivable machine. It generates knowledge by intuition, and also by inference, in a step-by-step fashion using long chains of deduction, in the manner of Euclid's theorems, to move from simple, easy statements to complex, difficult conclusions. Order and correct sequence are the essence of Cartesian thought. As long as we never take anything false to be true, and preserve the proper order of the steps, Descartes believed, "there can be nothing too remote to be reached in the end, or too well hidden to be discovered."

Descartes held that the mind, left to its own devices, is an infallible guide to truth. The set of rules for thinking that he presented as part of his new method was not, as was the system of modern logic conceived by Frege and Russell, an artificial procedure introduced because the natural workings of the mind are not to be trusted. Quite the opposite. For Descartes, the natural operations of the mind do not err unless they are disturbed by incidental and extraneous factors such as prejudice, passion, or impatience. The rules of the Cartesian method presuppose the basic reliability of the mind, and they keep it reliable by preventing the intrusion of distorting influences.

Echoes of this theory of the worldless mind as an autonomous agent, operating in an orderly, serial fashion, independent of all things physical, can be detected to this day among certain psychologists and those who try to model the mind with machines. It is not that modern researchers try to maintain the doctrine that mind-stuff is ineffable or anything as romantic as that. Instead, the new Cartesians argue that mental activities like thinking, judging, remembering, reasoning, and understanding language can be studied on their own terms and in their own right, without bothering too much about how they are realized in a physical device or "machine," such as a brain. They would not dream of denying that such a device is necessary, but they assume that since the same act of thinking can be executed by a variety of different machines, there is little to be gained by studying the details of any particular machine. Whereas Descartes asserted that the mind stands apart from the body and can never be imitated by any machine, many modern cognitive scientists assume that the machine is all but irrelevant because so many different types of machine can be used to realize a given act of cognition.

At a high enough level of abstraction—say, playing a game of tic-tac-toe—we can talk about the mental processes of a player in terms of a goal and the steps toward that goal, ignoring completely the question of how the brain implements those processes through its nerve cells and circuits. The brain's role is indispensable, but uninteresting. In the same way, it is possible to talk about "transport" in terms of a person changing his or her location, moving from this place to that place, brushing aside as irrelevant the question of whether the change was effected by car, bus, subway train, bicycle, or roller skates.

It was the invention of the computer that lent scientific depth to the idea that what matters are the "programs" of thought rather than the machine on which the programs are run. A theorem in logic could be proved by a Bertrand Russell, whose brain was made of carbon, or by one of Newell and Simon's Logic Theorist computers, which were constructed out of very different materials and operated on other principles entirely. The same goes for playing games of chess, in which the gap between computer programs and the best human chess players is closing at an alarming rate. Is it not, therefore, a waste of time to take the brain seriously, when it is only one of a large number of devices all capable of realizing the same program? Does it not make sense to treat thinking as a serial, symbolic, digital affair, which can ideally be described in terms of formal logic, since it is already being approached at a fairly high level of abstraction in any case?

Many of today's new connectionists refute this subtle form of Cartesianism, insisting that it does matter what kind of physical device is being used, and it does matter that thinking is embodied and not worldless, as Descartes believed. Consider a very simple example, from Balakrishnan Chandrasekaran of Ohio State University. We can multiply two numbers together by using one or other of two quite different physical devices: pencil and paper, or a slide rule. The first way involves writing down the numbers and manipulating them step by step according to the rules of ordinary school arithmetic, while the second calls for lining up the logarithms of the numbers on the slide rule and reading off the result. If the numbers are small, the two procedures will give the same result, and it makes little difference which one is used. But when the numbers are large, and the two physical devices are under more of a strain, an important difference does emerge. In the case of paper and pencil, large numbers mean more time spent in computation, more paper used, a greater expenditure of pencil lead. The slide rule, on the other hand, will compute the larger numbers in the same amount of time as it computes small numbers, but there will be a loss of precision. So while both "machines" perform the same task, their weaknesses and strengths are not the same, and, under duress, each exacts its own particular price for the large demands placed on its resources. Moreover, they represent the problem in entirely different ways.

Idealizing the mind, as Descartes idealized it, making it independent of the brain, can be a misleading exercise. Just because, when we think, we reach what seems to be a "logical" conclusion, we cannot conclude that the underlying cognitive machine cranked out a series of logical operations. The mind may have behaved more like a slide rule than a person using pencil-and-paper arithmetic, so that the limitation of the system will not show up until the system is under strain. Then, as we have seen in the four-card game, a change of representation may be enough to make highly intelligent people behave in "irrational" ways.

Paradoxically, the birth of modern logic put an end to the belief that ordinary human intelligence is rational in the sense of obeying formal rules of inference. It was the natural tendency of the mind to tolerate ambiguity, fill in missing information, construct plausible scenarios, generalize, and apply schemas and stereotypes, that made it necessary to invent a radically *unnatural* notation, a high-level, abstract language whose chief aim was to expose and thwart these natural ways of making sense of the world, which come so easily to us that we do not realize we are using them. Eventually this unnatural system of logic gave birth to the digital computer, which became a metaphor for mind, but a false and misleading one.

The very artificiality of logic showed that natural mind operates on different principles, even though it is often capable of thought which obeys certain rules of logic, as, in a much cruder way, a slide rule can arrive at the same result as pencil and paper. The mind follows different principles because many properties of thought, including some that are anathema to logic, such as the ability to make sense of ambiguous or contradictory information, arose as a result of the way the brain evolved, just as the computational properties of the slide rule are inseparable from the way it is designed. This shatters the Cartesian belief that thought can be studied and understood while ignoring the physical device that realizes thought. By putting the mind "under strain," as it were, modern psychologists like Amos Tversky and Daniel Kahneman have shown that irrational thinking, far from being a surface effect due to incidental errors and distractions, is actually so deep-seated and systematic that it can be captured in a set of universal principles. As they emphasize, it is very hard to rid ourselves of our irrational biases, because they are tied so closely to our knowledge of the world.

By taking seriously the question of what sort of computer the brain is, connectionism offers a new and different theory of what the mind does. As long ago as the 1890s, when modern logic was in its babyhood, William James developed his ideas of how human beings think by discarding, at the very outset, the Cartesian myth that intellect is disembodied. James began with the premise that psychology is the study of entire individuals living in a world of real space and time. "With any other sort of mind, absolute intelligence, Mind unattached to a particular body, or Mind not subject to the course of time, the psychologist as such has nothing to do," he declared.

In the worldly mind, James argued, thinking is not digital and local, a matter of putting one atomic fact after another. Rather, thought is a stream, fluid, continuous by its very nature, even though it may seem to consist of separate and distinct words, images, and symbols. This is related to activity in the brain. While we think, James said, our brain changes, and "like the aurora borealis, its whole internal equilibrium shifts with every pulse of change. The precise nature of the shifting at a given moment is a product of many factors." It may be convenient to express mental facts as separate items, encoded in words, but their separateness is only apparent, not real. Thought discriminates. But it also associates.

James was a connectionist extraordinary, nearly a century ahead of his time. Some of the diagrams in his masterpiece, *The Principles of Psychology*, are remarkably similar in spirit to those emanating today from such hotbeds of modern connectionism as the University of California at San Diego. James spoke of a "jungle of connections" in the mind that blends thoughts together. And the connections need not be logical. Prejudice, rather than reason, may be the web that links thought with thought in the mind. "Reason is only one out of a thousand possibilities in the thinking of each of us," he wrote. Descartes saw prejudice as an outside factor, leading astray an intellect that in itself is free from error. Today's cognitive scientists turn that idea on its head and recognize prejudice as a basic strategy of thought for a mind that must make imperfect sense of a complex world.

Connectionist models, being inspired by the architecture of the embodied brain, are Jamesian in certain respects. They capture some of the streaming quality of human cognition. They imply an intelligence that is highly fluid and adaptable, with information flowing continuously through the system, from higher to lower levels and from lower to higher, like a restless sea always on the move. A perception, a memory, a thought, leads to further processing immediately, without the need for a central executive to decide on the next step in a chain of computations.

At the same time, connectionism is especially suggestive in what it has to say about cognition as the means by which an entire person does things in the world. It blurs the distinction between the "intellectual" domain, where we solve puzzles, make inferences, and plan actions, and the more mundane activities of seeing, hearing, remembering, and moving about the world. The traditional school of artificial intelligence, based on the serial processing of symbols and the separateness of thoughts, has tended to keep these two aspects of our mental life distinct, so that there is now some disagreement as to what exactly intelligence is. For instance, can a cat think? The symbolic school might answer no. A cat, after all, cannot speak or play chess or prove theorems in *Principia Mathematica*. To a connectionist, however, a cat may be a cognitive creature, and a superbly efficient one at that, because it negotiates its world with such excellent mastery. It is an expert at purposeful doing. For connectionists, the dividing line between perception and thinking is becoming increasingly vague and uncertain.

A number of researchers believe today that everything the

mind does can, in principle, be described in terms of connectionist systems, and the reason for their belief is that the brain itself is such a system. Some are building hybrid machines that combine connectionist networks with serial symbol processes, but there is no pretense that this is how human intelligence actually works. A network that reads printed text and understands stories, for example, is taught to recognize patterns, but it is also provided with symbolic knowledge structures that are like the schemas, rules, and stored reasoning chains of the traditional symbolic school of artificial intelligence.

James Hendler, a computer scientist at Berkeley who is developing hybrid systems of this kind, insists that rules, schemas, and stored inference chains are indispensable if a machine is to understand a story. "Suppose I tell you that John is a detective hired by Bill to trail Mary," Hendler said. "John follows Mary into a hardware store. After a few moments, he thinks Mary is becoming suspicious of him. He picks up a rope and walks to the counter.

"Now a human reader knows at once that John picked up the rope because he wanted to look inconspicuous. Yet there is no particular fact in the story which by itself leads to the idea of inconspicuousness. Notice how indirect the inference is. It calls for a schema that operates at a fairly high level. You would think that this sort of interpretation would be a natural one for connectionist systems, but it turns out that connectionism can't touch that kind of high-level inference yet."

One of Hendler's machines was given the task of planning the purchase of a meat cleaver. The machine was clever enough to rule out the idea of taking a plane flight home after making the purchase, because it is forbidden to carry weapons on a plane. That decision was based on the knowledge that one of the possible uses of a cleaver is as a weapon. But what if the machine were told to buy a letter opener? Would it decide that letter openers are banned on planes because they are sharp enough to stab? Hendler was in a quandary. He did not want to have in his system the misleading fact that a letter opener is a weapon, but he did want to give the machine the ability to infer that a letter opener looks very much like a knife, which is a weapon. His answer was to build a connectionist network trained to recognize a number of similar objects, and this was linked to a standard, "old-fashioned" symbol system in which was stored a great deal of information about the various objects. The hybrid system was sophisticated enough to avoid taking the letter opener home on a plane, but not for the crude reason that it is a weapon. By combining the powers of recognition of the connectionist network and the specific knowledge in the symbolic domain, the system as a whole was able to solve a problem which neither old-fashioned serial symbol manipulators nor new-fashioned connectionist networks can solve on their own—yet.

Yet here is the crux of the matter. Hendler does not and cannot argue that his machine as it stands is a cognitive system. It consists of two separate pieces which look very different, and, more important, are developed out of different types of hardware. The system is too Cartesian to be useful as a model of mind. "I had to do some very clumsy stuff to make the two pieces talk to each other," Hendler said. He has come to believe that in actual cognition, as the brain-mind performs it, there must be systems in the middle, between the low level of perception and the higher level of explicit, factual symbolic knowledge, and these systems are neither symbolic in the traditional sense, nor strictly connectionist as the word is used today. "There has got to be more in the middle," he says.

Exactly what this middle medium may turn out to be that enables the symbolic to talk to the subsymbolic remains mysterious. Eventually the two domains must be reconciled, and this is one of the main research goals of cognitive science as it moves into the 1990s. A kind of wholeness will be achieved, or, at least, the implications of wholeness will be explored. The intelligent machines of the future must be more like William James's Psychological Man; more complete, more worldly than the science-fiction fantasy of a detached brain thinking in limbo.

Balakrishnan Chandrasekaran and his colleagues are working on a theory of how two styles of intelligence, the deliberate ordering of thoughts with full awareness, and the thoughts that well up into consciousness without disclosing whence they came or how they were formed, can be implemented in a machine that is only partly connectionist. His theory will lead to a next round of models in which connectionist networks simulate the kind of thinking whose origins are inscrutable, while symbolic systems model deliberative thought. "Our minds work in such a way that predeliberative mental processes come up with the most interesting ideas, and then deliberative processes tidy them up, put them in order," Chandrasekeran said. "Both types of thinking interact with each other very powerfully, so that, for example, learning at the level of awareness eventually ends up by strengthening the content of thoughts that are hidden from awareness." In these models, however, it should not be assumed that just because a process is serial, it can be described in terms of symbolic logic. That is an outsider's view of artificial intelligence, and is apt to lead to mistaken ideas about the nature of the subject. Relations between thoughts even in the early programs of Newell and Simon need not be logical; for example, they can be relations between items in a search space.

It seems extremely unlikely that the high-level knowledge structures in the mind—schemas and scripts, symbols, rules, and stored chains of inference—are like the software of a standard computer, programs that run on a von Neumann or a connectionist machine and can be understood completely in their own right, without reference to the hardware. Another possibility is that such structures simply "emerge" from the patterns of activity in connectionist networks, so that what may look like a hard-knowledge structure is really a simplified summary of the "vote" taken by a network that must satisfy an immense number of soft constraints all at once. In this view, the mind is a soft machine; there is only network activity, and everything else simply bubbles up from it.

Jerome Feldman, a Berkeley computer scientist who coined the term *connectionist*, thinks the relationship between these styles of intelligence—hard and serial versus soft and simultaneous—will become clearer when models are built that contain some of the rich internal structure that evolution has built into human brains. We do not start life with a brain that is like a book with blank pages, waiting for experience to write on them the messages that enable us to think and act intelligently. Instead, we come into the world in possession of specialized cognitive structures, little autonomous computers already organized to perform mental tasks that are much too difficult and technical to learn from scratch, by trial and error; tasks such as vision, recognizing speech sounds or a human face, perhaps even acquiring a theory of the syntax of our native language. These modular systems in the head are like the implicit knowledge of cause and effect that infants display almost at birth, systems that drive learning instead of letting learning drive them. They are processes which go on mostly below the level of awareness and are so important to survival that nature could not afford to let us simply pick them up haphazardly from experience. They are part of our inherent worldliness. And even those skills and knowledge structures we do learn by practice and observation eventually become automatic and unconscious, almost as if they were inborn, so little effort and attention do we need to pay to them. Tying a bow tie is painfully deliberate for a novice, but a practiced diner-out can do it while reading a book.

Some connectionist researchers do treat the brain as a blank book, largely because their chief interest is to find out how a network can learn. They may devote an entire career to that one question, since learning, a central theme of the new theory of the mind, is something that a connectionist system does much more easily and "naturally" than a von Neumann computer. These researchers realize full well that what they are trying to do cannot be done, namely to conjure up general intelligence out of pure learning on structureless, "empty" webs of units and connections. But they resist building structure into their networks, even though it is clear that nature "prewires" specific cognitive structures into the brain, because, for their purposes, this would be a kind of cheating; they might be building in exactly the expertise they are trying to make their systems learn. This is reminiscent of the dilemma of early artificial-intelligence pioneers, who did not want to install large amounts of knowledge in their problem-solving machines because that would be tantamount to telling the machine the answer to the problem in advance, as if a student were to copy his neighbor's work during an exam.

Feldman's own research program at Berkeley is different. The blank-book method he finds unlikely to lead to new insights about the mind, and, as a cognitive scientist, he is not particularly interested in the engineering approach, where results are of paramount importance and it therefore makes sense to build connectionist networks for part of a task such as speech recognition and to use a von Neumann machine for the other part. Feldman believes that the mind is connectionist entirely, and contains nothing resembling a von Neumann architecture. But he also insists on the importance of inherent structure in the network, perhaps in the form of modular subnetworks that contain specific knowledge, either innate or learned. That means knowledge structures do not simply emerge from the global activity of a single, huge network, but are actually present more explicitly in the system.

"I think very little behavior just emerges," Feldman said. "In the kinds of models that I work on, a script or a schema is really there. There is a structure that captures the relationships present in the script or schema. It is not some pattern over all the brain that bubbles up in some way. I believe that intelligence is due to the fact that there is not just any old network in the brain, but very specific networks that evolved and learned."

Whether large-scale knowledge structures emerge from the network as a whole, or are represented in smaller networks where the links between thoughts are already present in the connection strengths as a sort of permanent memory, they can no longer be regarded in the old way, as rigid, brittle "building blocks" of cognition. They are quite different from the hard rules and schemas of standard symbolic artificial intelligence.

In the connectionist system, a symbol is not a single, distinct object like an x or a y in algebra. On its own, cut off from its associations, it ceases to be a symbol. It represents nothing at all. A symbol in a connectionist device like the brain, therefore, may at some level be mistaken for the hard, digital entity of classical computer science, when it is looked at from above, on a scale so large that its small-scale underpinnings, the rich web of meanings that are essential to its very existence, are invisible. But that is an artificial, misleadingly constricted version of what such a symbol truly is.

The word *pen*, for example, can be regarded merely as a symbol for an instrument that writes. But in cognitive terms, it is the tip of an iceberg of brain-wide and body-wide implicit knowledge that is vast and various, and concerns not just the way we think, but also the way we act. It is linked to what we know about how to hold and open a pen, about ink, paper, surfaces that are smooth, rough, or slippery, motor systems that control the way the hand grasps a pen and moves it across the page, even the fact that a pen can be used to punch a hole in paper. By itself the symbol is empty, hollow, meaningless. It has power only by virtue of its connections to the whole "pen world" in which are engaged the mind, the senses, the body, the skills that were once slowly learned with full awareness but are now automatic and require no attention. The symbol is part of a stream of information flowing through many different parts of the brain, a flood of continuous, teeming, shifting activity.

This new approach to cognition is quite unlike that of standard artificial intelligence, where knowledge structures are large-scale models of aspects of the world, stored explicitly in memory and pulled out one by one like books from a shelf. Symbols are drenched in meaning, schemas are more flexible and active than they were in the conventional theory (a conventional schema of a pen would need a special "slot" for the information that it can punch holes in paper), categories are unstable and fluid, created ad hoc, "on the fly," to suit the circumstances of the moment. Lawrence Barsalou of the Georgia Institute of Technology has developed a theory of unstable categories of this kind, going beyond the work of Eleanor Rosch (who as we saw earlier, broke decisively with the notion that the mind forms categories along classical lines, as if it were a logician). Also, the old idea that a particular schema, symbol, or category is the same every time it is realized in the mind, may have to be thrown overboard. If a symbol is regarded as the global result of a network of many units and connections settling into a stable state, then its internal structure is unlikely to be duplicated exactly on each occasion. The parliament of connections in the microcosm of cognition may vote that the symbol *pen* is the one that best fits the perceptual evidence. But even though the final result may be *pen* each time a vote is taken, the debate may be different, and the margin of approval may be greater or less each time.

"Connectionism is strong in those parts of our mental life that traditional artificial intelligence has tended to ignore: pattern recognition, perception, content-addressable memory," said William Bechtel. "It strikes me that by exploring those aspects, we may discover a great deal about the mind, things we have simply passed over in trying to work with classical symbolic structures. Even if it turns out that many kinds of thinking are symbolic and serial, there may be large benefits to be won by simulating that style of thinking in a connectionist system.

"A stable state of a network is going to be very sensitive to a whole variety of other things happening in the network. And that means the state need not be exactly the same every time. If you then use that stable state as a symbol in a thought process, you will get some of the fluidity that is inherent in the connectionist system. You get around the brittle edges of symbolic structures. Even though you may want to manipulate a symbol in traditional ways, serially and with rules, it is not really a traditional entity. It has been softened. One way to make symbolic structures softer is to make them more complex. Another way is to realize them in connectionist networks. I suggest this second way should be taken seriously, because it may give us for free properties which otherwise would be very difficult to imitate. It may lead to more realistic models of human cognition."

The forms of thought, it is clear, are not independent of the nature of the brain, nor of our entanglements with the world. Perhaps the impossibility of understanding human intelligence as an absolute, torn from its worldly and bodily context, is one reason why writers of fiction take a view of the mind that is highly congenial to the new theories in cognitive science. They deal with characters of flesh and blood, who mostly muddle through life by the fitful light of the natural mind. Iris Murdoch says that the novelist has always understood implicitly what philosophers have grasped less clearly, "that human reason is not a single unitary gadget the nature of which could be discovered once and for all. The novelist has had his eyes fixed on what we do, and not on what we ought to do or must be presumed to do. He has as a natural gift the blessed freedom from rationalism which the academic thinker achieves, if at all, by a precarious discipline."

The early period of artificial intelligence was one in which researchers, to a greater or lesser degree, did think of human reason in terms of what it ought to be rather than what it is. Connectionism represents a clean break with that tradition. It replaces it with the belief that while reason may sometimes masquerade as a "unitary gadget," a magic box that needs only data to be intelligent, the surface appearance conceals an indescribable richness of activity that must be understood as the product of a history of living in the world that reaches back into the remotest mists of man's beginnings, and as the larger part of an intelligence that is worldly to its foundations.

NOTES

INTRODUCTION

10   *"recognizes no dividing line between man and brute"*
       John B. Watson, quoted in R. E. Fancher, *Pioneers of Psychology* (New York: W. W. Norton, 1979).

11   *the neuron conducts signals in one direction only*
       See D. O. Hebb, *Essay on Mind* (Hillsdale, N.J.: Lawrence Erlbaum Associates, 1980), 34–35.

16   *In an eloquent manifesto*
       Ulric Neisser, "The Limits of Cognition," in Peter W. Jusczyk and Raymond M. Klein, eds., *The Nature of Thought: Essays in Honor of D. O. Hebb* (Hillsdale, N.J.: Lawrence Erlbaum Associates, 1980).

17   *"The question of capacity looks very different"*
       Neisser, 116–117.

19   *If we, in our skeptical age*

I am grateful to Christopher Cherniak, Professor of Philosophy, University of Maryland, for this formulation, and for extremely valuable conversations.

I should also like to thank William Griffith, chairman of the Philosophy Department, George Washington University, and Wayne Davis of Georgetown University, Washington, D.C.

CHAPTER 1

23   *mechanical computers as labor-saving devices*
Paul E. Ceruzzi, *Reckoners* (Westport, Conn.: Greenwood Press, 1983).

24   *optimum size of a modern software-writing team*
David L. Waltz, "The Prospects for Building Truly Intelligent Machines," *Daedalus* 117, 1 (1986): 192.

24   *the "Galileo of artificial intelligence"*
Edward A. Feigenbaum: "We're still waiting for our Newtons and Einsteins in AI. But we've had our Galileo, and he was Newell and Simon." Quoted in Mitchell Waldrop, *Man-Made Minds: The Promise of Artificial Intelligence* (New York: Walker Publishing, 1987).

25   *Simon announced to a bemused class*
Pamela McCorduck, *Machines Who Think* (San Francisco: W. H. Freeman, 1979), 116.

29   *the "Dark Period"*
Patrick H. Winston, "Perspective," in Patrick H. Winston and Karen Prendergast, eds., *The Commercial Uses of Artificial Intelligence* (Cambridge, Mass.: MIT Press, 1984), 3–4.

29   *"Building intelligent machines has turned out to be a very hard problem"*
David Waltz, interview with the author.

31   *how evolution has "spent its time"*
Rodney Brooks, "Intelligence Without Representation," unpublished research report (Cambridge, Mass.: MIT Artificial Intelligence Laboratory, 1986), 3.

33   *took these plausible stories too seriously*
Waltz, "Prospects for Building," 195.

33   *"It is no accident"*
Hans Berliner, in Daniel G. Bobrow and Patrick J. Hayes, eds., "Artificial Intelligence: Where Are We?" *Artificial Intelligence* 25 (1985): 375–415 (403).

34   *"generally quick at every other kind of knowledge"*
Plato, *The Republic,* vol. 7 of *The Works of Plato,* ed. Benjamin
Jowett (New York: Dial Press), 282. Also see Richard E. Nis-
bett, Geoffrey T. Fong, Darrin R. Lehman, and Patricia W.
Chang, "Teaching Reasoning," *Science* 238 (1987): 625–631.

34   *like a student cribbing in an exam*
See Natalie Dehn and Roger Schank, "Artificial and Human
Intelligence," in Robert J. Sternberg, ed., *Handbook of
Human Intelligence* (Cambridge, England: Cambridge Uni-
versity Press, 1982), 361–362.

34   *logic simply a result of the way knowledge about the world is
organized in memory*
See for example Leon Cooper, "Source and Limits of the
Human Intellect," *Daedalus* 109 (1980): 1–17.

36   *information as a full-blown science*
See my *Grammatical Man* (New York: Simon & Schuster,
1982).

37   *"'passing over' the world as such"*
Stuart and Hubert Dreyfus, "Making a Mind Versus Modeling the Brain," *Daedalus* 117, 1 (1988): 24–25.

CHAPTER 2
39   *"is logic a natural kind of the mind?"*
Christopher Cherniak, interview with the author.

40   *a touch of fanaticism in his makeup*
Michael Dummett, *Frege: Philosophy of Language* (New York:
Harper and Row, 1973). Dummett found that Frege, at least at
the end of his life, was a fierce racist. A fragment of a diary, not
published with the rest of his papers, shows that Frege was
bitterly opposed to the parliamentary system, democrats, lib-
erals, Catholics, and the French. As for the Jews, he thought
they should be deprived of their political rights and if possible
expelled from Germany. Dummett remarks: "When I first read
that diary, many years ago, I was deeply shocked, because I had
revered Frege as an absolutely rational man, if, perhaps, not a
very likeable one." Frege died in 1925.

40   *Logic is not a "peep-show"*
Gottlob Frege, *The Basic Laws of Arithmetic: Exposition of the
System,* trans. and ed. Montgomery Furth (Berkeley and Los
Angeles: University of California Press, 1964), 24–25. The

Psychological Logician "looks into his psychological peep-show and tells the mathematician: 'I see nothing at all of what you are defining.' And the mathematician can only reply: 'No wonder, for it is not where you are looking for it.'"

40 *"infected" may be putting it too mildly*
W. C. Kneale, "Gottlob Frege and Mathematical Logic," in A. J. Ayer et. al., *The Revolution in Philosophy* (London: Macmillan, 1957).

40 *"bloated with unhealthy psychological fat"*
Frege, *Basic Laws of Arithmetic*, 24.

41 *The word* true *is the goal of logic*
Frege, "Logic" (1879–1891), in Hans Hermes, Friedrich Kambartel, and Friedrich Kaulbach, eds., *Gottlob Frege: Posthumous Writings* (Chicago: University of Chicago Press, 1979), 128. Frege wrote: "To sum up briefly, it is the business of the logician to conduct an unceasing struggle against psychology and those parts of language and grammar which fail to give untrammeled expression to what is logical. He does not have to answer the question: how does thinking normally take place in human beings? What course does it *naturally* follow in the human mind? What is natural to one person may well be unnatural to another" ("Logic," 6–7).

41 *"There is no reproach the logician need fear less"*
Frege, "Logic," 7.

41 *"our very noses rubbed into the false analogies in language"*
Frege, "Dialogue with Pünjer on Existence," in *Posthumous Writings*, 67.

42 *"a device for knowing what things are and why they are"*
Henry B. Veatch, *Aristotle: A Contemporary Appreciation* (Bloomington, Ind.: Indiana University Press, 1974), 165.

42 *the purity of a thought*
"Logic," 140.

42 *"a formula language of pure thought modelled upon the formula language of arithmetic"*
Frege, (1879), trans. Terrell Ward Bynum *Conceptual Notation and Related Articles* (Oxford: Clarendon Press, 1972).

42 *Logic is a microscope*
Frege, *Conceptual Notation*, 104–105. "I believe I can make the relation of my 'conceptual notation' to ordinary language clearest if I compare it to the relation of the microscope to the eye. The latter, because of the range of its applicability and because

of the ease with which it can adapt itself to the most varied circumstances, has a great superiority over the microscope. Of course, viewed as an optical instrument it reveals many imperfections, which usually remain unnoticed only because of its intimate connection with mental life. But as soon as scientific purposes place strong requirements upon sharpness of resolution, the eye proves to be inadequate. . . . Similarly, this 'conceptual notation' is devised for particular scientific purposes; and therefore one may not condemn it because it is useless for other purposes." In his "Introduction to Logic" (1906; *Posthumous Writings*, 195n), Frege said: "We are very dependent on external aids in our thinking, and there is no doubt that the language of everyday life—so far, at least, as a certain area of discourse is concerned—had first to be replaced by a more sophisticated instrument, before certain distinctions could be noticed. But so far the academic world has, for the most part, disdained to master this instrument." And: "It is the business of the logician to conduct an unceasing struggle against psychology and those parts of language and grammar which fail to give untrammelled expression to what is logical" ("Logic," 6–7).

43   *"One is a number"*
Bertrand Russell and Alfred North Whitehead, *Principia Mathematica*, vol. 1, (Cambridge, England: Cambridge University Press, 1950), 2. Russell and Whitehead decided that ordinary language is ill-equipped to represent the handful of simple, highly abstract ideas in their deductive system of reasoning. Language is good at expressing complex ideas compactly and tersely, but it fails when it comes to expressing very simple ones. See Alan Wood, *Bertrand Russell: The Passionate Sceptic* (London: George Allen and Unwin Ltd., 1957). Russell invented his own pet names for many symbols. In lecturing, he would refer to $E!$ as "E shriek" (Wood, 49).

44   *Russell knew only six people who had read the* Principia *all the way through*
Bertrand Russell, *My Philosophical Development* (New York: Simon & Schuster, 1959), 86.

44   *"I disliked the real world"*
Russell, *My Philosophical Development*, 210.

44   *"because generals are stupid"*
Russell, *My Philosophical Development*, 211.

45   *consistency and "unworldly" systems of thought*

See Murray Code, *Order and Organism* (Albany, N.Y.: State University of New York Press, 1985), 203. "Indeed, the more rigidly rigorous the pursuit of logical consistency, the more obscure becomes its relevance to actuality. For a high degree of consistency is obtainable only in those areas of knowledge which, like mathematics, approach a high degree of abstraction. But here pure logical consistency is what Whitehead calls 'an easy intellectual consistency,' i.e. questions about the relevance to actuality, which is where the real difficulties lie, are simply ignored."

45   *the idea that logic is rigorous "is so much moonshine"*
Frege, *The Foundations of Arithmetic* (1893), trans. J. L. Austin (Evanston, Ill.: Northwestern University Press, 1980), 112.

46   *"Alas, arithmetic totters"*
Russell, *My Philosophical Development*, 58.

46   *Bertrand Russell at a dinner party*
Jacob Bronowski, *The Origins of Knowledge and Imagination* (New Haven, Conn.: Yale University Press, 1978), 78–79.

47   *"The truth is rarely pure and never simple"*
Oscar Wilde, *The Importance of Being Earnest: A Trivial Comedy for Serious People* (Harmondsworth, England: Penguin), 259.

48   *we would have to adopt a completely literal frame of mind*
See George Miller, *Language and Speech* (San Francisco: W. H. Freeman, 1981), 136–137.

49   *The old idea that logic is the language of thought*
Miller, 136.

49   *"I found the inadequacy of language to be an obstacle"*
Frege, *Conceptual Notation*, 104.

50   *"Progress was first made by walking away from all that seemed relevant to meaning"*
Alan Newell and Herbert A. Simon, "Computer Science as Empirical Inquiry: Symbols and Search," *Communications of the Association for Computing Machinery* 19 (1976): 113–126.

51   *"flourish of romanticism" that surrounded the globalist research program*
Marvin Minsky and Seymour Papert, *Perceptions: An Introduction to Computational Geometry* (Cambridge, Mass: MIT Press, 1988), 4.

CHAPTER 3

54   *Early logic and the Athenian law courts*
For a discussion of this point see Chapter 1 of William Kneale and Martha Kneale, *The Development of Logic* (Oxford: Clarendon Press, 1986).

54   *Aristotle warned his readers to refrain from complaining*
Aristotle, *On Sophistical Refutations*, trans. E. S. Forster (Cambridge, Mass.: Harvard University Press/Loeb Classical Library, 1955), 155. Aristotle points out that in his theory of reasoning he had absolutely no earlier work to quote but was laboring at tentative researches, and adds: "If, therefore, on consideration it appears to you that in view of such original conditions, our system is adequate when compared with the other methods which have been built up in the course of tradition, then the only thing which would remain for all of you, or those who follow our instruction, is that you should pardon the lack of completeness of our system and be heartily grateful for our discoveries."

55   *"a genius for generalization"*
Kneale and Kneale, 405.

56   *there is in the human mind a mysterious source of knowledge*
Luis M. Laita, "Boolean Algebra and Its Extra-Logical Sources," *History and Philosophy of Logic* 1 (1980): 37–60. Mrs. Boole claimed after the death of her husband that his logic had a psychological, pedagogical, and religious origin and aim, not merely mathematical and logical, as scientists assumed.

56   *The discovery of some of Carroll's lost writings on logic*
William Warren Bartley, *Lewis Carroll's Symbolic Logic Together with Letters from Lewis Carroll to Eminent Nineteenth-Century Logicians and to His "Logical Sister," and Eight Versions of the Barber-Shop Paradox* (New York: Clarkson N. Potter, 1986).

58   *the Schoolboy Problem*
Bartley, 326–331.

58   *"they still tended to scamper off like white rabbits"*
Bartley, 25.

58   *content is of no real importance*
      See Margaret Boden, *Minds and Mechanisms* (Ithaca, N.Y.:
      Cornell University Press, 1981), 158.

58   *grocers on bicycles*
      Bartley, 381.

61   *Sir James Lighthill*
      Sir James Lighthill, "A Report on Artificial Intelligence"
      (UK: Science Research Council, 1972).

62   *"Generalizing is a matter of throwing away information"*
      Denise Cummins, interview with the author.

63   *"If you are going to ask about reasoning"*
      Cummins interview.

64   *Eurisko "stumbled" onto some of its discoveries*
      Douglas Lenat, "Computer Software for Intelligent Systems,"
      Scientific American, September 1984, 211.

65   *"Compared with human capabilities this is extraordinarily
      meager"*
      Lenat, 211.

65   *No compact, powerful, elegant methods exist*
      Douglas Lenat and R. V. Guha, "The World According to
      CYC," *MCC Technical Report* ACA-AI-300-88 (Austin, Texas:
      Microelectronics and Computer Technology Corporation,
      1988), 2–3.

66   *"isolated flashes of useful commonsense reasoning"*
      Lenat and Guha, 155.

66   *our gift for making analogies*
      Lenat and Guha, 8.

67   *"I think we are a long way from making a general-intelligence
      machine"*
      Daniel Bobrow, interview with the author.

68   *"We have no suitable science of cognition"*
      Waltz, "Prospects for Building," 192.

CHAPTER 4

70   *"seem to model a ghostly, ethereal world"*
      Bernard Meltzer, "Knowledge and Experience in Artificial
      Intelligence," *AI Magazine* (Spring 1985), 40–42.

71   *It is disastrous to succumb to the temptation of testing a robot in
      a highly simplified world*
      Brooks, "Intelligence Without Representation," 12.

72   *"fairylands"*
See Marvin Minsky and Seymour Papert, draft of a proposal
to ARPA for research on artificial intelligence at MIT (1970–
71), 39. Quoted in Hubert L. Dreyfus and Stuart E. Dreyfus,
Mind over Machine (New York: Free Press, 1986), 74: "Each
model—or 'microworld' as we shall call it—is very schematic; it talks about a fairyland in which things are so simplified that almost every statement about them would be literally
false if asserted about the real world."

72   *"You can invent anything you please"*
Quoted in Ernest J. Simmons, *Introduction to Tolstoy's Writings* (Chicago: University of Chicago Press, 1968), 78.

72   War and Peace *demands "eyes, ears, voice and all other organs
of sense"*
E. Lampert, "The Body and Pressure of Time," in Malcolm
Jones, ed., *New Essays on Tolstoy* (Cambridge, England:
Cambridge University Press, 1978), 136.

73   *"it was a sure sign of something wrong between them"*
Leo Tolstoy, *War and Peace* (1869; New York: New American
Library, 1968), 1406.

73   *the "endless labyrinth of links"*
Quoted in Lampert, 36: "...in which everything is connected with everything else, whether in harmony or dis-
cord."

73   *the knowledge medium "does what no science can claim to do"*
Isaiah Berlin, *The Hedgehog and the Fox* (New York: Simon &
Schuster, 1966), 70.

74   *rich, compelling discoveries about the everyday irrationality of
the human mind*
See, for example, Daniel Kahneman, Paul Slovic, and Amos
Tversky, eds., *Judgment under Uncertainty: Heuristics and
Biases* (Cambridge, England, and New York: Cambridge
University Press, 1982).

74   *All Russians are Bolsheviks*
R. Revlin, V. Leirer, H. Yopp, and R. Yopp, "The Belief-
Bias Effect in Formal Reasoning: The Influence of Knowledge on Logic," *Memory and Cognition* 8 (1980):584–592
(584); and J. Morgan and J. Morton, "The Distortion of Syl-
logistic Reasoning Produced by Personal Convictions," *Journal of Social Psychology* 20 (1944):39–59.

75   *the ordinary mortal "passes into a looking-glass world"*

Peter C. Wason and P. N. Johnson-Laird, *Psychology of Reasoning* (Cambridge, Mass.: Harvard University Press, 1972), 83. "In this world people talk to him of making deductions which are valid in virtue of logic alone, and of the distinction between true conclusions and valid inferences. These ideas are perplexing, not because they are contrary to his practice but because they are wholly alien to his habitual patterns of thought . . . he is undoubtedly handicapped, both by being unable to exercise his intuitions about the real world, and by being cut off from any natural recourse to those semantic skills which are normally integrated with his deductive powers. Far from isolating his true logical ability, it seems that one might as well hope to discern it in an individual surgically deprived of his linguistic ability."

75   *If Susan goes to her aerobics class*
See Wason and Johnson-Laird, 73–74.

76   *only a glimpse of the "deductive component"*
Wason and Johnson-Laird, 85.

76   *"I have not laid eyes on the man"*
Sylvia Scribner, "Modes of Thinking and Ways of Speaking: Culture and Logic Reconsidered," in P. N. Johnson-Laird and P. C. Wason, eds., *Thinking: Readings in Cognitive Science* (Cambridge, England: Cambridge University Press, 1977), 490.

77   *"It stirred me almost to ecstasy"*
Jean Piaget, *A History of Psychology in Autobiography*, vol. 4: 240. Quoted in Brian Rotman, *Jean Piaget: Psychologist of the Real* (Ithaca, N.Y.: Cornell University Press, 1977).

78   *Reality "is now secondary to possibility"*
Barbel Inhelder and Jean Piaget, *The Growth of Logical Thinking*, (1959), trans. Stanley Milgram and Anne Parsons (New York: Basic Books, 1959), 251. *"Possibility* no longer appears merely as an extension of an empirical situation or of actions actually performed. Instead, it is *reality* that is now secondary to possibility." Quoted in Margaret Boden, *Jean Piaget* (New York: Viking, 1980), 65. "Piaget held that the adolescent is able to think by extensive search of possibilities."

78   *"intoxicated" with logic*
Boden, 74. "Piaget sees the familiar adolescent idealism (including his own, expressed in his early novel and prose poem) as a 'belief in the omnipotence of reflection' that is a

natural result of the need to exercise one's developing logical powers.... It is as though the adolescent were intoxicated with logic."

79   *Piaget's conversion to logic*
See Piaget, *Six Psychological Studies* (New York: Random House, 1967), x.

80   *"C'est pourri, idiot, débile"*
Peter Wason, "The Importance of Cognitive Illusions," *Behavioral and Brain Sciences* 4 (1981):356. "It is a cardinal feature of the four-card problem that a fair proportion of subjects *conspicuously fail to correct their initial responses even when all the relevant information is made available to them to show that they are wrong.*" "The utterances of our subjects often resemble those of a hypnotized person. The subject talks as if he were deluded . . ."

82   *"Every time I go to Miami, I take a plane"*
P. Pollard, "Human Reasoning: Some Possible Effects of Availability," *Cognition* 12 (1982):65–96.

82   *"If I eat haddock, then I drink gin"*
K. I. Manktelow and J. St. B. T. Evans, "Facilitation of Reasoning by Realism: Effect or Non-Effect?" *British Journal of Psychology* 70 (1979):477–488.

83   *"But how can it be that they are getting married?"*
Margaret Donaldson, *Children's Minds* (New York: W. W. Norton, 1978), 76.

84   *"sustained by human sense"*
Donaldson, 75.

CHAPTER 5

85   *"the logician of Baker Street"*
Sir Arthur Conan Doyle, "The Boscombe Valley Mystery," in *Sherlock Holmes: The Complete Novels and Stories*, vol. 1 (New York: Bantam, 1986), 281.

85   *"the science of deduction"*
Doyle, *The Sign of Four*, chap. 1, in *Complete Novels and Stories*, vol. 1.

85   *like inserting "an elopement into the fifth proposition of Euclid"*
Doyle, *The Sign of Four*, 108–109. Holmes: "Detection is, or ought to be, an exact science and should be treated in the same cold and unemotional manner. You have attempted to

tinge it with romanticism, which produces much the same effect as if you worked a love-story or an elopement into the fifth proposition of Euclid."

86   *a walking encyclopedia*
Doyle, *A Study in Scarlet*, in *Complete Novels and Stories*, vol. 1: 11. Watson: "Within eccentric limits, his knowledge was so extraordinarily ample and minute that his observations have fairly astounded me. . . . His ignorance was as remarkable as his knowledge. Of contemporary literature, philosophy and politics he appeared to know next to nothing. Upon my quoting Thomas Carlyle, he inquired in the naïvest way who he might be and what he had done. My surprise reached a climax, however, when I found incidentally that he was ignorant of the Copernican Theory and of the composition of the Solar System."

86   *a "stalwart, plainly dressed individual"*
Doyle, *A Study in Scarlet*, 17.

87   *"It was easier to know it than to explain why I know it"*
Doyle, *A Study in Scarlet*, 18.

87   *Schemas as the building blocks of thought*
David E. Rumelhart, "Schemata: The Building Blocks of Cognition," in Rand J. Spiro, Bertram Bruce, and William F. Brewer, eds., *Theoretical Issues in Reading Comprehension* (Hillsdale, N.J.: Lawrence Erlbaum Associates, 1980), 33–58. "Once we have accepted a configuration of schemata, the schemata themselves provide a richness that goes far beyond our observations. . . . In fact, once we have determined that a particular schema accounts for some event, we may not be able to determine which aspects of our beliefs are based on direct sensory information and which are merely consequences of our interpretation" (38).

87   *Kant's theory of knowledge*
Immanuel Kant, *Critique of Pure Reason* (1781), trans. Norman Kemp Smith (New York: St. Martin's Press, 1965).

89   *a logically possible world*
See Rudolf Carnap, *An Introduction to the Philosophy of Science*, Martin Gardner, ed. (New York: Basic Books, 1966), 10–11.

89   *a contradiction in the world of Sherlock Holmes*
Loren Estleman, "On the Significance of Boswells," in Doyle, *Complete Novels and Stories*, vol. 1: viii.

91   *Schemas in their modern incarnation*
See Henry Head, *Aphasia and Kindred Disorders of Speech* (Cambridge, England: Cambridge University Press, 1926); and Sir Frederic C. Bartlett, *Remembering: A Study in Experimental and Social Psychology* (Cambridge, England: Cambridge University Press, 1954). Bartlett rejected the storehouse metaphor of memory, since "a storehouse is a place where things are put in the hope that they may be found again when they are wanted, exactly as they were when first stored away. The schemata are, we are told, living, constantly developing, affected by every bit of incoming sensational experience of a given kind. The storehouse notion is as far removed from this as it well could be."

91   *"Russian whispers"*
Sir Frederic Bartlett, *Thinking: An Experimental and Social Study* (London: George Allen and Unwin, 1958).

93   *Hamlet arrives at Elsinore with too many schemas*
Alasdair MacIntyre, "Epistemological Crises, Dramatic Narrative, and the Philosophy of Science" (1977), in Gary Cutting, *Paradigms and Revolutions* (Notre Dame, Ind.: University of Notre Dame Press, 1980), 55–56.

93   *"Rocky slowly got up from the mat"*
John D. Bransford, *Human Cognition: Learning, Understanding and Remembering* (Belmont, Calif.: Wadsworth Publishing, 1979), 153.

95   *an author must create gaps in the world of a novel*
Jerome Bruner, *Actual Minds, Possible Worlds* (Cambridge, Mass.: Harvard University Press, 1986), 26–27.

95   *"like a good scout whose job it is to blaze a new trail"*
Annie Dillard, *Living by Fiction* (New York: Harper & Row, 1982), 156. "Fiction elicits an interpretation of the world by being itself a worldlike object for interpretation" (155).

96   *"an exploration of the field of possibility"*
Morris R. Cohen, *A Preface to Logic* (New York: Dover Publications, 1944), 181.

CHAPTER 6
98   *keeps a cool head even in the bedroom*
Gary S. Becker, "A Theory of Social Interactions," *Journal of Political Economy* 82 (1974):1063–1093.

98   *the "buzzing, blooming confusion"*
      William James, *The Principles of Psychology* (1890), vol. 1
      (New York: Dover Publications, (1950), 488.

98   *old maids and the size of the clover crop*
      Herbert A. Simon, *Administrative Behavior*, 3d ed. (New
      York: Free Press, 1976), 82.

99   *"solutions" to economic questions that will not work*
      Herbert A. Simon, "Rationality as Process and as Product of
      Thought," *American Economic Review* 68 (1978):1–16 (12).

100   *the magician of Berkeley*
      William Kahan, "Mathematics Written in Sand," *Proceedings
      of the Joint Statistical Association Meeting*, Toronto, 1983.

100   *the magician of Lublin*
      Isaac Bashevis Singer, *The Magician of Lublin*, trans. Elaine
      Gottlieb and Joseph Singer (New York: Farrar, Straus and
      Giroux/Noonday Press, 1960).

101   *"Before a conference, computer people would come to his hotel
      room"*
      Christopher Cherniak, interview with the author.

103   *the proof of a conjecture in the theory of groups*
      Larry J. Stockmeyer and Ashok K. Chandra, "Intrinsically
      Difficult Problems," *Scientific American*, May 1979, 140–159.

103   *the four-color problem solved*
      Kenneth Appel and Wolfgang Haken, "The Four Color
      Problem," in Lynn Arthur Steen, ed., *Mathematics Today:
      Twelve Informal Essays* (New York: Vintage, 1980), 153–181.

104   *number of possible moves in the game of checkers*
      Michael R. Garey and David S. Johnson, *Computers and In-
      tractability: A Guide to the Theory of NP-Completeness* (San
      Francisco: W. H. Freeman, 1979).

105   *trying to match college freshmen sharing dormitory rooms*
      Stockmeyer and Chandra, 140–159.

105   *"Can crocodiles run steeplechases?"*
      Hector Levesque, interview with the author.

107   *"A lot of the properties of human reasoning"*
      Levesque interview.

109   *a toy or laboratory curiosity*
      Christopher Cherniak, "Undebuggability and Computer
      Science," *Communications of the Association of Computing Ma-
      chinery* 31, 4 (1988):402–412 (408).

109   *"a little like that of coral animals toward the vast reef they have built"*
Cherniak, "Undebuggability," 411.

CHAPTER 7
111   *Lippmann on stereotypes*
Walter Lippmann *Public Opinion* (1922; New York: Free Press, 1965).

112   *"in a coarse net of ideas"*
Lippmann, 60.

112   *"fill in the rest of the picture"*
Lippmann, 59.

113   *"Were there no practical uniformities in the environment"*
Lippmann, 60.

113   *forming opinions of political candidates*
Philip J. Trounstine, "The Remaking of the Candidates '86," *San Jose Mercury News,* October 26, 1986, 1A, 14A.

114   *"You would be amazed at how deep and rich"*
Trounstine, 14A.

115   *the work of Eleanor Rosch*
Eleanor Rosch, "Cognitive Reference Points," *Cognitive Psychology* 7 (1975):532–547; "Human Categorization," in N. Warren, ed., *Studies in Cross-Cultural Psychology* (London: Academic Press, 1977); "Principles of Categorization," in Eleanor Rosch and B. B. Lloyd, eds., *Cognition and Categorization* (Hillsdale, N.J.: Lawrence Erlbaum Associates, 1978), 27–48; and "Prototype Classification and Logical Classification: The Two Systems," in E. Scholnik, ed., *New Trends in Conceptual Representation: Challenges to Piaget's Theory* (Hillsdale, N.J.: Lawrence Erlbaum Associates, 1983), 73–86.

117   *prototypes of the whole-number system*
Rosch, "Cognitive Reference Points," 534.

117   *All the drinks on this table are martinis*
Cherniak, "Prototypicality and Deductive Reasoning," *Journal of Verbal Learning and Verbal Behavior* 23 (1984): 625–642. Cherniak writes: "The prototype theory of category structure is stronger than a classical theory, in that it suggests that making some valid inferences will be more difficult than making others, and that refraining from making some invalid

inferences will be more difficult than not making others."

118   *Freud and scarcity economics*
David Reisman, "The Themes of Work and Play in the Structure of Freud's Thought," *Psychiatry* 13 (1950):1–16. Philip Rieff in *Freud: The Mind of the Moralist* (Garden City, N.Y.: Doubleday/Anchor Books, 1961) remarks (p. 171): "Whether dammed up by social repressions or allowed, in a permissive society, more scope, the capacities of the individual for pleasure remain limited. What Freud termed his 'economic point of view' makes of sexuality not only a limited quantity but one which is always expended in a miserly way."

118   *the basic level*
Rosch, "Principles of Categorization."

119   *"Holding* Decades *in my trembling right hand"*
L. Garis, "The Margaret Mead of Madison Avenue," *Ms.,* March 1975, 47–48. Quoted in Rosch, "Principles of Categorization," 45–46.

120   *Linda the bank teller*
Amos Tversky and Daniel Kahneman, "Judgments of and by Representativeness," in Kahneman, Slovic, and Tversky, eds., *Judgment under Uncertainty*, 84–98.

121   *"All theorizing is flight"*
Iris Murdoch, *Under the Net* (New York: Penguin, 1954), 80–81. "What I speak of is the real decision as we experience it; and here the movement away from theory and generality is the movement towards truth. All theorizing is flight. We must be ruled by the situation itself and this is unutterably particular. Indeed it is something to which we can never get close enough, however hard we may try as it were to crawl under the net."

121   *"more full of rough contingent rubble"*
Iris Murdoch, *The Philosopher's Pupil* (New York: Penguin, 1983), 76. "Every human being is different, more *absolutely* different and peculiar than we can goad ourselves into conceiving; and our persistent desire to depict human lives as dramas leads us to see 'in the same light' events which may have multiple interpretations and causes. Of course, a man may be 'cured' (consoled, encouraged, improved, shaken, returned to effective activity, and so forth and so on) by a concocted story of his own life, but that is another matter."

CHAPTER 8

123 *a celebrated puzzle*
Daniel Kahneman and Amos Tversky, "Choices, Values and Frames," *American Psychologist* 39, 4 (1984):341–350.

123 *"For let men please themselves as they will"*
Francis Bacon "The Great Instauration" (1620), in Richard H. Popkin, ed., *The Philosophy of the 16th and 17th Centuries* (New York: Free Press, 1966), 87.

125 *presuppositions, themes, and points of view*
Gerald Holton, *Thematic Origins of Scientific Thought: Kepler to Einstein* (Cambridge, Mass.: Harvard University Press, 1973).

125 *Einstein joked about his transformation into a "metaphysicist"*
Albert Einstein, letter to Moritz Schlick, November 28, 1930. Quoted in Holton, 243: "You will be astonished about the 'metaphysicist' Einstein. But every four- and two-legged animal is de facto in this sense metaphysicist."

126 *"Themes force upon people notions that are usually regarded as paradoxical, ridiculous or outrageous"*
Holton, 63–64. He goes on: "I am thinking here of the 'absurdities' of Copernicus's moving earth, Bruno's infinite worlds, Galileo's inertial motion of bodies on a horizontal plane, Newton's gravitational action without a palpable medium of communication, Darwin's descent of man from the lower creatures, Einstein's twin paradox..."

127 *"free creations of thought"*
Albert Einstein, *Ideas and Opinions*, trans. and rev. by Sonja Bargmann (New York: Dell, 1954), 33.

127 *A scientist's themes identify him as surely as his fingerprints*
Gerald Holton, *The Advancement of Science, and Its Burdens: The Jefferson Lecture and Other Essays* (Cambridge, England, and New York: Cambridge University Press, 1986), 18.

128 *detection of cosmic radio static*
Steven Weinberg, *The First Three Minutes: A Modern View of the Origin of the Universe* (New York: Basic Books, 1977), 45–49.

128 *"This is often the way it is in physics"*
Weinberg, 49.

129 *the almost random gathering of facts*

Thomas S. Kuhn, *The Structure of Scientific Revolutions*, 2d. ed. (Chicago: University of Chicago Press, 1970), 16.

130   *Kuhn uses the word* stereotypes
Kuhn, 89.

131   *sending up mental trial balloons*
Karl Popper, "Conversation with Karl Popper," in Bryan Magee, *Modern British Philosophy* (Oxford and New York: Oxford University Press, 1986), 96: "The fact that our inborn knowledge may be disappointed shows that even this inborn knowledge is merely conjectural. Moreover, according to my view, we do not learn by observation, or by association, but by trying to solve problems. A problem arises whenever our conjectures or our expectations fail. We try to solve our problems by modifying our conjectures. These new conjectures are our trial balloons—our trial solutions."

131   *As a young man living in Vienna*
Karl Popper, *Unended Quest: An Intellectual Autobiography* (Glasgow, Scotland: William Collins Sons, 1976), 33. Popper decided that every theory can be "immunized" against criticism. In 1922, he made a conjecture that most, if not all, learning processes consist of theory formation, that is, in the formation of expectations. A theory always has an early "dogmatic" phase. This led him to see that "there is no such thing as an unprejudiced observation. All observation is an activity with an aim (to find, or to check, some regularity which is *at least* vaguely conjectured); an activity guided by problems, and by the context of expectations (the 'horizon' of expectations as I later called it). There is no such thing as passive experience."

132   *The three worlds of knowledge*
Karl R. Popper, *Objective Knowledge: An Evolutionary Approach* (Oxford and New York: Clarendon Press, 1986), 106–152.

133   *"nets in which we try to catch the real world"*
Popper, *Unended Quest*, 60.

CHAPTER 9

134   *we misunderstand the nature of experience*
Henry James, *The Art of Fiction*, (1884), in Morton D. Zabel, ed., *The Portable Henry James* (New York: Viking, 1968).

135   *"when you give an inch, takes an ell"*

Henry James, 398.

135 *an anecdote about an English woman novelist*
Henry James, 398.

135 *"a kind of huge spider-web"*
Henry James, 397.

136 *"conscious perception of reality"*
Webster's *Seventh New Collegiate Dictionary* (Springfield, Mass.: G. & C. Merriam Company, 1967), 293.

136 *a celebrated review of machine translation efforts*
Yehoshua Bar-Hillel, "The Present Status of Automatic Translation of Languages," in F. T. Alt, ed., *Advances in Computers*, vol. 1 (New York: Academic Press, 1960).

137 *"The box was in the pen"*
Bar-Hillel, 159.

137 *no "existing or imaginable" program*
Bar-Hillel, 159.

138 *The SHRDLU program*
Terry Winograd, "A Procedural Model of Language Understanding," in Roger Schank and Kenneth Colby, eds., *Computer Models of Thought and Language* (San Francisco: W. H. Freeman, 1973).

139 *"the meaning of a sentence 'is' the process it evokes"*
Terry Winograd, "What Does It Mean to Understand Language?" in Donald Norman, ed., *Perspectives on Cognitive Science* (Norwood, N.J.: Ablex Publishing, 1981), 240.

139 *It is a "perturbation" to an active cognitive system*
Winograd, "What Does It Mean?" 245.

139 *the reader "risks his personal world"*
Richard E. Palmer, *Hermeneutics* (Evanston, Ill.: Northwestern University Press, 1969), 7.

140 *a reader should not simply "bombard the text"*
Palmer, 250.

140 *the hermeneutic notion of "pre-understanding"*
Winograd, "What Does It Mean?" 245.

140 *Interpretation is "horizontal"*
Palmer, 24. "Explanation is contextual, is 'horizontal.' It must be made within a horizon of already granted meanings and intentions. In hermeneutics, this area of assumed understanding is called pre-understanding.... It might be asked what horizon of interpretation a great literary text inhabits, and then how the horizon of an individual's own world of

intentions, hopes, and preintepretations is related to it."

141   *"the unseen from the seen"*
William James, 398.

141   *"Is the Mekong river longer than the Amazon?"*
Terry Winograd, "Extended Inference Modes in Reasoning by Computer Systems," *Artificial Intelligence* 13 (1980):5–26.

142   *Miss America was prevented from playing the tuba*
Richard J. Harris, "Memory and Comprehension of Implications and Inferences of Complex Sentences," *Journal of Verbal Learning and Verbal Behavior* 13 (1974):626–637.

143   *comprehending "literal" text*
David E. Rumelhart, "Some Problems with the Notion of Literal Meanings," in Andrew Ortony, *Metaphor and Thought* (Cambridge, England, and New York: Cambridge University Press, 1979), 78–90.

143   *"I believe that the processes involved in the comprehension of nonfigurative language"*
Rumelhart, "Some Problems," 80.

144   *Business had been slow since the oil crisis*
Rumelhart, "Some Problems," 86.

144   *"When the sun sets the earth does drizzle dew"*
William Shakespeare, *Romeo and Juliet* III, 5, 127–129, in *The Complete Works* (Baltimore: Penguin, 1969), 882.

145   *"From the time you wake in the morning"*
Palmer, 8.

146   *"The alchemists said you can turn lead into gold"*
Terry Winograd, interview with the author.

CHAPTER 10

149   *"In the main, and from the beginning of time"*
G. K. Chesterton, "On Tolstoy's Fanaticism" (1903), in A. V. Knowles, ed., *Tolstoy: The Critical Heritage* (Boston: Routledge and Kegan Paul, 1903): "The only thing that has kept the race of men from the mad extremes of the convent and the pirate-galley, the night-club and the lethal chamber, has been mysticism—the belief that logic is misleading, and that things are not what they seem."

151   *Memory is logic*

Leon Cooper, "Source and Limits of Human Intellect," *Daedalus* 109 (1980):1–17 (9).

152   *cost of bringing a computer memory up to human size*
Waltz, "Prospects for Building," 207.

153   *a now celebrated working paper*
Arthur W. Burks, Herman Goldstine, and John von Neumann, "Preliminary Discussion of the Logical Design of an Electronic Computing Instrument," *Datamation*, September-October 1962.

158   *an analogy suggested by Earl Hunt*
Earl Hunt, interview with the author.

CHAPTER 11

163   *It is a ghost in the machine*
John Tienson, "An Introduction to Connectionism," *Southern Journal of Philosophy* 26 (1987):12.

165   *detecting WORK*
J. L. McClelland. D. E. Rumelhart, and G. E. Hinton, "The Appeal of Parallel Distributed Processing," in David E. Rumelhart, James McClelland, and the PDP Research Group, eds., *Parallel Distributed Processing: Explorations in the Microstructure of Cognition*, vol. 1: (Cambridge, Mass.: MIT Press/Bradford Books, 1986), 23.

166   *"Memory traces . . . are dynamic objects"*
James McClelland, interview with the author.

166   *"Say you are standing in a library"*
Scott Fahlman, interview with the author.

168   *standard artificial-intelligence programs spell out explicitly all the information the system is to use*
William Bechtel, "Connectionism and the Philosophy of Mind: An Overview," *Southern Journal of Philosophy* 26 (1988):17.

169   *representations as* responses *to incoming information*
Bechtel, 17.

169   *a machine called a Perceptron*
Frank Rosenblatt, *Principles of Neurodynamics* (New York, Spartan Books, 1962).

170   *Neural networks being considered by the Department of Defense*
DARPA Neural Network Study, October 1987 to February

1988, Executive Summary (Lexington, Mass.: Lincoln Laboratory, July 8, 1988).

170 *"Classification appears to be a rather ubiquitous information processing task"*
Balakrishnan Chandrasekaran and Ashok Goel, "From Numbers to Symbols to Knowledge Structures: Artificial Intelligence Perspectives on the Classification Task," *IEEE Transactions on Systems, Man and Cybernetics* 18, 3 (1988):416.

170 *"the ultimate furniture of the world"*
Henry B. Veatch, *Aristotle: A Contemporary Appreciation* (Bloomington, Ind.: Indiana University Press, 1974), 22.

171 *"man is a resonable two-foted beest"*
Poems of Geoffrey Chaucer (New York: Thomas Crowell and Co., 1900), 204.

CHAPTER 12

173 *able to tell an egg from a walnut*
Diane Ingraham, Gurmail Kandola, and Mark Pillon, "Neural Networks Learning Systems Based on the Brain," *Micro Cornucopia* 41 (1988):16–20.

173 *"A neural network acts like a small child"*
Diane Ingraham, interview with the author.

174 *"That gives neural networks all kinds of possible spooky uses"*
Ingraham interview.

176 *pattern recognition may indeed play a role in high-level intelligence*
Bechtel, "Connectionism," 29.

177 *members of two notorious New York street gangs*
McClelland, Rumelhart, and Hinton, "The Appeal of Parallel Processing."

177 *learned the past tense of English verbs*
D. E. Rumelhart and J. L. McClelland, "On Learning the Past Tenses of English verbs," in McClelland, Rumelhart, and PDP Research Group, eds., *Parallel Distributed Processing*, vol. 2.

178 *a network's memory as a hilly landscape*
David H. Ackley, Geoffrey E. Hinton, and Terrence Sejnowski, "A Learning Algorithm for Boltzmann Machines," *Cognitive Science* 9 (1985):147–169.

178 *"Suppose you see an elephant at the zoo"*

Fahlman interview.

179   *learning the family trees of an English and Italian family*
David E. Rumelhart, Geoffrey E. Hinton, and Robert J. Williams, "Learning Representations by Back-Propagating Errors," *Nature* 323 (1986):533.

180   *"The state of the art in neural networks"*
Ingraham interview.

182   *"There's not a snowball's chance in hell"*
Jerry Fodor, interview with the author.

183   *"The question is, how do you put the elements"*
Fodor interview.

183   *not the linguistic prodigy it appears to be*
Cummins interview.

184   *"multiplexing" in the visual system*
See Christopher Vaughan, "A New View of Vision," *Science News,* July 23, 1988, 58–59.

184   *"To assume that experience does everything in the brain is totally false*
Jack Cowan, interview with the author.

CHAPTER 13

187   *an economy cannot be run in a* logical *fashion*
Friederich von Hayek, "The Use of Knowledge in Society," *American Economic Review* 35 (1945):519–530.

187   *"never exists in a concentrated or integrated form"*
Von Hayek, 529–530.

187   *"the economy of knowledge with which it operates"*
Von Hayek, 526–527.

188   *"a conceptual abyss"*
Paul Smolensky, "Information Processing in Dynamical Systems: Foundations of Harmony Theory," in Rumelhart, McClelland, and PDP Research Group, eds., *Parallel Distributed Processing,* vol. 1, 197.

189   *"clutching a rope of symbolic logic anchored at the top"*
Smolensky, 197.

190   *a machine called NETtalk*
Terrence J. Sejnowski and Charles R. Rosenberg, "Parallel Networks That Learn to Pronounce English Text," *Complex Systems* 1 (1987):145–168.

191   *"like the Ptolemaic system of astronomy"*

Terrence Sejnowski, interview with the author.

192   *the kind of "thinking" a skilled basketball player does*
Terence Horgan and John Tienson "Settling into a New Paradigm," *Southern Journal of Philosophy* 26 (1987):97–113.

195   *"The world is your friend"*
Sejnowski interview.

196   *connectionist networks as "percolating" plausible patterns of activity upward*
Berliner, 403–404.

196   *"Although the answers are far from clear"*
Berliner, 404.

198   *Making schemas explicit without disembodying them*
Lokendra Shastri, interview with the author.

198   *disillusion with the conventional theory of schemas*
David E. Rumelhart, in D. E. Rumelhart, P. Smolensky, J. L. McClelland, and G. E. Hinton, "Schemata and Sequential Thought Processes in PDP Models," in Rumelhart, McClelland, and PDP Research Group, *Parallel Distributed Processing*, vol. 2.

CHAPTER 14

202   *the astronomer married the star*
David L. Waltz and Jordan B. Pollack, "Massively Parallel Parsing: A Strongly Interactive Model of Natural Language Interpretation," *Cognitive Science* 9 (1985):51–74.

203   *"What we are discovering"*
Sejnowski interview.

204   *"a mob, eager for enjoyment and destruction"*
Sigmund Freud, "My Contact with Josef Popper-Lynkeus" (1932) in *Collected Papers*, vol. 5 (London: Hogarth Press, 1956), 297. Quoted in Philip Rieff, *Freud: The Mind of the Moralist*, (Garden City, N.Y.: Doubleday/Anchor Books, 1961), 63.

205   *In some of Freud's later writings much of the ego is unconscious*
Sigmund Freud, *The Ego and the Id* (London: Hogarth Press, 1923).

205   *"a tumbling ground for whimsies"*
William James, 163.

206   *unconscious creation of categories and prototypes*
A. Marcel, "Conscious and Preconscious Recognition of

Polysemous Words," in R. S. Nickerson, ed., *Attention and Performance*, vol. 8 (Hillsdale, N.J.: Lawrence Erlbaum Associates, 1980).

207   *anesthetized patients can remember the chitchat of doctors during surgery*
H. L. Bennett, "Perception and Memory for Events During Adequate General Anaesthesia for Surgical Operations," in Helen Pettinati, ed., *Hypnosis and Memory* (New York: Guilford Press, 1987).

207   *"My God, they've dragged another beached whale up"*
Bennett, "Perception and Memory."

207   *a computer program to diagnose faults in Vermilion*
Frederick Rose, "an 'Electronic Clone' of a Skilled Engineer Is Very Hard to Create," *Wall Street Journal*, August 12, 1988, 1, 14.

209   *the richer associations of unconscious thought*
Donald P. Spence and Bert Holland, "The Restricting Effects of Awareness: A Paradox and an Explanation," *Journal of Abnormal and Social Psychology* 64 (1962):163–174; and Donald P. Spence, "Conscious and Preconscious Influences on Recall," *Journal of Abnormal and Social Psychology*, 68 (1964):92–99.

209   *the "presentiment of coherence"*
Kenneth Bowers, "On Being Unconsciously Influenced and Informed," in Kenneth S. Bowers and Donald Meichenbaum, eds., *The Unconscious Reconsidered* (New York: John Wiley and Sons, 1984).

210   *Einstein's "phenomenal intuitive instinct"*
Jeremy Bernstein, *Einstein* (New York: Viking, 1973).

210   *"I have a nose"*
Ernst G. Straus, "Memoir," in A. P. French, ed., *Einstein: A Centenary Volume* (Cambridge, Mass.: Harvard University Press, 1979), 31.

211   *"What is happening is that connections are being activated in the network"*
John Kihlstrom, interview with the author. And see John F. Kihlstrom, "The Cognitive Unconscious," *Science* 237 (1987):1445–1452.

212   *Intuition a matter of linking ideas*
Bowers, "On Being Unconsciously Influenced."

212   *"You really don't know why the network ended up where it ended up"*

James Anderson, interview with the author.

213   *Thought... "isn't primarily intended, I suppose, for introspec-*
       tion"
       "Dialogue with Jerrold Fodor," in Jonathan Miller, *States of*
       Mind (New York: Pantheon Books, 1983), 94.

214   *the "quest for universality of mechanism"*
       Seymour Papert, "One AI or Many?" *Daedalus* 117 (1988):
       1–14.

215   *the brain as a network of networks*
       Minsky and Papert, *Perceptrons*, 247–280.

215   *"what appear to us to be direct insights into ourselves must be*
       rarely genuine"
       Minsky and Papert, *Perceptrons*, 280.

216   *"as threatening and fascinating as Count Dracula"*
       Kenneth Bowers, "Intuition and Discovery," in Raphael
       Stern, ed., *Theories of the Unconscious and Theories of the Self*
       (Hillsdale, N.J.: Analytic Press, 1987), 71.

CHAPTER 15

218   *such a device would have no genuine insight*
       Berliner, 404.

218   *it does not matter that the order of the letters of the alphabet is*
       arbitrary
       Donald Norman, interview with the author.

219   *Humans are the explaining species*
       Cooper, 5.

219   *members of a jury reconstruct the scrambled, piecemeal, incom-*
       plete evidence
       Nancy Pennington and Reid Hastie, "Juror Decision-Making
       Models: The Generalization Gap," *Psychological Bulletin* 89
       (1981):246–287.

219   *new theories of turbulence applied to the stock market*
       Gary Hector, "What Makes Stock Prices Move?" *Fortune*,
       October 10, 1988, 69–76.

220   *the market is "neither rational nor irrational, but inscrutable"*
       Hector, 76.

220   *a study of blackjack players in an Amsterdam casino*
       Gideon Keren and William A. Wagenaar, "On the Psychology
       of Playing Blackjack," *Journal of Experimental Psychology:*

General 114 (1985):133–158.

220   *people tend to see an element of skill in situations which are governed by chance*
E. J. Langer, "The Illusion of Control," *Journal of Personality and Social Psychology* 32 (1975):311–328; and E. J. Langer, "The Psychology of Chance," *Journal for the Theory of Social Behavior* 7 (1977):185–208.

221   *A distinct mechanism in the brain for the idea of cause and effect*
Alan M. Leslie and Stephanie Keeble, "Do Six-Month-Old Infants Perceive Causality?" *Cognition* 25 (1987):265–288.

221   *babies of six months are shown films of causal sequences*
A. Michotte, *The Perception of Causality* (New York: Basic Books, 1963).

222   *a mental engine pushing the mind of the infant*
Alam M. Leslie, "Getting Development off the Ground," in P. van Geert, ed., *Theory Building in Development* (Amsterdam: Elsevier North-Holland, 1986), 405–437.

222   *the idea of intention as a primitive building block*
Bruner, 17–19.

222   *a big bully pursuing two lovers*
Bruner, 18.

222   *a new theory of dreaming*
J. Allan Hobson, *The Dreaming Brain* (New York, Basic Books, 1988).

223   *"The brain-mind may need to call upon its deepest myths"*
Hobson, 214.

224   *students asked to describe their dreams*
Martin Seligman and Amy Yellen, "What Is a Dream?" *Behavioral Research Therapy* 25 (1987):1–24.

224   *"Waking has many of the properties that dreaming has"*
Seligman and Yellen, 1–24.

225   *what qualities go to make a good firefighter*
C. A. Anderson, M. R. Lepper, and L. Ross, "The Perseverance of Social Theories: The Role of Explaining in the Persistence of Discredited Information," *Journal of Personality and Social Psychology* 39 (1980):1037–1049.

226   *a barrier to finding out why crime "really" happens*
James Q. Wilson and Richard J. Herrenstein, *Crime and Human Nature,* (New York: Simon and Schuster, 1985), 41.

226   *If a love affair breaks up*
See Christopher Peterson and Martin E. P. Seligman, "Causal Explanations as a Risk Factor for Depression: Theory and Evidence," *Psychological Review* 91 (1984):347–374.

227   *explanatory styles of politicians*
Harold M. Zullow and Martin E. P. Seligman, "Pessimistic Rumination Predicts Electoral Defeat of Presidential Candidates: 1948–1984, unpublished manuscript, University of Pennsylvania.

228   *good explainers, success, and health*
Christopher Peterson and Martin E. P. Seligman, "Explanatory Style and Illness," *Journal of Personality* 55 (1987):238–265; and Martin E. P. Seligman and Peter Schulman, "Explanatory Style as a Predictor of Productivity and Quitting among Life Insurance Sales Agents," *Journal of Personality and Social Psychology* 50 (1986):832–838.

229   *the encapsulated computer of visual perception*
Jerrold Fodor, *Modularity of Mind: An Essay on Faculty Psychology* (Cambridge, Mass.: MIT Press, 1983).

229   *One reason why reading is so difficult*
Lila R. Gleitman and Paul Rozin, "The Structure and Acquisition of Reading 1: Relations Between Orthographies and the Structure of Language," in A. S. Reber and Donald L. Scarborough, *Towards a Psychology of Reading: The Proceedings of the CUNY Conference* (Hillsdale, N.J.: Lawrence Erlbaum Associates, 1977).

230   *intelligence should be measured by "nonentrenched" tasks*
Robert J. Sternberg, *Beyond IQ: A Triarchic Theory of Human Intelligence* (Cambridge, England: Cambridge University Press, 1985), 69; and see: Robert J. Sternberg and Richard K. Wagner, *Topics in Learning and Learning Disabilities*, July 1982, 1–11.

CHAPTER 16
232   *a yellow-striped animal ate his friend*
James McClelland, interview with the author.

233   *writing pure nonsense may be an impossible task*
Anthony Burgess, "Let's Talk Nonsense," *New York Times Book Review*, August 9, 1987, 1, 24–25.

234   *a celebrated series of studies*

See Kahneman, Slovic, and Tversky, eds., *Judgment under Uncertainty*.

234   *immoderately inclined to make sense of "worthless" information*
Daniel Kahneman and Amos Tversky, "On the Study of Statistical Intuitions," *Cognition* 11 (1982):123–141.

234   *people more likely to think logically if given no information about a person*
Kahneman and Tversky, "On the Study of Statistical Institutions," 123–141.

235   *"I knew it all along"*
B. Fischoff and R. Beyth, "'I Knew It Would Happen': Remembered Probabilities of Once-Future Things," *Organizational Behavior and Human Performance* 13 (1975):1–16.

235   *in hindsight, the mind fancies itself an intellectual prodigy*
B. Fischoff, "Perceived Informativeness of Facts," *Journal of Experimental Psychology: Human Perception and Performance 3* (1977):349–358.

236   *the struggle between the British colonials and the Gurkhas*
Fischoff and Beyth, "'I Knew It Would Happen.'"

238   *the letter k appears about twice as often in third place*
Amos Tversky and Daniel Kahneman, "A Heuristic for Judging Frequency and Probability," *Cognitive Psychology* 5 (1973):207–232.

239   *the public is seldom won over by explanations of why nuclear power stations are safe*
Kevin McKean, "Decisions, Decisions," *Discover*, June 1985, 26.

239   *the random bombing of London*
Daniel Kahneman and Amos Tversky "Subjective Probability: A Judgment of Representativeness," in Kahneman, Slovic, and Tversky, eds., *Judgment under Uncertainty*.

240   *people unable to produce random strings of numbers or letters*
Lola L. Lopes, "Doing the Impossible: A Note on Induction and the Experience of Randomness," *Journal of Experimental Psychology: Learning, Memory, and Cognition* 8 (1982): 626–636.

240   *not even a single random number*
Michael Kubovy and Joseph Sotka, "The Predominance of Seven and the Apparent Spontaneity of Numerical Choices," *Journal of Experimental Psychology: Human Perception and Performance 2* (1976):291–294.

240   *"A fundamental problem facing extraplanetary eavesdropping"*
       Lopes, 628.

241   *the "hot hand" effect in basketball*
       Robert Vallone and Amos Tversky, "The Hot Hand in Bas-
       ketball: On the Misperception of Random Sequences," *Cog-
       nitive Psychology* 17 (1985):295–314.

242   *"Is it more representative for a Hollywood actress to be divorced
       more than four times than to vote Democratic?"*
       Amos Tversky and Daniel Kahneman, "Extensional Versus
       Intuitive Reasoning: The Conjunction Fallacy in Probability
       Judgment," *Psychological Review* 90 (1983):293–315 (296).

242   *"For a person with a firm belief in the deterministic character of
       the world"*
       Berndt Brehmer, "In One Word: Not from Experience," in Hal
       R. Arkes and Kenneth Hammond, eds., *Judgment and Decision
       Making: An Interdisciplinary Reader* (Cambridge, England,
       and New York: Cambridge University Press, 1986), 715.

243   *"Our faith in experience is far from well grounded"*
       Brehmer, 715.

243   *We behave like the eighteenth-century astronomers*
       See Gerd Gigerenzer and David J. Murray, *Cognition as Intu-
       itive Statistics* (Hillsdale, N.J.: Lawrence Erlbaum Associates,
       1987), 3.

244   *"Tom W. is of high intelligence"*
       Amos Tversky and Daniel Kahneman, "Causal Schemas in
       Judgments under Uncertainty," in Kahneman, Slovic, and
       Tversky, eds., *Judgments under Uncertainty*, 127.

245   *"the reluctance to revise a rich and coherent model"*
       Tversky and Kahneman, "Causal Schemas," 128.

CHAPTER 17
247   *the self as press agent*
       "Dialogue with Daniel Dennett," in Jonathan Miller, *States of
       Mind*, 79.

247   *"He can be wrong, he can be massively misinformed"*
       "Dialogue with Daniel Dennett," 79.

248   *"Even in our own individual, individuality escapes our ken"*
       Henri Bergson, *Laughter: An Essay on the Meaning of the
       Comic*, trans. Cloudesley Brereton and Fred Rothwell (New
       York: Macmillan Publishing Co., 1913).

248   *a glance, a few spoken words are sufficient to "tell us a story"*
Solomon Asch, "Forming Impressions of Personality," *Journal of Abnormal and Social Psychology* 41 (1946):258–290 (258).

249   *film of a man and a woman in an apartment*
E. B. Ebbesen and R. B. Allen, "Cognitive Processes in Implicit Personality Inferences," *Journal of Personality and Social Psychology* 37 (1979):471–488.

249   *the theory of cognitive dissonance*
Leon Festinger, *A Theory of Cognitive Dissonance* (Stanford, Calif.: Stanford University Press, 1957).

250   *American prisoners of war made false confessions*
Daryl Bem, *Journal of Personal and Social Psychology* 6 (1966):707–710.

250   *college students perform an excruciatingly boring task*
Leon Festinger and J. M. Carlsmith, "Cognitive Consequences of Forced Compliance," *Journal of Abnormal and Social Psychology* 58 (1959):203–210.

251   *Daryl Bem's theory of "inferences without insight"*
Daryl J. Bem and H. Keith McConnell, "Testing the Self-Perception Explanation of Dissonance Phenomena: On the Salience of Premanipulation Attitudes," *Journal of Personal and Social Psychology* 14 (1970):23–31.

252   *we become "experts" in certain domains of our own behavior*
Hazel Markus, "Self-Schemata and Processing Information about the Self," *Journal of Personality and Social Psychology* 35 (1977):63–78; and Hazel Markus, Jeanne Smith, and Richard Moreland, "Role of the Self-Concept in the Perception of Others," *Journal of Personality and Social Psychology* 49 (1985):1494–1512.

252   *how a chess player's mind works*
William G. Chase and Herbert A. Simon, "Perception in Chess," *Cognitive Psychology* 4 (1973):55–81.

253   *a cartoon version of masculinity*
Markus, Smith, and Moreland, "Role of the Self-Concept."

255   *the self as Big Brother*
Anthony Greenwald, "The Totalitarian Ego: Fabrication and Revision of Personal History," *American Psychologist* 35 (1980):603–618.

255   *the theory of possible selves*
Hazel Markus, "Self-Knowledge: An Expanded View," *Jour-*

nal of Personality 51 (1983):543–565; and Hazel Markus and Paula Nurius, "Possible Selves," *American Psychologist* 41 (1986):954–969.

256   *"does not harbor this hope in vague abstraction"*
Markus and Nurius, "Possible Selves," 954.

257   *we have opinions and other animals do not*
Daniel Dennett, *Brainstorms: Philosophical Essays on Mind and Psychology* (Cambridge, Mass.: MIT Press, 1981), 306–309.

257   *"there are all these sentences lying around"*
Dennett, *Brainstorms*, 306.

257   *"this is what happens, I think, when you follow an argument"*
Dennett, *Brainstorms*, 308.

258   *players of the four-card game show no insight into their own reasoning*
P. C. Wason and J. St. B. Evans, "Dual Processes in Reasoning?" *Cognition* 3 (1975):141–154.

258   *"as if caught between two conflicting processes"*
J. St. B. Evans, "Current Issues in the Psychology of Reasoning," *British Journal of Psychology* 71 (1980):227–239 (236).

CHAPTER 18

260   *Free will is an illusion*
See B. F. Skinner, *Beyond Freedom and Dignity* (New York: Knopf, 1971).

261   *it was necessary to enter "the den of philosophical wolves"*
Lawrence Kohlberg, "From Is to Ought," in Theodore Mischel, ed., *Cognitive Development and Epistemology* (New York: Academic Press, 1971), 153.

262   *"I had no moral conflicts about breaking British law"*
Lawrence Kohlberg, quoted in Gustav Niebuhr, "A Philosopher of Morality," *Atlanta Constitution*, February 18, 1987, B1–2.

262   *Kohlberg's theory on stages*
Lawrence Kohlberg, "The Child as Moral Philosopher," *Psychology Today*, September 1968, 2:27; and "Stage and Sequence: The Cognitive-Developmental Approach to Socialization," in D. Goodlin, ed., *Handbook of Socialization Theory of Research* (New York: Rand McNally, 1969).

262   *William Golding's novel* Lord of the Flies

Referred to in Kohlberg, "The Child as Moral Philosopher."

265   *a provocative and stimulating failure*
Richard Shweder, "Liberalism as Destiny," *Contemporary Psychology* 27 (1982):421–424.

267   *Carol Gilligan's studies of real-life experiences*
Carol Gilligan and John Michael Murphy, "Development from Adolescence to Adulthood: The Philosopher and the Dilemma of the Fact," *New Directions in Child Development* 5 (1979):85–99.

268   *"the dilemma of the fact"*
Gilligan and Murphy, 85–99.

269   *Jake and Amy decide the Heinz problem*
Carol Gilligan, *In a Different Voice* (Cambridge, Mass.: Harvard University Press, 1982), 24–39.

270   *"First, virtue is ultimately one"*
Quoted in Kohlberg, "From Is to Ought," 232.

271   *Criticisms leveled at Robert Bork*
David Lauter and David G. Savage, *Los Angeles Times*, September 13, 1987, 1, 6–7.

272   *Martin Luther King as stage-six thinker*
Kohlberg, "The Child as Moral Philosopher."

272   *liberalism . . . is not powerful enough to satisfy*
R. M. Unger, *Knowledge and Politics* (New York: Free Press, 1975). Quoted in John C. Gibbs, "Kohlberg's Stages of Moral Judgment: A Constructive Critique," *Harvard Educational Review* 47 (1977):43–61. Gibbs remarks that the classical idea of the social contract "makes assumptions about human nature, which, although valid as far as they go, are primitive in relation to the highest achievements of the human moral and social development."

273   *"Socrates realized the difficulty"*
Raziel Abelson, "History of Ethics," in *The Encyclopedia of Philosophy*, vol. 3 (New York: Free Press, 1967), 82.

CHAPTER 19

275   *"feign that I had no body, that there was no world"*
René Descartes, *Discourse on the Method*, in Elizabeth Anscombe and Thomas Geach, eds., *Descartes: Philosophical Writings* (Indianapolis: Bobbs-Merrill, 1971), 32.

275   *"there can be nothing too remote to be reached"*

Descartes, *Discourse on the Method*, 21.

277   *multiplying with pencil and paper or with slide rule*
Balakrishnan Chandrasekaran, "What Kind of Information Processing Is Intelligence? A Perspective on AI Paradigms and a Proposal," *Technical Research Report* (Columbus, Ohio: Ohio State University Laboratory for Artificial Intelligence Research, July 1987), 7.

279   *psychology is the study of entire individuals*
William James, *Principles of Psychology*, vol. 1, 183.

279   *"like the aurora borealis"*
William James, 234.

279   *a "jungle of connections"*
William James, 551.

280   *"Reason is only one out of a thousand possibilities"*
William James, 552.

281   *"Suppose I tell you that John is a detective"*
James Hendler, interview with the author.

282   *"I had to do some very clumsy stuff"*
Hendler interview.

283   *"Our minds work in such a way that predeliberative mental processes come up with the most interesting ideas"*
Balakrishnan Chandrasekaran, interview with the author.

285   *"I think very little behavior just emerges"*
Jerome Feldman, interview with the author.

286   *categories created "on the fly"*
L. W. Barsalou, "Ad Hoc Categories," *Memory and Cognition* 11 (1983):211–227; and Lawrence Barsalou, "The Instability of Graded Structure: Implications for the Nature of Concepts," in Ulric Neisser, ed., *Concepts Reconsidered: The Ecological and Intellectual Bases of Categories* (Cambridge, England: Cambridge University Press, 1987).

287   *"Connectionism is strong in those parts of our mental life"*
Bechtel interview.

288   *"human reason is not a single unitary gadget"*
Iris Murdoch, *Sartre: Romantic Rationalist* (New Haven: Yale University Press,) 8.

INDEX